Teamwork Models and Experience in Education

Teamwork Models and Experience in Education

Howard G. Garner
Virginia Commonwealth University

Allyn and Bacon
Boston · London · Toronto · Sydney · Tokyo · Singapore

Library of Congress Cataloging-in-Publication Data
    Teamwork models and experience in education/ Howard G. Garner, editor.
        p. cm.
    Includes index.
    ISBN 0-205-13783-0
        1. Teaching teams—United States. 2. Child care services—United
    States. 3. Work groups—United States. 4. Community and school—
    United States. I. Garner, Howard G.
    LB1029. T4T43 1995   94-32869
    371. 1′48—dc20   CIP

Printed in the United States of America
10 9 8 7 6 5 4 3 2 1   99 98 97 96 95

Dedicated to my parents,
Ernestine Wynne Garner
and
Walter Glenn Garner

Contents

PART I   Models and Benefits of Teamwork

**PART II   Establishing the Structure and Culture
            for Teamwork**

Preface

Teamwork among professionals and parents who are working with the same children and youth is no longer just an ideal to be pursued. Today it has become a necessity. The helping professions are confronting and attempting to solve serious human problems that are increasingly complex and that cross the traditional dividing lines between the various professions. Society can no longer afford the inefficiency of a service delivery system in which children and families are passed back and forth among a variety of schools, programs, and professionals who sometimes give inconsistent and even contradictory recommendations for change.

The problems being experienced by an increasing number of young people today result from the interactive effects of poverty, child abuse, crime, drug and alcohol abuse, dysfunctional families, disabilities, distorted values of society, and a human service system that is grossly underfunded and uncoordinated. In attempting to respond to these difficult problems and complex causal factors, schools and child care programs are utilizing the knowledge and skills of various helping disciplines, including regular education, special education, child care, social work, counseling, psychology, physical therapy, occupational therapy, speech therapy, recreation therapy, nursing, and medicine. The challenge and urgent need is for the professionals from these disciplines to learn to work successfully with one another and with parents in assessing problems, developing plans for intervention, coordinating the implementation of these plans, and then evaluating the effects and outcomes. Teamwork provides both a structure and a process to meet these goals.

Across the nation, schools and child care programs are adopting the teamwork philosophy and restructuring their organizations according to the team model. Some have implemented these changes because they were required by federal and state special education regulations. Many others have done so because the team model promised higher-quality services for children and families as well as higher morale and increased job satisfaction for the professionals and parents working together.

Over the past 25 years, helping professionals in the fields of education and child care have gained a great deal of experience in organizing, supervising, and participating in teams. Much of this experience has not been shared with others on a large scale. This book is designed to allow some of these professionals to communicate their experience and knowledge in four areas: (1) the various team models and their benefits, (2) the process of organizational change to achieve teamwork, (3) administrative leadership in supporting and monitoring teams, and (4) teams in action. The teams described work in settings from early intervention programs for infants and toddlers, to special education programs, to middle school education, and to transition programs for youth with disabilities from high school to the world of independent living. As the reader explores the experience and knowledge of these professionals from across the country, it will be useful to look for patterns and themes that cut across the different programs and settings described. Although there are differences among programs based on the needs of the individuals being served, the team approach brings a number of benefits and challenges that are common to all.

The authors of the book's chapters deserve sincere thanks for their willingness to accept the challenge of communicating in writing their experience with teams while continuing their respective jobs in teaching, consulting, supervising, and serving on teams. Their rich and diverse experience will serve as a helpful and much needed guide both to practicing professionals who are currently working with teams and to graduate students who are receiving training prior to becoming active team members.

Acknowledgments

This book represents a team effort, and I want to express my appreciation to the members of that team. The idea for this book emerged over dinner with Rochelle Haimes at Barium Springs Home for Children in North Carolina. We recognized that a number of people across the country were using teams to make significant differences in the lives of children and youth and in the organizations that served them, and a forum was needed to allow these professionals to share their rich experience with others. This book is that forum.

The authors of the book's chapters deserve special recognition for their innovative contributions to the application of teamwork in diverse settings. They deserve credit for their willingness to take risks in making organizational changes and empowering their employees to play a significant role in solving problems and making decisions. I am sure these national leaders in teamwork would join me in recognizing the professionals who serve on teams serving children and youth who have been our colleagues and teachers in pioneering the use of teams in education and child care.

I also want to acknowledge the folks at Allyn and Bacon for their vision in recognizing the importance of this book and for their support in the long process of planning, writing, editing, reviewing, rewriting, and printing. My special thanks to Mylan Jaixen, Executive Editor, and to Susan Hutchinson, Editorial Assistant, for their encouragement, assistance, patience, and professional expertise. In addition, I want to thank our field readers, Richard Quigley, CEO at Woodland Hills in Duluth, Minnesota; Douglas E. Harris at Franklin Northwest Supervisory Union in Swanton, Vermont; and Charles Sharman, professor and colleague here at Virginia Commonwealth University. They read the manuscript carefully and provided excellent feedback and suggestions to me and the authors that resulted in a much improved final product.

On a more personal note, I would like to acknowledge the importance of my family in both my work and this long-term effort. My wife, Ann Sarratt Garner, and my children, Glenn and Kristin, have been the pillars of my life. My son-in-law, Danny Zorn, has encouraged my work and shared his own experience with teams in his work.

Finally, I appreciate the lessons I have learned about teams from my Men's Group that has met weekly for 16 years and from my basketball teammates who play together on Thursday and Sunday nights. Learning how to work, live, and play together is the challenge and joy of being human.

Howard Glenn Garner

Biographical Sketches

Howard G. Garner, Ph.D., is Professor of Education at Virginia Commonwealth University in Richmond. From 1985 to 1990 he served as the Director of the Virginia Institute for Developmental Disabilities, an interdisciplinary program for training, service, technical assistance, and dissemination. He is the author of three books, *Teamwork in Programs for Children and Youth: A Handbook for Administrators* (1982), *Helping Others Through Teamwork* (1988), and *Teamwork in Human Services* (1994). In addition three educating teachers of children with disabilities, he serves as a consultant to public schools, residential programs, and hospitals.

A native of Greenville, North Carolina, Dr. Garner graduated with a bachelor's degree in European History from the University of North Carolina at Chapel Hill. He received his master's and Ph.D. degrees from the University of Florida. His work career has included high school teaching, administration of a residential treatment program, university teaching, and university administration.

Christine Ameen, Ph.D., is currently Director of Program Evaluation and Planning for Starr Commonwealth in Michigan. She also provides consultation and training to agencies interested in program evaluation and planning. She has written numerous documents including: "Program Evaluation: A Blueprint for Program Excellence" and "Program Evaluation: A Tool for Program Development and Management."

Joan Bacon, Ph.D., Assistant Professor of Special Education at Augustana College in Sioux Falls, South Dakota, uses cooperative learning to develop future teachers' teaming skills. A former special educator and school district coordinator, she has led school-based and interagency teams for preschoolers, youth, and adults. She earned her doctorate at the University of South Dakota.

Larry Brendtro, Ph.D., Professor of Special Education at Augustana College in Sioux Falls, South Dakota, developed team models to complement the Positive Peer Culture approach of working with troubled youth. He currently is co-editor of the *Journal of Emotional and Behavior Problems*, which is a collaboration of the various disciplines involved in reclaiming youth at risk.

James Cunningham has since 1989 held the position of Assistant Director of a residential village at Starr Commonwealth Schools in Albion, Michigan, where he had served as a child care worker for 14 years. He holds a master's degree in Counseling Psychology from Western Michigan University and is a licensed professional counselor. He has also trained in residential treatment issues for the past 6 years.

Mary Drees is the Program Supervisor at the Youth Development Center in Milwaukee, WI. She has six years experience as a team member and is an active participant in the effort to professionalize the field of child and youth care.

Thomas O. Erb, Ph.D., is a Professor of Curriculum and Instruction at the University of Kansas. He began teaching on an interdisciplinary team 26 years ago. Dr. Erb has co-authored *Team Organization: Promise—Practices and Possibilities* (NEA, 1989) and written the often reprinted "What Team Organization Can Do for Teachers" (*Middle School Journal,* 1987).

Jane M. Everson, Ph.D., is the Director of the Helen Keller National Center–Technical Assistance Center (HKNC–TAC) housed in Sands Point, New York. She is also an Associate Professor with the Human Development Center, Louisiana State University Medical Center, School of Allied Health Professions, New Orleans, Louisiana. She is an experienced educator of high school students with severe disabilities and has authored many articles, book chapters, and books on transitional services for these youth. In her current position she directs state and local partnerships providing technical assistance in 12 states to programs serving young adults who are deaf-blind.

Michael Gamel-McCormick is an Instructor in the Early Childhood Special Education Masters Program at Virginia Commonwealth University. He has been a team member serving children with and without disabilities in the role of elementary school counselor and teacher. He has also supervised a transdisciplinary team serving infants and young children with disabilities and their families. He received his master's degree from the University of Wisconsin and two bachelor's degrees from the University of Delaware. He is currently working on his dissertation for his Ph.D. at Virginia Commonwealth University.

Corinne W. Garland, M.Ed., is the Executive Director of Child Development Resources in Lightfoot, Virginia. Ms. Garland is experienced in the administration of early intervention and early childhood services in the public, private, and university sectors. She has been involved in the development and implementation of inservice training and technical assistance for early intervention providers with emphasis on a family-centered, transdisciplinary approach. She has served as President of the International Division of Early Childhood of the Council for Exceptional Children and is currently the division's governor. She served a three-year term as a Governor's appointee to the Virginia Interagency Coordinating Council and as chair of its Service Delivery Committee.

Rochelle Haimes, ACSW, is the former Vice President, Services, at Barium Springs Home for Children in North Carolina. She is now an independent consultant in Charlotte, North Carolina. A former child care worker, social worker, and program supervisor in residential and community-based programs, her focus now is program development and organization. Since 1982 she has been "cheerleading" the evolution of teams in the agency's residential services. She is active nationally as a trainer, consultant, and peer reviewer.

Mark Krueger, Ph.D., is a professor and Director of the Child and Youth Care Learning Center, University of Wisconsin–Milwaukee. He worked as a member of a treatment team for 11 years and has authored several articles and books on teamwork and child and youth care.

Martin Mitchell, Ph.D., is currently Vice President of Program for Starr Commonwealth, Michigan. He has written numerous documents related to teamwork including "The Organizational Ethos: From Tension to Teamwork" and the "Mitchell/Ameen Treatment Environment Surveys." He has served as a trainer and consultant on teamwork throughout the United States and Canada.

Abraham Nicolaou, Ph.D. is a Professor of Special Education at Western Michigan in Kalamazoo, Michigan. Professional interests and responsibilities have been in the fields of autism, emotional impairment, and transdisciplinary teacher training at graduate levels. He has authored and co-authored a number of articles in these fields and for over a decade directed an educateur training program in cooperation with Starr Commonwealth Schools in Albion, Michigan.

Fred P. Orelove, Ph.D., is the Executive Director of the Virginia Institute for Developmental Disabilities at Virginia Commonwealth University. Dr. Orelove's primary interest is individuals with severe disabilities, and he has taught children, directed training and demonstration projects, and prepared teachers for 15 years. He is the co-author (with Dick Sobsey) of *Educating Children with Multiple Disabilities: A Transdisciplinary Approach.*

Steven A. Roy, SCJ, is currently President and CEO of St. Joseph's Indian School in Chamberlain, South Dakota. He works in the fields of education and child and youth care as a practitioner and a consultant. His latest contributions have been in the area of organization restructuring for successful teamwork.

Charles Sharman is the Director of the Central Virginia Leadership Academy at Virginia Commonwealth University in Richmond, Virginia. During the past decade he has developed programs and conducted training in teambuilding and the usage of teams to foster school improvement in over 400 schools in Virginia and other states.

Maxine M. Smith is the Education Coordinator at Thompson Children's Home in Charlotte, North Carolina. Currently working within a team model, she also had prior experience in working with teams as the Assistant Director of Residential Services at Barium Springs Home for Children. She graduated from Utica College Syracuse University with a bachelor's degree in Psychology and Social Studies, from the State University of New York at Cortland with a master's degree in Education, and from the University of Alabama with an Education Specialist's degree. She holds a Certificate of Advanced Standing in Educational Administration from the University of North Carolina–Charlotte.

Abe M. Wilkinson is Executive Director of the Georgia Elks Aidmore Children's Center in Conyers, Georgia. In addition to having implemented a team model with this agency, he had previous experience in working with teams as Director of Residential Services for Barium Springs Home for Children in Barium Springs, North Carolina. He graduated from Arkansas State University with a bachelor's degree in Communications and a master's degree in Counselor Education.

Harold S. Wright, Jr. is an Assistant Principal at Patrick Henry High School in Hanover County, Virginia. He received a B.A. from Randolph-Macon College and an M.Ed. and Ph.D. in Educational Leadership from Virginia Commonwealth University. He is actively involved with teams and the teaching process through school renewal and special education.

▶ 1

Teamwork in Education and Child Care

Howard G. Garner

RHETORIC AND REALITY

The idea that professionals should cooperate, communicate effectively, and be "team players" has been discussed, advocated, and accepted by educators and human services professionals for a long time (Garrett, 1955; Whitehouse, 1951). In fact, it is impossible to find anyone working with children and youth who is against "team-work." In the fields of education and child care, how can anyone oppose sharing information, developing common goals, collaborating in planning and implementing programs, and sharing responsibility for the achievement of quality services for children and youth? Clearly, teamwork is compatible and congruent with the goals of all organizations devoted to educating students, helping people, and facilitating change. And yet, is it not ironic that a concept, a value, and a way of working together, such as teamwork, can receive such universal support and still remain a goal rather than an expected and common reality?

In spite of the rhetoric in support of the "team concept," many helping profes-sionals still work in organizations where competition occurs more frequently than cooperation, where protecting one's turf is more important than providing coordinated services, and where professionals feel trapped and frustrated instead of creative and powerful. In such schools and programs, faculty and staff members ally themselves with their departmental or unit colleagues and collectively blame the problems on "those other people in those other departments" who seem to put their needs for resources, status, credit, power, and control over the best interests of the students and clients. Because the values of teamwork are so synonymous with the values of education and child care, they are perhaps taken for granted and the essentials required to achieve teamwork are overlooked.

Fortunately, over the past two decades, helping professionals, and the schools and programs in which they work, have gradually begun to recognize that teamwork is more than a set of platitudes that everyone accepts unconsciously but no one actually lives. But these changes have come slowly and sporadically. The status quo has a way of perpetuating itself as people hold onto the known and resist the unknown that change represents. Often, change only occurs when forces from outside the school or the organization present challenges, demands, and new standards that cannot be met using the old structures and procedures. In the fields of education and child care these challenges and demands have come from several sources, including radical changes in the management of American businesses, the public demand for school improvement, and public laws regarding services to persons with disabilities.

Changes in American Business Management

While schools and child care programs have struggled and stumbled along, maintaining the traditional administrative hierarchies and ways of organizing and managing employees, the American business community has recently been forced to adopt new ideas about organization and management in order to improve quality, productivity, and profits (Deming, 1982; Peters & Waterman, 1982). Spurred not by humanistic descriptions of "teams helping others" but by the demands of the marketplace, American businesses in the 1970s began to reorganize, establish clear mission statements and goals, and create smaller units of employees who were given radical amounts of responsibility and power to solve problems and make decisions around the issues of quality, consumer satisfaction, and productivity. Challenged and threatened by the Japanese, who after World War II applied the quality control ideas of the American statistician W. Edwards Deming to achieve an economic miracle (Mann, 1985), a number of large bureaucratic companies that once seemed entrenched in a top-down, chain of command of organization and administration began to implement major changes in their organizational structures and decision-making processes. These businesses followed Deming's basic principles for effective management, including his advice to "Break down barriers between departments" (Deming, 1982, p. 24). The pursuit of quality and the effective use of their human resources brought companies dramatic financial successes as well as a new sense of purpose, high morale, and creative energy among employees. Apparently, what was good for customers and companies was also good for those who did the work (Deming, 1982; Mann, 1985; Scherkenbach, 1991).

The public demand for quality in the private sector was inevitably applied to the public sector. Public criticism of the public schools and their failure to provide a "world-class education" for America's children was accompanied by comparisons between the American education system and those of other industrial nations, especially Germany and Japan. Calls for school reform and school improvement came from small towns and the U.S. Congress, along with a wide range of proposed solutions and experiments. The restructuring of schools using some of the principles from the business community followed.

Teamwork and the School Reform Movement

The principles of teamwork and collaboration are currently being used extensively in the school reform movement in the United States. These applications of the team approach are called by various names, including site-based management and school restructuring.

Most school divisions and individual schools continue to be administered and operated using hierarchical, bureaucratic decision-making structures and processes. Decisions about changes in procedures and daily practice usually come from the top of the organization, the superintendent or the board of education, and are passed down a military-style "chain of command" to principals and then to teachers. The teachers in most schools are organized in separate departments with high degrees of role differentiation and specialization, and they often see themselves as belonging to competing territorial units within the school and not as members of a cooperative team. Especially in secondary schools, subject area specialists who teach the same students rarely, if ever, communicate directly with one another regarding individual student needs, instructional strategies, or even curriculum.

In contrast, the advocates of school restructuring propose the use of site-based, participatory management, allowing each individual school and its personnel and parents to assume primary responsibility for shaping their school's mission, goals, and procedures (Maeroff, 1993). These direction-setting decisions are often addressed by a new school council that includes representatives of all constituent groups including parents, teachers, administrators, and support personnel. In addition, restructured schools also form teams of teachers around intact groups of pupils, allowing those teachers and students to develop identity, loyalty, and ownership for their learning environment and experience. These same principles have served as the basis for the middle school movement in the United States (Erb & Doda, 1989).

Whitaker and Moses (1990) described the restructuring of schools in the 1990s as a paradigm shift in education, moving far beyond the 1970s and 1980s attempts at educational reform. They stated: "A few examples of paradigm shifts needed in education include multiple interactions rather than one way directives, leadership by knowledge rather than authority, and inquiring behavior rather than mandated behavior" (p. 4). School restructuring is viewed as following the dramatic organizational changes that have been occurring in the world of business and industry. "Examples of ways that the private sector has restructured include creating performance improvement programs, developing human resources, job sharing, establishing work teams, eliminating waste, flattening the organization, and incorporating new technology" (p. 5).

Moses and Whitaker (1990) detailed 10 key components of restructuring divided into three categories: visionary, productivity, and collaborative elements. The visionary elements included setting a new mission for the schools; reorganizing the school to fit the mission; and realigning the curriculum, instruction, and assessment to fit the mission. The productivity elements included enhancing the teaching profession, implementing school-centered decision making, expanding the use of technology, and providing excellent service. The collaborative elements included increasing parent and community involvement, building collaborative relationships, and providing extended health and social services in the school.

Comer (1987) reported impressive changes in school climate, student achievement, and even educational achievement of parents in certain New Haven, Connecticut, schools as a result of collaboration among Yale University, mental health, public school, and community personnel. These changes were achieved in schools with the worst combination of poverty, racial and cultural isolation, and low parental achievement.

As participatory models of school change and decision making are being applied, educators are learning from their experiences. Harrison, Killion, and Mitchell (1989) reported four major mistakes they made in trying to implement site-based management in a Colorado school division. They identified as their first mistake the failure to define terms precisely at the outset and to avoid confusing site-based management with other school improvement strategies. Their second mistake had to do with the definition of roles, especially those of central office personnel and those in the schools. The third mistake concerned the absence of training for both principals and teachers. Principals needed training in how to involve others in making significant decisions, and principals and teachers needed training in how to facilitate team meetings, resolve conflicts, and achieve consensus decisions. The final mistake was their lack of preparation in managing the change process. They said, "If we were to begin the process tomorrow with the benefit of hindsight, we would be more conscious of the impact of change on individuals, and we would offer a wide variety of intervention strategies" (p. 58).

Timar (1989) stated that the movement to restructure schools in America is threatened by a number of factors. These include the perception that restructuring is the agenda of a small group of educators. A second threat is potential fragmentation and competition among individual projects or programs as each pursues a different aspect of the reform agenda. Some restructured schools have suffered because of the absence of administrative and financial support from the central office of the school division (Maeroff, 1993). In some states, restructuring has become politicized and regulated to the point that policy proliferation creates a familiar bureaucratic wet blanket that inhibits real change from occurring.

Maeroff (1993) noted that "[t]eam building for school change is still a curiosity, carried out on a modest scale and sustained largely by outside funds" (p. 519). Using a circus image, he argued that the use of teams to effect educational change in schools is probably dependent upon their maintaining a focus on the educational needs of pupils and that to become diverted to side issues runs the risk of their becoming a sideshow to the performance going on in the main ring.

Teamwork in Programs for Students with Disabilities

Spurred by federal and state mandates in special education since the late 1970s, multidisciplinary teams that include parents have been formed in school divisions across the country to identify children who are eligible for special education and related services, to develop individualized plans, and to evaluate individual student progress over time (Losen & Losen, 1985). In some schools these teams have become the basis for ongoing consultation and collaboration among professionals and parents, responding to the changing and complex needs of children.

Interactive Teaming.   Morsink, Thomas, and Correa (1991) described "interactive teaming" in special programs for children with disabilities and special needs. Such teamwork allows team members to understand the contributions of each team member, to share their knowledge and experience, to establish and pursue common goals, and to make changes in the program and the school. They identified five key decision points where a special education team of professionals, working closely with parents, is needed. These decision points include referral for special assistance, screening to help determine eligibility, classification after meeting criteria for special services, instructional planning, and evaluation of student progress. Team decision making in these areas was federally mandated by Public Law 94-142 in 1975, PL 99-457 in 1986, and PL 101-476 in 1990. As a result, school divisions across the country have more than fifteen years of experience using teams in making major decisions regarding students with disabilities and the programs needed to serve them.

Early intervention programs for preschool children with developmental delays and disabilities have pioneered the use of a new model of teamwork called "transdisciplinary teamwork" (Woodruff & McGonigel, 1988). This model moves beyond the sharing of information and decision making typical in interdisciplinary teams to a level of interaction and collaboration that allows for what is called "role transition or role release." Team members develop a high level of understanding and skill that allows them to release to one another professional interventions that previously were guarded and protected by each discipline. In this model each child's parents are full-fledged team members who are expected to participate in all decisions throughout the course of the intervention process.

Collaborative Teams.   Rainforth, York, and Macdonald (1992) analyzed the use of collaborative teams for students with severe disabilities. These students with the most severe and complex problems require services from a number of professionals, including physical, occupational, and speech therapists; psychologists; social workers; special educators; and medical professionals. Each professional, along with the student's parents, brings a unique perspective and specific skills that are needed in the design and implementation of a comprehensive and integrated intervention program.

The integrated therapy model (Giangreco, York, & Rainforth, 1989) was proposed as an effective means of providing services within functional contexts. This means that a child who needs to develop a specific skill, such as mobility, receives instruction during those times of the day when that skill is needed, such as when transitions from one area to another are required. Thus, therapy is not provided in an isolated setting leading to problems of transfer of the training but is integrated within the child's daily life and routine. To achieve this, the integrated therapy model utilizes aspects of the transdisciplinary team model, with team members teaching one another their discipline's intervention techniques and providing consultation and support as these are applied by professionals from other disciplines. In this approach, parents become important partners with professionals in making decisions about how best to integrate the therapy within the child's daily routine and in providing therapeutic support and interventions.

In analyzing the benefits of collaborative teams for students with severe disabilities, Rainforth, York, and Macdonald (1992) cite the utilization of information and perspectives from different disciplines for improved decision making, the integration of therapeutic interventions into the students' daily lives, and the design of relevant and effective curricula and instruction. A second set of benefits accrues to the members of the team. These include a sense of belonging to a group pursuing common goals; positive interpersonal relationships; overcoming competition and isolation; mutual support in coping with stress, anxiety, and failure; and developing new professional knowledge and skills.

Residential Child and Youth Care.   In many residential programs, interdisciplinary teams, including child care workers, teachers, social workers, and therapists, are now organized around small groups of children and youth. In residential programs based on the team model, administrators delegate significant amounts of power and responsibility to these teams and provide them with appropriate support and training. As a result, the young people receiving services only interact with staff who are members of their team. Each of these adults has complete information regarding the children's individual needs and has participated in the development of individualized treatment plans that are being implemented consistently across the whole day.

Since the 1960s the team model has been applied in residential programs for youth using the positive peer culture (PPC) model of treatment (Vorrath and Brendtro, 1974). Arguing that the management system of a human service organization should be matched to the treatment methodology, Vorrath and Brendtro (1985) proposed the concept of "teamwork primacy," which bases all treatment decisions on the group of staff who provide direct services to the clients. They called the model "a radical departure from traditional systems of organization and administration" (p. 128). Teamwork primacy eliminates traditional departments and organizes the staff into interdisciplinary teams around intact groups of youth. The model minimizes the role of middle management and empowers teams by giving them significant amounts of responsibility and power. Vorrath and Brendtro (1985) stated: "This structure is clearly in contrast with traditional notions of 'teamwork' in which the supervisor conducts a meeting from the end of the table while others listen politely, deferring to his greater authority and supposedly greater wisdom" (p. 129). Moreover, the PPC model believes in the empowerment of the peer group, as well as the adult team, in accomplishing changes in values, self-concept, and behavior among youth who have previously exhibited extremely challenging and hurting behaviors.

A number of other authors have described the effective use of teams in residential programs for children and youth (Brendtro & Mitchell, 1983; Garner, 1982; Krueger, 1990). Garner (1982) described a "total team model" for residential child care in which all staff who work directly with the clients are organized in teams around groups of children and youth. In this model, staff do not belong to traditional departments of education, child care, and social work. Instead, all personnel who provide direct services to children and youth belong to teams that are given significant amounts of power and responsibility in planning and implementing individual and group treatment programs. In the total team model, Garner recommends the participation of teams in making both budgetary and personnel decisions in order to ensure the use of complete information in reaching these decisions and to promote commitment and followthrough in their implementation.

Commentary

Teamwork appears to be a "wave of the future" that is now pounding the beaches of all types of organizations, from businesses to human services organizations to schools and residential programs. This new way of doing business requires both new structures and new skills on the part of administrators and direct service personnel. Significant changes are needed in how administrators and team members relate to one another and how decisions are made. The shift from a top-down way of operating to a bottom-up approach creates changes in patterns of communication and leadership. Teamwork experience has shown that much can be achieved when everyone is working together in pursuit of the same goals. However, in order to achieve this promise, a number of critical issues have to be faced.

CRITICAL ISSUES IN TEAM FUNCTIONING

Having made an overview of the various settings in which teamwork is being employed, it is appropriate now to turn to some of the issues and factors that seem to affect the success or failure of the team model and specific teams in action. Experience has shown that a group of people do not work together successfully or achieve real teamwork just because the group is called "a team" (Garner, 1988). Given the fact that some teams are successful and others are not, it is important to explore and understand the essential components of effectively functioning teams.

Eight Characteristics of Effectively Functioning Teams

Larson and LaFasto (1989) conducted research over a three-year period to identify the unique characteristics of effectively functioning teams. They interviewed the members of a wide variety of teams in diverse settings, from schools to hospitals to businesses to sports. In this research they found eight consistent patterns and characteristics that distinguished successful teams from unsuccessful ones. These included the following:

1. A clear, elevating goal
2. A results-driven structure
3. Competent members
4. Unified commitment
5. A collaborative climate
6. Standards of excellence
7. External support and recognition
8. Principled leadership

Each of these eight characteristics of successful teams is briefly discussed in the following sections, with commentary on how these factors are experienced in educational and child care settings.

1. *Goals:* Larson and LaFasto found that successful teams had a clear understanding of their objective, while unsuccessful ones became unfocused and politicized, lost their sense of urgency, or had individual members' goals taking priority over team goals. Teams with elevating goals that were challenging and worth pursuing created a sense of urgency and of making a difference.

Professionals who work in education and child care can cite examples of where teams have maintained their focus on the needs of the children and youth being served and other examples where teams lost their focus, resulting in the team members' becoming discouraged and withdrawing from the team process. This undermines the whole purpose behind individualized planning, which is to establish clear goals that everyone working with a child can pursue consistently.

2. *Structure:* The structure of a team needs to be designed around the results to be achieved. Larson and LaFasto identified three types of teams that require different structures. They found that the structure of a *problem resolution team* needs to promote trust, the structure of a *creative team* needs to promote autonomy, and the structure of a *tactical team* needs to promote clarity.

Teams in education and child care frequently pursue all three results—problem resolution, creativity, and tactical planning. In many programs not enough attention is paid to the specific results a team is to achieve, and therefore issues regarding team structure are not properly addressed. Trust issues affect team members' ability to be open in discussions and to gather the information needed for appropriate planning. Teams frequently do not know how much autonomy they have in devising creative solutions and become immobilized in the process. Similarly, when teams are implementing their plans, there is too often a lack of clarity regarding what is possible and what is prohibited.

3. *Competent Members:* Everyone agrees that successful teams need competent members; however, the researchers discovered that competence is needed in both technical skills and in personal skills to work in collaboration with others. Again, the skills that are needed may vary depending on the type of team. For example, problem-solving teams require members who have a high degree of integrity and who engender trust, while creative teams need members who have a high degree of confidence and tenacity and who can be both independent thinkers and self starters.

In education and child care many people expect that everybody should be able to do everything, and they are often disappointed with the performance of both individuals and teams when they are unable to meet this expectation. Another false assumption is that all helping professionals already possess interpersonal skills in communication and conflict resolution. Again, this unfulfilled assumption leads to criticism and cynicism. The need for advanced training in these critical areas should not be viewed as a sign of inadequacy but as an ongoing process of personal and professional growth. Participation in teams does demand the development of high-level, human interaction skills on the part of all team members.

4. *Unified Commitment:* The members of a successful team feel a strong identification with and commitment to their team and share a strong sense of "who we are" and "what we are about." Larson and Lafasto stated: "[G]roup spirit and teamwork come about as a result of identification with a team. In that identification there is a relinquishing of the self—not a denial of the self, but a voluntary redefinition of the self to include membership in the team as an important aspect of the self" (pp. 76–77).

In education and child care, professionals have often viewed themselves as individuals engaged in difficult and lonely work. This working in relative isolation has been perpetuated in the past by the structure and schedules of schools and child care programs in which one adult was placed in charge of a group of children or youth in a classroom, residential unit, or activity area. When that individual finished his or her time with the group, the children were then either passed on to the next adult (with a sigh of relief) or sent home to the parents. There seldom was a sense that "we have a shared responsibility for this group of children and we need to stick together as a team."

A lack of identification with one's team is also caused by professionals being assigned to a unworkable number of different teams. For example, in some special education programs, psychologists, social workers, and therapists have membership on as many as 10 different teams in 10 different schools. Under these conditions it is not surprising that these professionals do not feel a unified commitment with all of their teams. Instead, they naturally fall back on their identification with their colleagues who share their same job title and responsibilities, which is the basis of the departmental model.

5. *A Collaborative Climate:* A climate that fostered teamwork was described by Larson and LaFasto as including clear roles, responsibilities, and lines of communication. This climate also promoted a feeling of trust among the members, which allowed for open, direct, and problem-centered discussion and decision making.

In education and child care the perception of a collaborative climate varies depending on a number of other factors including size, leadership, and organizational structure. For example, professionals who have worked primarily in departmentalized organizations are more accustomed to competition and distrust among the various subgroups than to an atmosphere of openness and trust. In some elementary schools, teachers on the same grade level often become allies and compete with other grade-level groups for control of the curriculum, access to limited resources, and the principal's attention.

6. *Standards of Excellence:* How clear and consistent are the team's expectations for the work of the whole team and its individual members? Larson and LaFasto stated that standards of excellence may come from four sources: (1) from within the individual, (2) from the team itself, (3) from the consequences of success and failure, and (4) from sources outside the team.

Unfortunately, in education and child care there is not a strong consensus regarding what constitutes excellence. What is the relative importance, for example, of higher test scores in reading and math and improved self-concept or the relative importance of an orderly classroom and creative learning? Whereas the business community has a clear, numerical bottom line (called profit) to measure success and failure, the helping professions often have difficulty measuring and demonstrating the effectiveness of their work.

Where the team model has been used in education and child care the standards of excellence have usually been clearly articulated by both teams and administrators following a period of open discussion and consensus decision making about values, goals, and approaches. Teams function best when there are clear standards that everyone can use to evaluate the team's success and failure.

7. *External Support and Recognition:* Teams need resources to achieve their goals, support from key individuals and related organizations, and recognition and rewards for their performance. Successful teams see themselves as working in a way that is compatible with the organization's philosophy and values. They receive support from their supervisors and are given recognition and rewards when they achieve their goals.

It has been noted that in the helping professions the importance of working together is accepted so routinely and casually that it has become a cliché without meaning (Garrett, 1955). Teamwork loses its meaning and importance when external resources, support, and recognition for teams are not forthcoming from the organization and from the administrators who oversee the work of the teams. Team members can become discouraged and cynical when no one seems to care whether the teams meet or not or whether they achieve their goals. In such an environment, "teamwork" can quickly become another one of those trends that are eventually discarded on the junk heap of outlived, educational fads.

8. *Principled Leadership:* Larson and LaFasto discussed three behaviors of effective leaders that they found consistently in the extensive literature on management and leadership: Effective leaders establish a vision, create change, and unleash talent. Also, two deficits of ineffective leaders were analyzed, including the unwillingness to confront and resolve issues related to inadequate performance of team members and the tendency to dilute the team's efforts with too many different priorities.

Education and child care have a long history of the superintendent and principal as the primary authority figures, the ones with all the power who made the major decisions. In that tradition, teachers were expected to exercise leadership in their own rooms with their own children but not very much outside their classrooms. The team model requires a different style of leadership. In order to achieve the benefits of participatory decision making and management, administrators have to learn to share power and to delegate decision making to those who will have to carry out the decisions. Teachers, parents, and other professionals have to learn how to exercise and share leadership with their fellow team members, how to conduct a team meeting, and how to reach consensus. In the team model, principled leadership is required on the part of both the program administrators and the members of the teams.

These eight characteristics of effectively functioning teams provide criteria that can be used in evaluating teamwork in schools and child care settings. If an organization is having difficulty in achieving the desired level of effectiveness on the part of its teams, it may be helpful to examine the degree to which these eight characteristics are present. As has been noted previously, teamwork does not occur just because a group of adults are called a team instead of a committee, a task force, or a department. Teamwork is a complex process of interactions among persons working together. And even when conditions support teamwork, it does not occur automatically but develops over time as teams move through a number of predictable stages.

STAGES OF TEAM DEVELOPMENT

Teams progress through various stages of development that affect their ability to facilitate communication, make decisions, implement plans, and resolve conflicts (Brill, 1976; Francis & Young, 1979; Tuckman, 1965). Professionals who work in organizations using the team model have observed that teams differ from one another in their level of performance, even when they operate within almost identical environments. Even though the external structure and support system for teams may be very similar, team function will vary significantly based on each team's stage of development. Brief descriptions of the style of the meetings of two teams demonstrate how teams at different stages of development might function.

Team A conducts meetings that are energizing to its members. During these meetings, information is shared efficiently, and everyone participates. As a result, all team members have a shared awareness of the issues and concerns that the team needs to address. Before engaging in detailed discussions and problem solving, the team prioritizes the various issues on the agenda through a consensus decision-making process. Open and lively discussions lead to creative team solutions to complex problems, and assignments are made to implement the team's decisions. During the process of the meeting, team members give encouragement and support to one another. Leadership is shared and shifts among team members as the topics change. The members leave the meeting with a renewed sense of the team's goals and awareness of what each person needs to do to help the team achieve its objectives. Team A has been working together for quite a while and has not experienced any turnover of staff in the past year. The members are proud of their team and its accomplishments.

Team B conducts meetings that are often tiring, boring, and stressful to its members. During these meetings, team members are careful about what they say and how they say it. In this team one has to be sensitive to the different turfs being protected around the table. A number of hidden agendas keep the team from being able to make decisions about even small issues. Sometimes team members compete with one another for control of the meeting, while others withdraw and do not participate in the team process. During such meetings, team members wonder why the team was ever formed and why somebody does not do something to make it work better. Team B has existed almost as long as Team A but has experienced a great deal of staff turnover in the past six months. The members of this team are somewhat discouraged, but they are not giving up. Two team members have been through this before and know that things will improve as soon as the team works through this difficult stage of its development.

In reading the descriptions of these two team meetings, one might be tempted to simply label Team A as "a functioning team" and Team B as "a dysfunctional team." However, such labels do not adequately account for the fact that teams that are currently functioning at high levels of effectiveness have previously gone through stages of development that were typified by some of the problematic interactions being experienced by Team B. Teams, like individuals, grow and change over time in ways that are predictable and deserving of the term "stages of team development."

Tuckman (1965) described four stages of team development: forming, storming, norming, and performing. During the first stage, which Francis and Young (1979) called "testing" and Brill (1976) called "orientation," the team members seek a shared sense of the team's purpose and identity as well as their individual roles on the team. At this point the trust level is low, and members are guarded in what they say, staying on the topic, and not expressing strongly held, personal points of view. During the forming stage, team members are getting to know one another, developing relationships and alliances, and testing the environment for what is and is not acceptable behavior in the team.

The second stage of team development includes behaviors described as storming or infighting (Francis & Young, 1979), in which the team seeks group values, norms, and procedures. During this stage some team members express their confusion regarding the team's purpose and authority. Someone usually suggests that an administrator be called in to clarify matters. As conflict is experienced, some members may begin to feel stuck or to withdraw from the team's process. The interaction pattern at this stage of group development has been described as distorted, angry, and confrontive (Stanford & Roark, 1974). However, the open expression of differences can serve to increase the trust level of the group, especially when it becomes clear that the team provides a safe place where differences can be discussed and common ground explored. Some teams may need additional training or an outside consultant to assist them in working through the storming stage, which is clearly the most difficult stage for teams to work through.

A transition period leads to the "norming" stage, where the whole team has a shared sense of their purpose, procedures, expectations, and traditions. During this stage all members of the team begin to share their perspectives and concerns. A greater balance is now achieved between the tasks the team has to achieve and group maintenance concerns, such as how the team goes about making decisions. During this stage of team development, team members begin to take more risks and to give and receive feedback during the team meetings. The norming stage builds the pride and confidence of the team members and lays the groundwork for the performing stage.

Teams in the performing stage experience high levels of cohesiveness and team identity. These teams are both efficient and effective. They can get the job done, and the team members enjoy the process of working together. Teams at this highest stage of development are characterized by their flexibility, being able to move easily from team tasks to individual issues to team concerns. Leadership is shared in conducting the team meeting and in providing expertise on specific issues. In the performing stage, team members are more willing to take risks and to express their appreciation and affection for one another. During this stage the team provides a supportive environment in which team members can further develop their individual personal and professional skills.

This description of teams moving through various stages of team development communicates the highly interactive nature of teamwork as well as some of the skills that team members need to develop in order to achieve the full benefits of teamwork.

SUMMARY AND CONCLUSIONS

In the 1990s, teamwork is emerging as the preferred means of organizing and managing businesses, schools, child care organizations, and other human services programs. The team model brings together people who share responsibility for achieving common goals and objectives. It breaks down the territorial barriers created in hierarchical, departmentalized organizations. Schools are being restructured, using teams that increase participation in and ownership for the change process. Parents and teachers and other professionals are coming together to build collaborative relationships and to establish a shared vision for the future of neighborhood schools.

Teams now play a central role in school programs for students with disabilities. Multidisciplinary teams that include parents have responsibility for major decisions such as eligibility for services, instructional planning, and evaluation of progress. Teams are being used to provide integrated therapy so that children can receive services within the context of their daily lives instead of in isolated settings. Early intervention programs are using a transdisciplinary approach to teamwork that allows role release among the team members.

Many residential schools and programs that provide 24-hour-a-day programming and supervision are using the team model to structure their organizations and to ensure that the children and youth have consistently therapeutic experiences. Programs using the PPC model of intervention have demonstrated the power of a united group of adolescents and staff in effecting change with youth who have in the past shown extremely challenging behaviors.

The application of the team model in such a wide variety of educational and child care settings has provided experience that can serve as the basis for future developments. The characteristics of effective teams have been identified as well as the stages that teams progress through as they develop and change over time. Different models of teamwork have been developed to meet different goals and to adapt to the specific needs of children and youth.

The following chapters of this book explore the rich and exciting experiences of professionals who have directly implemented the team approach in education and child care. In the process of writing their respective chapters the authors were encouraged to speak from their experience, even if they did not always have hard research to "prove" their points. As a result, the reader has the opportunity to benefit from professionals who have worked directly with teams serving children and youth, who have completely reorganized large programs according to the team model, who have taken risks in trusting teams to make decisions in areas that were previously "for administration only," and who have provided consultation and training to others in the exciting, and sometimes scary, process of change.

REFERENCES

Brendtro, L., & Mitchell, M. (1983). The organizational ethos: From tension to teamwork. In L. Brendtro & A. Ness (Eds.), *Re-educating troubled youth: Environments for teaching and treatments* (pp. 94–120). New York: Aldine.

Brill, N. I. (1976). *Teamwork: Working together in the human services.* Philadelphia: J. B. Lippincott.

Comer, J. (1987). New Haven's school-community connection. *Educational Leadership, 44*(6), 13–16.

Deming, E. (1982). *Out of crisis.* Cambridge, MA: Massachusetts Institute of Technology, Center for Advanced Engineering Study.

Erb, T., & Doda, N. (1989). *Team organization: Promise—practices and possibilities.* Washington, DC: National Education Association.

Francis, D., & Young, D. (1979). *Improving work groups: A practical manual for team building.* San Diego, CA: University Associates.

Garner, H. G. (1982). *Teamwork in programs for children and youth: A handbook for administrators.* Springfield, IL: Thomas.

Garner, H. G. (1988). *Helping others through teamwork.* Washington, DC: Child Welfare League of America.

Garrett, J. G. (1955). Social psychology of teamwork. In M. R. Harrower (Ed.), *Medical and psychological teamwork in the care of the chronically ill* (pp. 67–70). Springfield, IL: Thomas.

Giangreco, M., York, J., & Rainforth, B. (1989). Providing related services to learners with severe handicaps in educational settings: Pursuing the least restrictive option. *Pediatric Physical Therapy, 1*(2), 55–63.

Harrison, C., Killion, J., & Mitchell, J. (1989). Site-based management: The realities of implementation. *Educational Leadership, 46*(8), 55–58.

Krueger, M. (1990). Promoting professional teamwork. In J. Anglin et. al., *Perspectives in professional child and youth care* (pp. 123–131). New York: Haworth Press.

Larson, C. E., & LaFasto, F. M. (1989). *Teamwork: What must go right/what can go wrong.* Newbury Park, CA: Sage.

Losen, S., & Losen, J. (1985). *The special education team.* Boston: Allyn & Bacon.

Maeroff, G. (1993). Building teams to rebuild schools. *Phi Delta Kappa, 74*(7), 512–519.

Mann, N. (1985). *The keys to excellence: The story of the Deming philosophy.* Los Angeles: Prestwick Books.

Morsink, C., Thomas, C., & Correa, V. (1991). *Interactive teaming: Consultation and collaboration in special programs.* New York: Macmillan.

Moses, M., & Whitaker, K. (1990). Ten components for school restructuring. *The School Administrator, 47*(10), 28–29.

Peters, T., & Waterman, R. (1982). *In search of excellence: Lessons from America's best-run companies.* New York: Harper & Row.

Rainforth, B., York, J., & Macdonald, C. (1992). *Collaborative teams for students with severe disabilities: Integrating therapy and educational services.* Baltimore, MD: Brookes.

Scherkenbach, W. (1991). *The Deming route to quality and productivity: Road maps and roadblocks.* Washington, DC: Ceepress Books.

Stanford, G., & Roark, A. (1974). *Human interaction in teaching.* Boston: Allyn & Bacon.

Timar, T. (1989). The politics of school restructuring. *Phi Delta Kappa, 71,* 265–274.

Tuckman, B. W. (1965). Developmental sequences in small groups. *Psychological Bulletin, 63,* 384–399.

Vorrath, H., & Brendtro, L. (1974). *Positive peer culture.* Chicago: Aldine.

Whitaker, K., & Moses, M. (1990). Beyond the rhetoric of restructuring. Paper presented at the annual meeting of the University Council of Educational Administration, Pittsburgh, PA.

Whitehouse, F. (1951). Teamwork: An approach to a higher professional level. *Exceptional Children, 18*(1), 75–82.

Woodruff, G., & McGonigel, M. (1988). Early intervention approaches: The trandisciplinary model. In J. Jordan, J. Gallagher, P. Hutinger, & M. Karnes (Eds.), *Early childhood special education 0–3* (pp. 163–182). Reston, VA: Council for Exceptional Children.

▶ 2

The Power and Use of Teams in Schools

Charles C. Sharman   Harold S. Wright, Jr.

INTRODUCTION

Even though most people associate teams with sports and games and not with business, industry, or education, the reality is that teams have become the centerpiece of organizational change. Many of our top organizations today use teams not only to increase productivity but also to solve complex problems, to create a sense of direction for the organization, and to help the organization increase its chances of surviving in an increasingly competitive world.

For the past century the primary means of managing and leading formal organizations did not involve teams but instead relied heavily on "top-down management." In this system, leaders, those at the top, made most of the critical decisions, and workers, those lower in the hierarchy, were expected to carry out those decisions. In the military, the automobile industry, service industries—virtually all organizations— there was a sharp demarcation between leaders and followers. Followers, especially, were not expected to play any major role in the leadership or decision-making aspects of the organization. This model was relatively successful until the mid-1960s for most U.S. organizations.

Prior to the mid-1960s, American companies were dominant throughout the world with respect to leadership, product development, market share, and productivity. Products from countries such as Japan, Germany, and Taiwan were perceived to be inferior to U.S. products and were thought to pose little threat to our companies or country. Then a funny thing happened on the way to the twenty-first century. In a relatively short period of time, products manufactured in numerous foreign countries became not only competitive with products from the United States but in many instances surpassed the quality of goods and services produced by their U.S. competitors. For the first time in over a century some of our leading companies began to lose market share and profitability. This happened in industries ranging from automobile manufacturing to those producing steel, television sets, and electronics. The overwhelming question for most American companies became, "What happened?" This was not a question with an easy answer or answers, but the Japanese, Germans, and others clearly had begun doing some things differently than many of their U.S. competitors. One difference was that these successful foreign companies had begun to build a sense of ownership of and commitment to performance excellence among their employees that our threatened U.S. companies were unable to match. One major way these foreign companies built this sense of ownership and commitment was by developing and using teams in their organizations.

Teamwork in the Animal Kingdom

When asked to think about teamwork, many people think of teamwork as a human invention. In reality, teamwork occurs in the animal kingdom as well. For example, geese are marvelous practitioners of teamwork. By flying in a *V* formation as a team, geese are able to fly 71 percent farther than if each bird flew alone. This occurs because, as each bird flaps its wings, an updraft is created for the bird following. When the bird flying lead in the formation gets tired, it rotates out of that position and lets another bird lead until that bird tires, at which point the leadership is rotated again, and again, and again. Geese also have enough sense to stay focused on their common goals. When they are flying toward a destination, their common goal, all birds stay in formation. If a bird drops out of the formation, it immediately loses the support of its teammates in front and begins to drop back behind the team. When this happens to a smart goose, it quickly rejoins the team to benefit from the team's coordinated efforts. Otherwise, in a very short period of time, it will be a lonely flock of one.

Geese are very protective and supportive of one another, also. When a bird is wounded and falls out of formation, two other birds leave the formation and follow the wounded bird down. They then stay with the downed bird until it is able to rejoin the flock or dies. Another way geese support one another is through their oral communication skills via honking. The geese in the back of the formation honk to encourage those in front. When we work with others, do we honk, and if we do honk, is it to encourage our teammates? This concept of teamwork in the animal kingdom is observable in many other higher developed species such as porpoises and gorillas.

Teamwork Makes the Difference

Teamwork is not a human invention, but humans have taken the concept to new levels. Teamwork has always been used in varying degrees in families, sports, business, and schools, but in recent years it has become increasingly clear that teamwork is essential in all of the aforementioned if they are to reach their greatest potential.

While many U.S. businesses have had great difficulty remaining competitive on a worldwide basis, and others have even gone out of business, a number of U.S. businesses have prospered during the same period of time. Companies such as Ford, AT&T, 3M, and John Deere have not only withstood attacks from worldwide competitors but have managed to thrive. These successful companies have numerous similarities. One thing they all have in common is their use of teams; many people in these organizations attribute much of their success to their building and using teams in creative and innovative ways (Tucker, 1988; Herrick, 1985).

One early question then becomes, "How do teams make such a difference in some organizations?" While there are many possible answers to this question, one set of responses includes the concepts of involvement, commitment, and responsibility. By using teams it is possible to actively involve large numbers of people in making critical decisions. Active, meaningful involvement in decision making is the first step in building ownership and commitment. Under top-down management, people working at lower levels were basically told what to do, how to do it, when to do it, and to what level of quality. In this atmosphere it was difficult to build a strong sense of responsibility and commitment among workers. Without commitment and responsibility many workers just did what they were told, no more, and often a little less. Where teams are involved in making critical decisions, however, team members are much more likely to assume responsibility for their decisions and actions and to be committed to improving the organization in meaningful ways. And this is precisely what has been missing in many of the past efforts to change and reform America's schools.

THE NEED FOR EDUCATIONAL CHANGE

A Crisis in American Education

Schools, like other U.S. organizations, have traditionally been managed in a top-down fashion. School boards hired the superintendent who hired and supervised the principals who hired and supervised the teachers. This system seemed to work fairly effectively for schools until the late 1950s to 1960s. Since then, however, the schools have come under increasing attack from a variety of sources. For example, in 1983 the National Commission on Excellence in Education published *A Nation At Risk,* which was very critical of the public schools and attributed many of the negative happenings in the country to a decline in public school effectiveness. A recent National Assessment of Educational Progress report (Applebee, Langer, & Mullis, 1989) also castigated the schools when it noted that among all 17-year-olds in the United States, only 17 percent were prepared for college-level science, only 6 percent were prepared for college-level math, and only 5 percent were able to read at the college level. In the same light, Albert Shanker (1990), a long-time advocate of education and head of the

American Federation of Teachers, stated: "After more than six years of intensive effort, public education in America is still on the verge of disaster" (p. 345). One could cite other criticisms, but it suffices to say the schools have received their share of negative attention, particularly since the late 1950s.

Top-Down School Reform

In response to these criticisms the schools, just like their business counterparts, have gone through numerous waves of reform. For those who have been around long enough, do you remember Sputnik? In 1957 the U.S.S.R. launched the first successful, orbiting, nonmanned space satellite. The United States' responded to this highly technical and complicated achievement with dismay and anger. Politicians and the American public placed much of the blame for Russia's gaining a space advantage over the United States on the public schools. Many believed that the schools should have been more efficient in developing the quality and quantity of scientists and mathematicians needed to be the first to place a satellite in space.

As a result of the Russian space success the U.S. government took the most direct action it had ever taken with respect to the public schools. One major federal response was the development of a series of curricular programs that became known by titles such as BSCS Biology, CHEM Study, and SMSG math. The federal government spent an enormous amount of money on these and similar science and math programs that were marginally successful in the long run. In developing these new curricula the government hired noted experts in their respective fields and put them together on special committees, such as biology or chemistry, and then charged them with developing state-of-the-art curricula for the nation's public schools. After the curricula were developed and packaged, they were then presented from the "top down" to the schools as finished products. It should be noted that these curriculum committees had very few or no public school teachers on them, especially in the early developmental stages. As a result, many of the science and mathematics curricula, especially the initial versions, had limited use in the schools without being significantly modified and adapted (Meade, 1991).

The critical point here is the top-down approach of developing and disseminating these federally initiated programs. Teachers had little or no input in conceptualizing and producing the programs or in planning how to use them in their schools. Consequently, teachers had limited understanding of the programs and little sense of commitment or ownership for them. The programs were therefore either modified by teachers to make them more effective in the schools, or they were abandoned. Although these federal efforts to intervene in the schools were intended to be helpful, the programs met with limited success (Meade, 1991). These 1950s–1960s reform efforts were followed by other change movements such as the British Primary School movement, the Open School movement, Back-to-Basics movement, and so on.

Why weren't these reforms more successful? As always, there are numerous answers to this question, but one response focuses on this issue of programs' being developed at the top and then imposed on those below. In all of the previous attempts at reform, teachers and administrators on the front lines were not appropriately involved and were left out of the decision-making loop at critical points. As a result, they had less than optimal commitment to the change effort and felt limited responsibility for implementing the proposed innovations and making them work.

To this point we have looked at some businesses that were faced with major problems and how they began using teams to help them overcome obstacles. We have also looked at how schools have been subjected to a plethora of criticisms over the past three decades and some attempts to respond to these criticisms. Now, let's shift our focus to how teams are today being developed and used in educational settings.

TEAMS IN SCHOOLS

Traditionally teams have not been heavily used in public schools. However, the tendency to use teams meaningfully in schools has been increasing, especially during the last two decades. For example, many site-based–management schools have made teams a key component of their school improvement efforts. Also, teams are used extensively in a variety of special education settings.

School accreditation is another area of education that has begun to recommend and advocate the use of teams as a means for bringing about school improvement. School accreditation affects virtually all schools in the United States and plays an extremely significant role in the school improvement movement. The following look at school accreditation's impetus for teamwork provides a tangible vehicle for demonstrating how teams can be useful in bringing about school improvement.

Teams and the School Accreditation Process

Seven regional accrediting agencies serve the United States. One of them is the Southern Association of Colleges and Schools (SACS). This regional accrediting agency serves 11 southern states, and it is the team-based accreditation model developed by this agency that will be explored in detail here. SACS, like all the accrediting agencies, has been heavily involved in school reform and restructuring for many years, but especially since the early 1980s. Much of the reform and restructuring efforts since the early 1980s have been based on John Goodlad's work *A Place Called School* (1984).

Briefly, in the past, SACS used (and still offers) a traditional method for accrediting schools that involved six steps: (1) schools "working as usual" for several years, (2) an intensive year of self-study, (3) an on-site visit by a team created by SACS, (4) several more years of "working as usual," (5) an interim visit, and (6) a repetition of the entire cycle. The evaluative criteria for this traditional method involved questions such as: Were teachers certified for their respective assignments, did the pupil-teacher ratio meet predetermined criteria, and was there sufficient support staff available? This approach focused primarily on inputs and not outputs. Incidentally, this process is the one that has been and/or is still being used by many accrediting agencies and state departments of education for accrediting schools.

During the early 1980s, however, SACS and other national accrediting agencies interested in school reform studied alternative methods of school accreditation. As a result of these efforts, SACS developed an alternative approach to school accreditation that focuses much less on inputs and much more on outcomes (A School Renewal Project, 1990). Although most schools currently accredited by SACS may choose between the traditional method or the newer, method, since the late 1980s, an increasing number of schools have abandoned the traditional approach and are adopting the alternative method for their accreditation process. This approach has a number of features that are essential to the discussion of teams and school improvement. Some key elements of the SACS alternative approach to accreditation are based on the following assumptions and assertions:

- Continuous school improvement is a key component of the movement. Meaningful school improvement is a never ending process.
- School improvement results from involvement of the professional staff at the local school level in planning and implementing programs designed to address the needs of that school.
- Each school has the professional capability to make key decisions affecting the quality of education provided by that school.
- To successfully meet accreditation standards, each school must show continuous progress and gains with respect to specified areas of the school program. SACS identified five such areas for their schools, and those wishing to be accredited under the new program are required to show continuous growth in each area over an extended period of time. These growth areas are:

1. Curriculum and instruction
2. Communication
3. Planning
4. School climate
5. Staff development

Progress of the schools involved in the alternative accreditation process is reviewed informally on a regular basis and formally every five years. Each local school faculty has the responsibility for setting its own agenda for improvement during this five-year period.

A program such as the SACS alternative accreditation process raises some entirely new issues with respect to optimal school structure and function. For such programs to be effective, schools must have involvement and commitment from all members of the faculty, not just from the formal leadership and/or a chosen few. To obtain this type of involvement and commitment, the team concept must become much more prevalent in a school than was previously the case.

When schools are given the freedom and responsibility to design and implement their own structures and programs, many differences emerge. However, there are (fortunately) also some major similarities found in different schools, especially those that are using the team concept. Let's now focus on schools that are using team approaches to continuous school improvement and review several aspects of these schools.

There are two basic types of teams used in schools today—the leadership team and the action team. Both types of teams are critical for continuous school improvement.

The Leadership Team

The *leadership team* is the most critical team found in schools using the team concept. This team may also be called the planning team, the school improvement team, or similar names. For this team to achieve its potential, the following minimal steps and actions must take place.

1. Appropriate members of the major constituents or stakeholders in the school and community must serve on this team. Leadership teams that seem to be having the most success are composed of teachers, administrators, parents, specialists, support staff, business partners, and other involved persons.

2. Once the categories of major stakeholders have been identified, the major "movers and shakers" in these various groups are identified and recruited. The "movers and shakers" are the leaders and the doers—the people who are able to get things done in a school. Among their many attributes, "movers and shakers" have the requisite expertise to be contributing team members and have credibility with the school community and are therefore able to provide quality leadership.

3. After the team has been assembled, the team must have the time, resources, and training necessary to learn to function as a team. Leadership teams that seem to experience considerable difficulty in functioning productively are often those teams that have not received adequate team-building training. "Teams" without requisite team-building skills may actually be nothing more than committees and function at a relatively low level of productivity. Team members without teamwork skills usually exhibit considerable confusion, frustration, and anxiety during team meetings and dealings. Team building is never finished and is an ongoing process that must be revisited and renewed on a regular basis.

Once the leadership team is in place and functioning, the team has a number of duties and actions it needs to perform. With respect to some of these duties and actions, successful leadership teams:

- Play a leadership role in developing a clear sense of direction for the school. Specifically, the leadership team is responsible for developing the school's vision and mission and for determining the specific goals the school will strive to achieve over the short and long term.
- Are responsible for building support from the entire school community for the school's vision, mission, and goals.
- Are responsible for clarifying, refining, and explaining the decision-making process used by the school to all members of the school community, especially the professional staff.
- Strive to have all the teams in the school focus on instruction and children and not dissipate their efforts on trivial or routine matters.
- Actively support team building at all levels throughout the school and community.
- Create implementing or action teams that will assume responsibility for achieving the specific goals developed by the leadership team.
- Coordinate the work of all the teams and keep them focused instead of permitting them to go off on tangents.
- Monitor, measure, and report the work of all the teams on a regular basis.

Action Teams

Like leadership teams, action teams go by a variety of names such as the implementing teams or design teams. *Action teams* will be the name used in this chapter. Action teams are the teams that are responsible for doing all the things that are necessary to actually achieve a given goal or goals.

After the leadership team has identified the major goals for the school, the first task for the leadership team involves creating an action team for each goal. In doing this the leadership team goes through the same four steps that were followed when they were created. Starting with the particular goal, the leadership team:

- Identifies the constituencies, i.e., parents, teachers, students, etc., required if the team is to be successful
- Determines the number of people needed to adequately represent each constituent group
- Determines the particular method or methods they will use for selecting people, i.e., using volunteers, "drafting" people, or using the election method
- Strives to obtain commitment from those invited to join the action team

As leadership teams address the most important issues in a school, especially those that relate to instruction and students, they need to identify a relatively small number of goals, usually three to five, for action teams to pursue. When schools try to work on a large number of goals all at the same time, it becomes very difficult to keep the teams focused and coordinated. For example, all types of vital resources tend to be scarce in most schools, and when large numbers of teams start competing for the same resources (e.g., people, time, money, meeting space), cooperation among teams often turns into unhealthy competition. In these dysfunctional, competitive situations the support, commitment, and responsibility people have worked so hard to build often become dissipated. It is at this stage that some schools revert to top down management and give up on the team concept.

With the aforementioned caveats in mind, assume that the leadership team has identified three major goals for the school to achieve. It is time to now see an "action team" in action.

A CASE STUDY: SPRINGFIELD MIDDLE SCHOOL

Springfield Middle School has a diverse student body of approximately 900 students. Sixty-five percent of the students are on free lunch, and student achievement is far below state standards. The Springfield leadership team worked long and hard exploring how to improve student performance and developed several goals designed to achieve this goal. After an extensive review of the literature, the leadership team felt that it was critical that the entire school community work to increase parental involvement in the school, and they established one of their goals as follows: "We will increase all aspects of parental involvement in Springfield Middle School at least 5 percent per year for the next three years." The leadership team developed other goals, but for discussion purposes let's focus on this one goal; increasing parental involvement. Once the leadership team developed this goal, their next task was to create an action team that would strive to achieve it.

Creating an Action Team

The Springfield leadership team took this aspect of the school improvement process very seriously. When creating this action team, the first task involved identifying the stakeholders who should be involved in pursuing the "increasing parental involvement" goal. The team used brainstorming to do this, creating a list of stakeholders: parents, teachers, administrators, students, social workers, clergy, and representatives from the central office. All these groups were identified as having a vested interest in the goal of increasing parental involvement in the school.

After identifying the stakeholders, the leadership team next determined how many people were needed from each of the categories identified. They decided that the action team needed five parents, three teachers, one local school administrator, two students, two social workers, three members of the clergy, and one representative from the central office who had considerable expertise in school-community affairs. The key criterion for determining the number of participants from each category was balance. It seemed obvious that the goal of increasing parental involvement called for a relatively large number of parents on the team. If the goal had been oriented toward instruction, they would have had a relatively larger number of teachers on the team.

After identifying the stakeholders and the number of stakeholders, the Springfield leadership team turned its attention to determining how it would actually select people. The leadership team discussed three ways of selecting members: (1) asking for volunteers, (2) using the election method, or (3) selecting people. Volunteers were solicited first, but it became clear that many of those who volunteered did not fit the criteria established earlier. They lacked the needed expertise or required credibility with their peer group. As a result, some volunteers were selected for the team and others were not. Perhaps an election was the way to go? The team realized that elections might be useful in another situation, but after considerable discussion the team decided not to use the election method. There were some key players the team needed but who had not volunteered. These people had the expertise and credibility needed, and the team took it upon themselves to select or "draft" these people.

Getting commitment from team members was another critical part of putting together an effective team. As individuals were invited to participate on the action team, the leadership team felt it was vital to discuss with them the issue of commitment. The leadership team worked hard to ensure that all members of all the teams in the school were committed to attending all meetings and would strive to be on time, follow team rules, and be prepared for team meetings.

Team Building

A group of people representative of all the constituencies necessary to increase parental involvement in Springfield Middle School had been identified and assembled, but they were still not a true team. One major mistake that many organizations make is to form a new group and put them to work immediately on solving real problems. Where this occurs, team members often do not know one another well, they have not built trust, they have not developed the essential skills required to be an effective team member, and they have not built a team knowledge base. Teams that do not build trust, develop essential skills, and form a necessary knowledge base are "teams at risk." Team members must have some essential understandings of themselves, how to relate to one another, and how to function as a team if they are to be reasonably effective. The Springfield action team still had to complete the early stages of team development before it could become an effective team.

Early in its development the Springfield "Parental Involvement Action Team" went on a two-day retreat with a consultant who specialized in team building. During these two days the team worked on three critical elements of team building: building *trust*, developing essential teamwork *skills*, and building a common *knowledge base*.

Building Trust. The consultant began the retreat by emphasizing that trust was the most critical element in team building. After a brainstorming activity the team developed the following statements about trust:

- Trust is fragile.
- Building trust is a never ending process.
- Trust comes from knowing and understanding ourselves, the others we work with, and how we all interrelate to improve learning for students at Springfield Middle School.

During the retreat the team engaged in a number of activities designed to build trust. Several commercial assessment instruments were used to help team members build increased understandings of themselves, their teammates, and their strengths and weaknesses.

Developing Skills. During the retreat the consultant also helped the team identify several skills essential for them to function effectively and worked with them to sharpen these selected skills. The skills identified as critical were:

- Communication—oral and written
- Brainstorming
- Consensus building
- Conflict resolution
- Conducting effective meetings
- Understanding the change process and how to foster change

In working on these critical skills, the consultant emphasized that they were in a safe environment and that it was important to practice these skills in this safe environment before using them on real issues. Numerous simulations were used during the two days to build/sharpen these critical skills.

Building a Knowledge Base. The third focus of the retreat involved building and expanding a common knowledge base. The team discussed the importance of everyone being exposed to a common knowledge base and then using that knowledge when making critical decisions. After another brainstorming session, the team came up with the following statements:

- Team decisions should be based on the most current research available.
- Best practice should be considered when making team decisions. For example, if another school was using a current innovation, Springfield team members would contact the school and solicit their input with respect to the effectiveness of the innovation.

- If the team decided to use a totally new innovation they had developed, the innovation should be tested, where possible, before being fully implemented.

Through brainstorming the team also developed a variety of means for building and expanding the team's knowledge base. Some methods they identified were:

- *Shared Reading:* It was decided that the team would select key articles and books and then set up a reading and discussion schedule where all members became familiar with major subjects pertinent to Springfield's needs.
- *Videotapes:* Team members felt that certain videotapes would be helpful to the team; a list of videos was actually started at the retreat to be expanded later.
- *Visitations:* It was decided that various team members would visit sites of activities and programs the Springfield team wished to learn more about. It was also decided that they would invite people to come to Springfield when appropriate to learn about ways of using innovations.
- Professional conferences and workshops were also listed as ways to increase the knowledge base.

At the end of the two day retreat, team members felt they had developed enough rapport and trust through team building to begin, in earnest, to address the issue of increasing parental involvement. Therefore, during the last two hours of the retreat, the action team developed a framework for a strategic plan to achieve their goal.

Space does not permit a full description of the next steps in this team's development. However, the reader might want to know that this "Springfield" team is not fictitious but a real team. Since their inception two years ago they have taken major steps toward increasing parental involvement in their school. For example, in two short years the team accomplished the following: They created a parent center; they now provide transportation for adults without transportation to back-to-school activities; and they have increased security around the school for evening functions to provide a safer environment for returning adults. As a result of these and similar activities, they have increased parental involvement significantly. They continue to work together in pursuit of this goal.

Before leaving this section, please remember that there were other action teams operating in the Springfield school, such as the Curriculum and Instruction Team, that worked similarly to bring about improvements in their respective areas. These teams had the same training and support the case study team had. Although each team had somewhat different experiences, they all followed a similar pattern and could have been reported on here.

Some final points need to be made and emphasized before closing. The case study team discussed here realized at the outset that building an effective team was a task that was never completed. As the team and situations changed, such as veteran team members leaving the team and new members coming on board, the team had to revisit the areas of trust, improving skills, and upgrading their knowledge base if they were to maintain their effectiveness. A second major point was that of focus. Early in the process the case study team determined its purpose and then stuck to achieving that purpose. They realized the need to resist pressures to try to solve a multitude of problems that were outside their primary purview. Instead, they maintained their focus on their primary goal—increasing parental involvement in the school. As evidenced by this example, teams have tremendous potential to improve schools, but this is only possible where team members have been carefully selected, developed, and used to achieve well-defined purposes.

SUMMARY AND CONCLUSIONS

During the past two decades the concept of teamwork has been actively employed by many U.S. companies to improve their productivity and competitiveness and has made a considerable difference in how these organizations operate and function. So, too, the idea of teachers, parents, students, and administrators working together as teams to solve the complex problems that face our nation's schools has become increasingly important. Teams are being used in such arenas as site-based–management schools, in a variety of special education settings, and as part of the school accreditation process as a vehicle to bring about school improvement.

The teamwork idea is exemplified in the school accreditation process, where SACS has offered an alternative to the traditional accreditation methods. The focus is on continuous school improvement by addressing curriculum and instruction, communication, planning, school climate, and staff development issues.

The process typically involves a leadership team and action teams. The leadership team's role encompasses developing clear direction for the school, building support, clarifying the decision-making process, actively supporting team building, creating action teams, and monitoring and measuring the outcomes of all teams. Action teams are responsible for doing all the things that are necessary to achieve a particular goal.

Finally, one must not forget that change is a slow process that takes place over a long period of time. In order for team building to be successful, trust must be developed among all the stakeholders, skills must be learned, and a knowledge base must be formed. Whether the school accreditation process is the focus at your school or whether another area is the focus, teachers, parents, students, and administrators working together to bring about improvement is a powerful force for change.

REFERENCES

Applebee, A., Langer, J., & Mullis, V. (1989). *Crossroads in American education: A summary of findings.* Princeton, NJ: National Assessment of Educational Progress and Educational Testing Service.

Goodlad, J. (1984). *A place called school.* New York: McGraw-Hill.

Herrick, N. (1985). Is the time finally ripe for educational democracy? *Social Policy, 16,* 53–56.

Meade, E. (1991). Foundations and the public schools: An impressionistic retrospective, 1960–1990. *Phi Delta Kappan, 73,* K1–12.

National Commission on Excellence in Education. (1983). *A nation at risk; The imperative for educational reform.* Washington, DC: U.S. Government Printing Office.

A school renewal project: An alternative route to regional accreditation. (1990). A joint project by the Commission on Elementary Schools and the Commission on Secondary Schools of the Southern Association of Colleges and Schools. DeKalb, GA: DeKalb County School System.

Shanker, A. (1990). The end of the traditional model of schooling and a proposal for using incentives to restructure our public schools. *Phi Delta Kappan, 71,* 345–357.

Tucker, M. S. (1988, February). Peter Drucker, knowledge work, and the structure of schools. *Educational Leadership, 45,* 44–46.

▶ 3

The Transdisciplinary Model in Educational Programs for Students with Severe Disabilities

Fred P. Orelove

Consider the following two individuals:

Luis is a 7-year-old boy who lives with his parents and younger brother. He responds to other people, especially children, through changes in his facial expression and eye movements. He also communicates through making sounds and by crying and laughing. Luis likes to eat noodles, oranges, and cookies, which are cut into small pieces and fed to him. He gets around by others pushing him in his wheelchair. He has limited use of his arms and needs some help with washing, dressing, and other daily routines. Luis enjoys music, his cat, his brother, and the Chicago Cubs. He is enrolled in a second-grade class in his neighborhood school, where he receives special education support services from a variety of professionals.

Ramona is an 18-year-old girl who attends a combined high school class with other students with disabilities. She sits in the cafeteria at a table with other children from her class. Sometimes she reaches over and takes food from other students' trays. When she is frustrated, she will try to hit staff or herself or will run out of the room. Ramona has two or three manual signs but does not use them accurately or reliably. Ramona is the only child of a single mother, and her grandparents also live with her. She especially enjoys dancing and looking at magazines.

Like millions of other youngsters in the United States, Luis and Ramona have particular learning, social-emotional, and health needs that require the specialized services and support of professionals. These needs present challenges: How should we get this child to communicate more effectively what he or she wants? What can we do to reduce this child's propensity to hit other people? How should we deal with the social impact of this child's gastrostomy (feeding) tube? What should we do to prepare this child for a job?

Consider that these questions may all be legitimately asked about the *same child*, and that the answer to one question affects the strategies for answering the others, and that no one person has all the information or skills to answer them or to put answers into practice. It becomes easy to appreciate that the most difficult challenge is not responding to the questions themselves but, rather, doing so in a way that maximizes the sharing of information and skills of all participants to solve complex problems with creativity, flexibility, and accountability. This is the purpose behind transdisciplinary teamwork and the reason why this model evolved.

This chapter examines the transdisplinary model in some detail. It looks at the organization, features, and benefits of the model and explores some of the challenges of applying the model within educational settings.

ORGANIZATION, FEATURES, AND BENEFITS

Contrast with Other Models

To appreciate the framework of the transdisciplinary model, it may be helpful to contrast it with two other well-known team approaches, the multidisciplinary and the interdisciplinary models.

Multidisciplinary. The multidisciplinary approach evolved from the medical model, in which various persons with expertise in diverse areas bring their particular knowledge to a specific patient (Hart, 1977). In educational settings this approach has been used chiefly to conduct an initial evaluation of a child with a disability. Professionals within this model work in isolation, not only to evaluate, but to provide services (Orelove & Sobsey, 1991). For example, Luis's teacher may be working on methods for teaching him to wash his face, while the occupational therapist is determining ways to get Luis to grasp objects and to increase the flexibility and range of his arm movements. In this situation neither person considers the ways in which these two activities overlap or how they can be combined into a more useful, more efficient approach. Moreover, Luis's parents need to talk separately with the teacher and the therapist to get information on Luis's progress, and the two professionals may offer contradictory information.

Interdisciplinary. The interdisciplinary model, in contrast, is designed to allow team members to communicate among themselves and to share information. However, although programming decisions are made by the group, assessment and implementation remain discipline-specific (McCormick & Goldman, 1979). In Ramona's situation, for example, the teacher and the vocational specialist may have talked over their frustration with Ramona's hitting and even come up with a plan, but the two interpret the strategies for dealing with the behavior quite differently, resulting in varying degrees of success and a confused child and mother. Thus, both the multidisciplinary and interdisciplinary approaches promote either isolation or competition, with program implementation being, at best, disjointed (Giangreco, York, & Rainforth, 1989).

Organization of Transdisciplinary Model

As suggested earlier, the transdisciplinary approach was developed to deal in a more unified way with the multiple needs of individuals (originally infants with cerebral palsy and other developmental delays). The term *transdisciplinary* is defined as being "of, or relating to a transfer of information, knowledge, or skills across disciplinary boundaries" (United Cerebral Palsy, 1976, p. 1). In practice, one team member typically acts as a coordinator or "synthesizer" (Bricker, 1976), with all members contributing to the overall effort, both in formulating and implementing decisions.

Features of Transdisciplinary Model

Role Release.   The sharing, or transfering, of information and skills across disciplines is an essential feature of the transdisciplinary model. The term *role release* was coined to refer to a releasing of some functions of one's primary discipline to other team members (Lyon & Lyon, 1980; United Cerebral Palsy, 1976). The practice of role release is viewed as enhancing both services to the individual with a disability and the skills of the team members.

Several steps or processes are involved in role release. Woodruff and McGonigel (1988) termed this sequence "role transition," which includes the following processes (incorporating examples based on Luis and Ramona):

1. *Role Extension*: This is self-directed study and other efforts to increase one's understanding, knowledge, and skills in one's own discipline. The speech therapist, for example, might enroll in a special seminar on the assessment and implementation of nonverbal communication strategies to assist Ramona.

2. *Role Enrichment*: This stage involves team members developing an awareness and understanding of the terminology and basic practices of other disciplines. Luis's physical therapist, for example, might deliver a workshop to the teacher and other related services staff on disordered movement, including the technical terms used to describe movement and posture.

3. *Role Expansion*: This suggests that a team member will acquire sufficient information from other disciplines on the team to make knowledgeable observations and program recommendations outside his or her discipline. The paraprofessional, for instance, might determine that Ramona needs to have her visual acuity tested and mentions it to the teacher, who in turn makes a referral to the vision specialist.

4. *Role Exchange*: In this stage the team member learns the theory, methods, and procedures of other disciplines and begins to implement the techniques *under the observation of the appropriate team member*. Luis's teacher, for instance, might attempt a new technique for helping Luis eat while the occupational therapist sits nearby and offers feedback.

5. *Role Release*: Similar to the preceding stage, this involves more independence for the team member, with the accountable discipline offering consultation but not constant supervision. For instance, Ramona's mother shows the staff a technique for calming Ramona when she is frustrated, and, after the staff get the hang of it, they use the technique with success.

6. *Role Support*: This involves informal encouragement from fellow team members and, when necessary, backup support and assistance by the team member from the relevant discipline. For instance, the calming technique with Ramona begins to lose effectiveness for a particular team member, and another team member observes and offers suggestions for fine-tuning the technique.

As might be expected, giving up part of one's functions, even temporarily, can be threatening. The degree to which someone can do this is a good measure of that individual's own confidence and of his or her trust in and from the other team members. Clearly, role release is a process that must be actively worked on by the team, with support from the administration.

It is important also to understand that role release, when operating most effectively, involves a fluid, multidirectional sharing of responsibilities across team members. Teams in which one particular individual always gives up control to another (in educational settings, usually the therapist to the teacher), with no reciprocity, do not represent a true transdisciplinary model.

Finally, releasing one's role does not entail relinquishing one's accountability. "The [transdisciplinary approach] is not preparing 'unitherapists' who can be all things to all people. . . . Each team member remains accountable for what is taught, to whom it is taught, how well it is learned, and the resulting child and family centered benefits of the teaching" (United Cerebral Palsy, 1976, p. 3).

Integrated Therapy.   The multidisciplinary and interdisciplinary models described previously share a common weakness within educational settings: *All* therapy services are provided directly by therapists, usually apart from other team members (Orelove & Sobsey, 1991). This results in two problems. First, the multiple needs of the learners require the knowledge and skills of professionals working together across a variety of disciplines. Second, requiring therapists to provide direct therapy at all times assumes incorrectly that a therapist will be available to teach learners during natural learning opportunities (Rainforth, York, & Macdonald, 1992).

An alternative is to integrate therapy services into the daily instructional context. For instance, a team that wanted to help Luis develop mobility skills might teach him during times when he needs to make transitions, such as moving between activities in the classroom or when traveling to or from the cafeteria. The goal of integrated therapy in general is to create services that enhance the student's participation in daily life. The important issue is not necessarily *where* services are provided—therapy can be just as isolated within the classroom—but rather that the techniques are *integrated into the instruction* across the day.

As with role release, the concept of integrated therapy is sometimes misunderstood. It is not the case that all services are to be provided indirectly and that therapists stop working directly with students. While the transdisciplinary model does rely more heavily on consultative and indirect approaches, it would be very unwise for therapists to cease hands-on interaction with students (Giangreco, York, & Rainforth, 1989; York, Rainforth, & Giangreco, 1990). Dunn (1988, 1991) has clarified the distinctions among three models of service provision for occupational therapists—which hold true for many other related services staff. Arguing for a role for all three models, Dunn (1988) states:

> *Direct service* is time consuming and therefore costly, but can address very complex problems and be quickly adapted to meet the student's changing needs. *Monitoring* is more time efficient, since others carry out the programs, but the student's health and safety must be considered. *Consultation* is an effective mechanism for providing ongoing environmental support, but requires special skills to be administered properly. (p. 721, emphasis added)

Another misconception about integrated therapy is that the approach leads to loss of professional identity. This does not happen in well-functioning transdisciplinary teams. Speaking of therapists who share and become an integral part of educational programs, York, Rainforth, and Giangreco (1990) note that "their teammates repeatedly comment about how much they value [them], [and] how therapy input and therapist collaboration has benefited students and families . . ." (p. 78).

Benefits of Transdisciplinary Model

Benefits for Professionals.   The transdisciplinary model is a collaborative model. As such, it results in promoting ". . . caring and committed relationships and skills critical for psychological health" (Rainforth, York, & Macdonald, 1992, p. 21). These skills include helping others achieve, coping with failure, managing conflict, confiding feelings, and so forth. Ideally, a team within a transdisciplinary model should be less territorial and competitive, realizing that success is measured by the degree to which the team works together to design and implement effective strategies.

The transdisciplinary model also enriches each team member's professional skills and contributions. Not only does each person learn *from* others, but—as teachers well know—there is much learned through *teaching* others.

Benefits for Students.   Naturally, the major benefits of any approach should accrue to the individuals with whom the professionals are working. The transdisciplinary model benefits students in several ways. First, the sharing of skills and information among team members yields a richness of problem solving and support for the learners. Second, the model views the learner holistically, rather than along disciplinary lines, resulting in an educational program that is more cohesive and beneficial to the student. Third, when combined with a particular approach to curriculum and instruction, the transdisciplinary model can be used to reduce the problems that learners with more severe disabilities have in acquiring new skills or in synthesizing, maintaining, and generalizing skills already gained (Orelove, in press). Fourth, transdisciplinary teams support unified, coordinated—and, it is hoped, more humanistic—approaches to dealing with students' challenging behaviors, resulting in more effective outcomes (Orelove, in press). Finally, by incorporating "therapy" in regular routines in typical settings during the day (e.g., the classroom rather than a therapy room), students preserve dignity and continuity of learning by not being removed from the flow of activities, and achieve the same skills more efficiently and through practice in functional (i.e., naturally occurring) activities.

Benefits for Families.   It has been suggested already that families benefit from the transdisciplinary approach through the designation of a team member to serve as a "synthesizer" of information, reducing the need for family members to "shop around" for information by having to speak to each team member separately. In addition, families gain new information and skills to better understand their children's learning and behavior. Most importantly, however, the best transdisciplinary teams treat parents with respect, including them in the decision-making process to the extent to which they desire to be involved. Teams best prepared to include parents in decision making are those that adhere to basic components of effective team functioning (Carney & Atwood, in press). Family involvement has long been a hallmark of effective early intervention programs (Hanson, 1985; Warren, Alpert, & Kaiser, 1986; see also Chapter 10 of this book).

CHALLENGES TO IMPLEMENTING THE TRANSDISCIPLINARY MODEL

Considering all the benefits of the transdisciplinary model, why don't more teams adopt the approach? One reason is that the approach is still not well known among school personnel. Despite the growing body of literature supporting and advocating transdisciplinary teams (e.g., Dunn, 1991; Giangreco, York, & Rainforth, 1989; Orelove & Sobsey, 1991; Rainforth, York, & Macdonald, 1992; York, Rainforth, & Dunn, 1990), the approach is not part of most university training programs and has not been incorporated into many textbooks. Another reason for the nonproliferation of the approach is that it requires a shift in values and philosophy and a great deal of work among individuals. Transdisciplinary teams—like all other teams—are made, not born, and require individual and collective reflection and consensus building, attributes that do not come easily to most people or groups. This section examines some of the challenges to implementing the transdisciplinary approach, grouped under the following three areas: (1) those that are largely *philosophical or professional*, (2) those that relate to *personal or interpersonal* issues, and (3) those that represent *logistical* problems.

Philosophical and Professional Challenges

Differences in Philosophy and Orientation.　Professional training has grown increasingly more specialized. It certainly is important for the school nurse to know how to perform suctioning of a child with a tracheostomy and for the special educator to develop individual transition plans. Learning the skills of one's own discipline without developing an ethic of and skills in collaboration, however, can perpetuate barriers to transdisciplinary teamwork.

The emphasis in specialized training, at the expense of cooperative teamwork, extends well into practice within school-based teams. If Luis's physical therapist, for example, focuses on measuring Luis's muscle tone and the teacher emphasizes the functional outcomes of Luis's arm movements, it will be more difficult to develop a coherent and successful intervention strategy. Similarly, if one team member insists on the term "upper extremity" to the confusion of Ramona's mother—who thought Ramona had "arms"—then communication becomes strained.

While it clearly is possible to overcome inadequate professional training, the more desirable route is to modify the approach to preservice preparation. To this end, Orelove (in press) offers several recommendations:

1. Provide models for teamwork within the classes and training programs, including faculty from various disciplines designing and delivering courses.
2. Teach skills of collaborative teamwork, including resolving conflicts, sharing decisions, and solving problems in groups.
3. Teach about the change process, including the role of team members within the educational system.
4. Select and develop field placements that support collaboration, including those that offer good models of transdisciplinary teaming.
5. Include consumers and family members within university curriculum development and instruction.
6. Involve university-affiliated programs (those interdisciplinary organizations sup-

ported through the federal Administration on Developmental Disabilities) to help support and secure funding for programs that involve faculty and service providers from a variety of disciplines.

Diminishment of Professional Status.   Although teams like to think of themselves as operating democratically, the reality is that some members view themselves as members of the Senate or Supreme Court. These individuals may feel their perceived status is threatened by a transdisciplinary model. Administrators who care about a smoothly operating team would do well to try to discern this kind of attitude during the interview or probationary period. Beyond that point the principal or other supervisor will need to use persuasion, a system of rewards, and continuing professional development activities to shape the team more along transdisciplinary lines.

A different type of status problem arises when a team perceives one member as being inferior. For example, an inexperienced teacher may be hired to work in an early intervention program at a salary significantly lower than that of the clinicians on the team. Landerholm (1990) suggests several reasonable solutions, including hiring experienced teachers at higher salaries and increasing staff training.

Professional Ethics and Liability.   Some fear that relying on indirect services may contribute to negligent behavior by not ensuring sufficient supervision by appropriately licensed or certified professionals (Geiger et al., 1986). One clear example involves the restrictions imposed by a given state's Nurse Practice Act. Most such acts specify the activities in which the licensed nurse can legally engage (Sobsey & Cox, 1991).

Unquestionably, some highly specialized or potentially risky procedures should be performed by specifically designated, trained professionals (or parents). The reality, however, is that therapists and nurses are not available all the time in schools. Schools need to develop and monitor policies and practices that ensure the safety and well-being of the child and staff without rigidly restricting the freedom of either party to make intelligent decisions. For a description of planning for health-related procedures, the reader is referred to Sobsey and Cox (1991).

Personal and Interpersonal Challenges

Threat of Training Others and of Being Trained.   Many individuals feel threatened by holding themselves up to close scrutiny. Engaging in role release, however, demands just that, revealing the gaps or uncertainties in a person's knowledge and skills. It also may be difficult for someone who has trouble accepting help or advice in general to be taught by another team member.

One step that administrators can take to reduce some of the fear is to ensure that the staff member is competent and comfortable in his or her own field. This can be done, of course, by hiring such individuals to begin with, but any team member needs opportunities and encouragement to attend seminars, workshops, courses, and other training events to keep current. It is also important to remember that transdisciplinary teams develop over time and in somewhat predictable stages; they need to be trusted and encouraged.

Attitudes and Approach Toward Families.   With families being such a significant part of the transdisciplinary model, it is incumbent upon professionals to examine their own practices and attitudes toward families. The chapter previously noted that using jargon can obscure communication with the family. Professionals may also engage in one or more of the following practices that reduce their effectiveness (Salisbury, 1992): (1) limiting their communication to administrative tasks, such as academic progress reports or reports of problem behaviors; (2) being insensitive to differences among families—their structures, ideologies, beliefs, and so on; (3) viewing parents as adversaries rather than partners; and (4) viewing parents as less observant, perceptive, or intelligent than themselves.

Cory Moore (1993), a parent, suggests that "to maximize family participation in the team process asks only for professionals to listen, to understand, and to respect us" (p. 48). She goes on to provide a variety of practical, helpful suggestions for putting this into practice. Some of the suggestions, worded in question format to professionals, include: (1) How are parents included in team meetings? Do they have a voice? Are they looked to as experts on their own children? Are they asked to share their thoughts and wishes. . . .? (2) Is the [Individualized Educational Program] truly a team effort? (3) Do you suggest or do you decree? (4) Do you take time to prepare for meetings? (5) Where do you hold meetings? (Some parents would like to meet in their homes, others on neutral ground.) (6) Do you use a round table to contribute to a sense of partnership? (7) Do parents know why the meeting is happening, who will be there, and what to expect? (8) Is everyone seated around a table when parents are ushered in (which can be overwhelming)?

Logistical Challenges

While interpersonal and professional barriers may pose the most significant barriers to adopting the transdisciplinary approach, it would be unfair to ignore day-to-day practical concerns. Team members need time to meet regularly and to give one another feedback and support. Therapists need to be scheduled carefully to make full use of their available time.

Rainforth, York, and Macdonald (1992) deal thoughtfully and thoroughly with several of these pragmatic concerns. While it is not feasible to go into these issues in depth, it seems useful to reiterate the authors' guidelines to increase the efficiency of scheduled meetings:

1. Begin and end the meetings on time.
2. Identify a facilitator and recorder for each meeting and rotate the roles among the team.

3. Generate an agenda prior to the meeting and review it at the beginning of the meeting.
4. Limit meetings to a set period of time, usually 30–60 minutes.
5. Determine followup activities for each item, assign people responsible for completion, and determine a timelime for followup.
6. Copy and distribute team minutes to each member within a few days following the meeting.

SUMMARY AND CONCLUSIONS

This chapter has focused on the organization of the transdisciplinary model and its application to learners in school programs. To date the model has been used most extensively with infants and young children and school-age children with severe disabilities. However, there is growing support for the approach, and three major professional organizations have issued guidelines on the provision of related services that support collaborative teamwork (American Occupational Therapy Association, 1989; American Physical Therapy Association, 1990; American Speech-Language-Hearing Association, 1991).

While no one model can be advocated for all teams in all situations, the transdisciplinary model does appear to have promise in situations in which individuals work closely together and have the ability to share with one another to help resolve common problems. The real test of the value of such teams is reflected in students such as Luis and Ramona. If we are truly successful, Luis and Ramona will have achieved the goals established by the team (in concert with the family), they will be valued by and feel the warmth and friendship of their peers, they will be prepared to live in their home communities, and they will feel good about themselves. A team that works together to help create those kinds of outcomes should feel very good about itself.

REFERENCES

American Occupational Therapy Association. (1989). *Guidelines for occupational therapy services in the public schools* (2d ed.). Rockville, MD: Author.

American Physical Therapy Association. (1990). *Physical therapy practice in educational environments*. Alexandria, VA: Author.

American Speech-Language-Hearing Association, Committee on Language Learning Disorders. (1991). A model for collaborative service delivery for students with language-learning disorders in the public schools. *American Speech-Language-Hearing Association, 3*(33) (Suppl.).

Bricker, D. (1976). Educational synthesizer. In M. A. Thomas (Ed.), *Hey don't forget about me!* (pp. 84–97). Reston, VA: Council for Exceptional Children.

Carney, I., & Atwood, B. (in press). Beyond good intentions: Full inclusion of parents on decision-making teams. In H. G. Garner & F. P. Orelove (Eds.), *Teamwork in human services: Models and applications across the lifespan.* Storeham, MA: Butterworth Heinemann.

Dunn, W. (1988). Models of occupational therapy service provision in the school system. *American Journal of Occupational Therapy, 42*(11), 718–723.

Dunn, W. (1991). Integrated related services. In L. H. Meyer, C. A. Peck, & L. Brown (Eds.), *Critical issues in the lives of people with severe disabilities* (pp. 353–377). Baltimore, MD: Brookes.

Geiger, W. L., Bradley, R. H., Rock, S. L., & Croce, R. (1986). Commentary. *Physical and Occupational Therapy in Pediatrics, 6*(2), 16–21.

Giangreco, M. F., York, J., & Rainforth, B. (1989). Providing related services to learners with severe handicaps in educational settings: Pursuing the least restrictive option. *Pediatric Physical Therapy, 1*(2), 55–63.

Hanson, M. J. (1985). An analysis of the effects of early intervention services for infants and toddlers with moderate and severe handicaps. *Topics in Early Childhood Special Education*, 5(2), 36–51.

Hart, V. (1977). The use of many disciplines with the severely and profoundly handicapped. In E. Sontag, J. Smith, & N. Certo (Eds.), *Educational programming for the severely and profoundly handicapped* (pp. 391–396). Reston, VA: Council for Exceptional Children.

Landerholm, E. (1990, Winter). The transdisciplinary team approach. *Teaching Exceptional Children,* 66–70.

Lyon, S., & Lyon, G. (1980). Team functioning and staff development: A role release approach to proving intergrated educational services for severely handicapped students. *Journal of the Association for the Severely Handicapped, 5*(3), 250–263.

McCormick, L., & Goldman, R. (1979). The transdisciplinary model: Implications for service delivery and personnel preparation for the severely and profoundly handicapped. *AAESPH Review, 4*(2), 152–161.

Moore, C. (1993, May). Maximizing family participation in the team process. In L. Kupper (Ed.), *The second national symposium on effective communication for children and youth with severe disabilities* (pp. 43–54). McLean, VA: Interstate Research Associates.

Orelove, F. P. (in press). Transdisciplinary teamwork. In H. G. Garner & F. P. Orelove (Eds.), *Teamwork in human services: Models and applications across the lifespan.* Storeham, MA: Butterworth Heinemann.

Orelove, F. P., & Sobsey, D. (1991). *Educating children with multiple disabilities: A transdiciplinary approach* (2d ed.). Baltimore, MD: Brookes.

Rainforth, B., York, J., & Macdonald, C. (1992). *Collaborative teams for students with severe disabilities: Integrating therapy and educational services.* Baltimore, MD: Brookes.

Salisbury, C. (1992). Parents as team members: Inclusive teams, collaborative outcomes. In B. Rainforth, J. York, & C. Macdonald, *Collaborative teams for students with severe disabilities: Integrating therapy and educational services* (pp. 43–66). Baltimore, MD: Brookes.

Sobsey, D., & Cox, A. W. (1991). Integrating health care and educational programs. In F. P. Orelove & D. Sobsey, *Educating children with multiple disabilities: A transdisciplinary approach* (pp. 155–185). Baltimore, MD: Brookes.

United Cerebral Palsy, National Organized Collaborative Project to Provide Comphrehensive

Services for Atypical Infants and Their Families. (1976). *Staff development handbook: A resource for the transdisciplinary process.* New York: United Cerebral Palsy Association.

Warren, S. F., Alpert, C. L., & Kaiser, A. P. (1986). An optimal learning environment for infants and toddlers with severe handicaps. *Focus on Exceptional Children, 18*(8), 1–11.

Woodruff, G., & McGonigel, M. J. (1988). Early intervention team approaches: The transdisciplinary model. In J. B. Jordan, J. J. Gallagher, P. L. Hutinger, & M. B. Karnes (Eds.), *Early childhood special education: Birth to three* (pp. 164–181). Reston, VA: Council for Exceptional Children.

York, J., Rainforth, B., & Dunn, W. (1990). Training needs of physical and occupational therapists who provide services to children and youth with severe disabilities. In S. Kaiser & C. McWhorter (Eds.), *Preparing personnel to work with persons with severe disabilities* (pp. 153–180). Baltimore, MD: Brookes.

York, J., Rainforth, B., & Giangreco, M. F. (1990). Transdisciplinary teamwork and integrated therapy: Clarifying the misconceptions. *Pediatric Physical Therapy, 2*(2), 73–79.

▶ 4

The Educateur:
A Transdisciplinary
Profession

Abraham Nicolaou   James Cunningham
Howard G. Garner

INTRODUCTION

What is an *educateur?* A child care worker, an educator, a social worker, a counselor? The answer to this question is, "Some of all of these, and maybe more." Educateurs receive training in each of these well-established disciplines and develop skills that cut across the traditional, professional dividing lines. The educateur may offer a new answer to another old question: "How do you overcome the barriers that divide professionals who are trained in separate disciplines with different values, philosophies, and skills?" Some say you have to overcome these barriers through teamwork, whether it be multidisciplinary, interdisciplinary, or transdisciplinary. Others say you overcome the barriers by training professionals to fulfill transdisciplinary roles.

Schools and child care agencies have often experienced tension and competition among professionals who were trained in the separate fields of education, child care, social work, counseling, and psychology. When these professionals work with the same children and youth, they often devote considerable energy to protecting their respective roles, responsibilities, and skills. As a result, a number of problems result, such as inconsistent treatment goals and decisions being made without complete information (Garner, 1982). In order to overcome such problems and to achieve higher-quality services, schools and agencies have begun organizing their staffs into

teams of various types. Initially, *multidisciplinary teams* brought together representatives from each of the disciplines providing services to children and youth.
Multidisciplinary teams facilitate communication and information sharing, but each
discipline remains relatively autonomous and continues to conduct its own assessments, develops its own intervention plans, and provides services independently
(Garner, 1994).

Interdisciplinary teams were formed in programs where it was important to attain
a high level of intensity and consistency in the pursuit of specific treatment goals for
individual children and youth. Like the multidisciplinary model, interdisciplinary
teams also include professionals trained in different disciplines, but they work for more
integration of the knowledge and interventions from each of the various disciplines.
Interdisciplinary teams typically use consensus decision making to establish common
goals and carefully coordinate their interventions to achieve greater consistency and
effectiveness. Each professional works directly with the children and youth, striving
to provide services unique to his or her respective discipline while at the same time
acknowledging and accepting the significant amount of overlap among the different
helping disciplines on the team.

Transdisciplinary teams were formed primarily in programs serving either preschool children with disabilities or students with severe and profound disabilities. The
transdisciplinary team usually includes members from special education, physical
therapy, occupational therapy, speech therapy, and social work. These team members
conduct assessments together, work closely with parents in selecting appropriate
goals, and then assign one team member to be the primary service provider. *Role
release* allows this person to provide services to the students that cut across the lines
separating the disciplines represented on the team. The other team members provide
support and consultation to the primary service provider. Role release thus allows an
individual team member to use knowledge, treatment interventions, and professional
skills from several disciplines.

This overview of the different models of teamwork allows one to understand why
it has been said that "the educateur" is truly a transdisciplinary professional.

BACKGROUND OF THE EDUCATEUR MODEL

European Roots

The educateur model embodies holistic training and treatment principles that origi-
nated first in Europe and subsequently found varying applications in Canada and the
United States. The educateur concept was propelled into prominence in Europe as
a consequence of the practical exigencies of war, that is, the necessity to respond to
massive human needs created by the destructive forces of World War II that left
orphaned and displaced children and youth in urgent need of immediate and direct
assistance (Mitchell & Nicolaou, 1988). In this context, traditionally relied upon

forms of service delivery were rendered ineffectual and inoperative. The result was a gradual implementation of a new form of service delivery for which a growing cadre of trained care providers and treatment methods would need to be developed. The philosophical focus of this emerging delivery system was holistic in that individuals directly responsible for providing immediate care to those in need were few in number, and they were compelled to attend to the total needs of individuals, including physical, mental, psychological, social, and spiritual needs. Additionally, any assistance given was frequently done in the natural context of the environmental surroundings. Thus, the seminal qualities that would eventually characterize the educateur professional were being established. Most notably, these included an emphasis on as complete an understanding of the full range of human function and need as possible, working with individuals in naturally occurring and functional contexts, and, finally, maintaining a primary and consistently available adult care giver.

The educateur concept became pervasive throughout many European countries following the war, and training institutes were developed to prepare this type of professional. These training institutes became sufficiently extensive so that, as of 1988, it was reported that over 50,000 educateurs existed in France alone which meant there was one such trained person for every thousand people in that country. While variations exist in the actual titles ascribed to such a professional within different European countries, nevertheless, the core practice and training received are quite similar and intensely rigorous (Mitchell & Nicolaou, 1988). Essentially, preparation is broad-based and includes skill development in theoretical, technical, and manual areas with training occurring in actual treatment settings (for example, residential, halfway homes, and families). Thus, the educateur is contrasted to the types of professionals whose training is more specialized and concentrated in the knowledge base of a particular discipline. Further, the practice arenas in which the educateur learns and works range from more restricted settings (e.g., residential programs) to open milieus (e.g., community-based program activities). It is noteworthy that admission to the educateur training program in most European countries follows attainment of a baccalaureate degree, which in the United States is equivalent to a two-year associates degree.

As the educateur concept spanned the ocean to the North American continent, it became established in Canada principally through the figure of Jeannine Guindon (1973; Morse, Bruno, & Morgan, 1971), who first applied what she referred to as the "re-education" process to delinquent youth in France and then later established a four-year undergraduate "Psychoeducateur" training program at the University of Montreal based on holistic training and treatment principles similar to those that had evolved in Europe. Others, such as Tessier and Girouard (1974), who also were working in the context of the Canadian child care system, continued further applications of the concept in various treatment and training settings in their country. Whether attributable to the somewhat socialized nature of child care in Canada and in some all of the European countries in which the Educateur concept flourishes, it is known that this individual generally enjoys a professional stature that engenders both respect and decent salaries.

Development of the Concept in the United States

The first major attempt to introduce educateur principles in the United States was undertaken by Nicholas Hobbs (1965), who, after studying programs in Europe and particularly in France, became the principal force in conceiving and implementing Project Re-Ed, a short-term residential school for emotionally disturbed children that was based "roughly on the European patterns" that he had observed. As he noted, a need existed for a bold new effort to provide mental health and educational services not only to alleviate acute manpower shortages, but also to emphasize assistance based on a positive model of education. Since Hobbs's conception of the Re-Ed idea in 1956 and its initiation in 1961 through a National Mental Health Council grant, the program continues to gather research information as to the efficacy of the approach. Essentially, Project ReEducation is currently credited to be the origin of the ecological model in the special education of individuals with emotional disturbance (Swap, 1991).

The first major treatise on the educateur concept was developed and published by Linton, whose comprehensive monograph on the subject appeared in 1971. In contrast to the holistic orientations emerging in foreign countries based on the potential for positive development and living, he characterized prevailing mental health practices in the United States as a medical model dominated by efforts focused on underlying disease processes. He proposed a general model for training a new reeducation professional that consisted of three possible training levels (paraprofessional, bachelors, and graduate), each level having curriculum focusing on areas of theory, application, and re-educational methods. Albeit theoretical, Linton's discussion served at the very least as an indication of the mounting interest in the educateur movement and reinforced the need for the establishment of systematic training programs. The period during which he wrote was not only one of unprecedented social unrest, but also one of equally unprecedented experimentation in the human services profession and education. As more traditional mental health treatment practices were being increasingly called into question and established delivery systems were being transformed to be more in accord with these views, the prospect for adoption of innovative approaches such as that of the educateur in various treatment facilities as well as in university-level training programs was enhanced. For instance, a number of residential treatment centers began to reorganize practices along team concept and interdisciplinary lines (Vorrath & Brendtro, 1985) and established psychoeducational models and methods in their treatment practice (Brendtro & Ness, 1983; Brendtro, Ness, & Nicolaou, 1983). Similarly, several universities developed and offered educateur training programs during this period—at Southern Connecticut University, University of California at Northridge, University of Virginia, Ohio State University, and, more recently, Western Michigan University.

In 1980 Brendtro issued a clarion call for an "American Educateur" curriculum as a means of forging a much needed alliance between the human service profession and education in order to close the gulf that had historically existed between the two entities. He not only advocated that such cooperative alliances be formed between the two, but he provided the leadership impetus for initiating such a linkage between an exemplary human service facility, The Starr Commonwealth Schools, of which he was then president, and that of a major multipurpose university, Western Michigan University. Somewhat coincidental with establishment of the joint educateur training effort was the formulation of the psychoeducational view and its major operational tenets as a holistic practice model that, in effect, provided the conceptual framework for the training and the work of the educateur (Brendtro & Ness, 1983; Brendtro, Ness, & Nicolaou, l983).

Beginning with the initial planning contacts in 1979 and implementation of the actual program in 1980, the two institutions forged a training alliance that lasted through 1991 and led to approximately 84 educateurs being trained. The structure and content of the program was thoroughly described in a previous article (Nicolaou & McCauley, 1991). In brief, the training experiences were designed to be as consistent as possible with the primary features of the educateur concept as it had evolved to this point and as embodied in the works and writings of European, Canadian, and American leaders discussed earlier in this chapter. Its two major components included a breadth of training experiences in manual, technical, and theoretical areas as well as in clinical areas that involved guided hands-on work with children and youth in treatment settings. However, the educateur in this program was distinguished from his or her European/Canadian counterparts by the fact that training and credentialing were specifically and directly linked to the field of special education. Further, the actual work sphere of the educateur, during the internship portion of training, was confined almost exclusively to a residential treatment setting. These departures enabled training to occur within an already well-developed psychoeducational framework oriented to the needs of socially-emotionally impaired persons, while also providing a subsequent market niche for the specially trained "educateur" within the extant delivery system of employment opportunities for special needs or high risk persons.

ROLE OF THE EDUCATEUR

The educateur may be described as a transdisciplinary specialist whose broad skill and knowledge base enable him or her to function in various ecologies in order to meet the total life needs of troubled children and youth. This concept presupposes a commitment and responsibility to teamwork practices through which the educateur contributes directly to daily "on-line" care in addition to serving a coordinating function to integrate the program goals and objectives from various sources, disciplines, and professions. It further presupposes that the educateur's sphere of operation is ecologically limitless and unrestricted provided human need(s) can be identified and barriers to service delivery overcome. Thus, the educateur may function in the full range of traditional service delivery options that extend from institutionalized settings on the one hand to more normalized and integrated settings on the other extreme. Additionally, the educateur in this regard is able to assume a preventative role by actively mobilizing the needed resources and effecting the appropriate interventions early in the child's need cycle. A description by Barnes (1987) provides an apt illustration as to the role of the educateur:

> *Thus, the educateur, a specialist in working with youth as "constant contact practitioner" or generalist, engages with his clients in the thick of whatever they are doing. He can relate purposefully during a wide range of life space incidents or program events, and it is his expertise to structure the nature and operation of these events so that they are therapeutic and growth-inducing for the youngsters involved. The skill of the educateur is in relating directly to children and youth and helping them over the total range of their experience. Through making conscious use of the available milieux, individual, and peer relationships, his own personality, and appropriate outside resources, the educateur transforms the whole experience of everyday life, whether in community or residential programs, into an educational and rehabilitative program. (p. 164)*

The Educateur in Practice: A Personal View from Starr Commonwealth Schools

The concept of the educateur was introduced at Starr Commonwealth Schools in the late 1970s, when two educateurs were hired as teachers for two of the treatment teams. The two were just out of college, and the staff were told that they were the first of a new breed of child care workers called "educateurs." Many of the staff viewed these two suspiciously. Part of the problem was the word *educateur* itself, literally "foreign" in spelling and pronunciation. The treatment staff frowned and squinted in an attempt to figure out what this new concept was about.

Later the staff read the book *Re-Educating Troubled Youth* by Brendtro and Ness (1983), which explained the theoretical framework for the re-educative process and some of the management techniques. As the other members of the staff began to develop a better understanding of the concept of the educateur via training and reading, it became easier to understand that this was not a new program idea developed at the college level and presented as a panacea for managing and dealing with troubled youth. Instead, these two educateurs were hard workers with a great deal of training.

A former child care worker and current teacher on a residential treatment team talked about how demanding the educateur training program was at Western Michigan University. As an educateur intern she had classes at the university on Monday, Tuesday, Thursday, and Friday. She received practical training in all different areas of child care skills for a half day on Wednesdays on campus. Then on Saturday or Sunday she worked a 10-hour shift in the cottage with the children alongside an experienced child care worker. This educateur stated that during this training she learned more and grew more as a professional child care worker than at any other time in her career.

She was on her way to becoming not only a competent technician but also a professional. She was able to explain why her child care practices were successful. According to Carbone (1980), part of being a professional child care worker is the ability to not only understand the theoretical basis for your success with children, but also to be able to articulate the theories and how they manifest themselves in practice. There was a growing understanding of the need for older, experienced worker to articulate and teach the skills and knowledge that result in effective care to new child care workers.

The interns, as noted earlier, were involved in an inter-disciplinary treatment team in which they had full-fledged membership with all the power and responsibilities that went along with it. Because this program was a Teamwork Primacy Model, there were no supervisory relationships on the team as articulated by Vorrath and Brendtro (1985). It was a very difficult process for the interns to be thrust into a situation in which they were, at least in theory, on the same responsibility level as the veteran staff. Initially it was a scary feeling to be on teams. It was very confusing, but as the educateurs gained experience in the teamwork process, it began to make sense. The interns, who were being trained in the educational, psychological, emotional, and social theories regarding intervention with troubled children, interfaced with the veteran treatment staff, who were experienced in the practice of child care. Initially they attempted to fit into the teams by conforming to "standard" practice instead of questioning practice and ideas. This, however, began to change as the interns gained experience in the treatment modality and the teamwork process.

The strength of the educateur training program is that the interns are able to get practical experiences simultaneously with classroom and theoretical work. Lectures and readings generally make more sense when there is an experiential background on which to base an understanding. An example of this is the application of one of the six tenets of the psychoeducational model (Brendtro & Ness, 1983), which states that "crisis is opportunity." It is one thing to discuss in a university class how a crisis can become an opportunity, but it is quite another to be on your way home at the end of your shift and encounter one of your children up in a high tree refusing to come down. This is definitely a crisis. How do you make it into an opportunity? It was the working through of these types of experiences that truly helped the interns to bridge the theory-practice abyss and develop the confidence necessary to work with troubled children.

The educateurs are with the children during those critical "other 23 hours" (away from the one-hour therapy session) and are in a position to guide and support children during times of crisis. Kaplan (1961) talks about the ability of significant people in a child's life to maximize the impact they have on the child with minimum effort on their part when a child is in crisis. These adults are more effective because they can intervene immediately in the child's life space as the crisis is occurring. The educateur can work very directly with feelings and events as they occur. There is no questioning of what occurred, how the child responded, or how the child felt, as can happen when the issues are not "dealt" with until the therapist or the social worker sees the child.

A worker shared an experience he had with a child who had an extremely difficult time controlling his temper, especially when interacting with his peer group. Because of the worker's therapeutic relationship with this child, the adult and child were able to work out a system in which the child care worker would "cue" the child that he was becoming angry by winking at him. This proved effective in helping the child to immediately begin to exercise control over this area and reduce the instances of temper tantrums. Coupled with talks the staff and the group had with him, this helped the child to become aware of his own internal and external cues. The child was able to develop self-discipline and control much faster because of the ability of the educateur to intervene immediately when the issue was "hot" and the child's internal system was in disequilibrium and vulnerable to change.

Potentialities of the Educateur Model

Hood (1983) discusses the inefficiency of the traditional methods used to help troubled children. They have been very narrow in their focus, which has been defined more often than not by professional consideration rather than what best meets the need of the child. Comer (1980) talks about the need of innovative programs to deal with the whole person (social, emotional, moral, psychological, as well as intellectual). The importance of transdisciplinary training of educateurs cannot be overemphasized with regard to working in the therapeutic milieu. The roles of the educateur during a given day may range from planning a recreational activity for the group to conducting a family conference or dealing with an acting-out child or group. The educateur must not only be an initiator and predictor of behaviors but must also be able to respond or react therapeutically. In order for educateurs, in the words of Redl and Wineman (1952), to engage in "the clinical exploitation of life events," they must be capable of doing whatever is necessary to help the child or the group at any given moment. They must be unimpeded by the limitations of staff roles, academic dogma, and professional chauvinism. The child care provider of the future must be a generalist, not a specialist. The educateur model provides a guide to the future of child care in the United States.

CHALLENGES FOR THE FUTURE

Formidable obstacles relating to the widespread preparation of the educateur and the adoption of the concept in the human services field must be confronted and surmounted if the educateur approach is to be a practical working reality. First, the absence of an overall national policy or legal mandate directly aimed at protecting and enhancing the fundamental human rights and welfare of children supports perpetuation of fractionated and decentralized approaches to meeting their treatment needs.

Conversely, a more social perspective is adopted in European countries and Canada that appears to place a greater value on children as a precious generational resource to be nourished and whose needs are to be addressed. This perspective and commitment were dramatically illustrated by the role of European countries (particularly Poland) and Canada in spearheading the drafting of a Convention on the Rights of the Child in November 1989, which "when, and if, signed and ratified by 20 countries will become a binding instrument of international law" (Lewis, 1990, p. 150). The United States may sign and ratify this document, which would be a significant and unusual event.

The more universal acceptance of the educateur in foreign countries is evident in the statement by Serge Ginger, who noted that they are not only highly regarded and better paid than most professionals, but their treatment influence is pervasive and extends beyond the confines of institutional settings to open milieus and even in-home care areas (Mitchell & Nicolaou, 1988). In a subsequent address at a world congress representing an international organization of growing influence (viz. the International Association for Workers of Maladjusted Children) he described the increasing geographic diversification of the educateur's role and function within the various European countries (Ginger, 1990). In the United States there has been a continued reliance on manpower pool resources that continue to draw heavily from traditionally trained and highly specialized personnel. Not only have multidisciplinary rather than holistic treatment practices been thus perpetuated, but, as an unintended result, elitist hierarchies are frequently established among treatment specialists that often have detrimental effects on direct care practices and the welfare of children.

Second, more general acceptance and implementation of the educateur concept nationwide are impeded by certification procedures and requirements that exist in different states. Public Law 94-142, the Education for All Handicapped Children Act of 1975, represented landmark legislation at the national level in behalf of the civil rights of handicapped persons. However, it stipulates provisions for services and qualifications for personnel that are basically categorical and provides little, if any, philosophical, financial, or regulatory incentive for states to pursue certification of personnel with the qualities of an educateur. Further, mental health codes vary from state to state and hence would not present a viable vehicle or uniform basis of support for development of the educateur professional.

Third, university training programs are generally committed to attempting innovative approaches such as that represented by the educateur model, but their continued maintenance and longevity is often subject to the limitations of sufficient critical student mass and external sources of funding. Currently only a handful of university programs exist that train educateurs; others have been discontinued for the reasons mentioned. It is imperative that training programs go beyond exclusive attention to practitioner levels of preparation and include in their efforts the development of leadership personnel who will be imbued with the philosophy and skills to spawn new treatment practices and programs that utilize the educateur concept. Also, universities must become proactive in seeking vital community and field service linkages for the development of "best practices" as well as training resources and sequences. Such a direction may hasten more widespread adoption and integration of the educateur philosophy and methods within the current system of child care.

Finally, as global interdependence accelerates on all levels of human activity, holistic approaches become an increasingly viable means for responding to the rapid socio-political changes that affect people's lives on a daily basis. In fact, the next important challenge to confront the educateur is that

> *by the year 2000 [he] will have to widen his horizons and be located in the geometric area between youth, his family, his region and the world; one will have to surpass pedagogy and the traditional cleavages and take into consideration the systemic interrelations between the five principal dimensions of every human being: the physical . . .; the affectionate . . .; the rational. . .; the social . . .; the spiritual . . .; the individual . . .; the sociological. . . ." (Ginger, 1990, p. 262)*

Ginger's observation may very well forecast the urgent need that will exist for human care providers to transcend traditional disciplinary lines in both training and function in order to operate in multiple environments and capacities to effectively respond to the total needs of children and youth.

SUMMARY AND CONCLUSIONS

The educateur profession is a relatively new one, developed in Europe at the end of World War II in response to the critical need for teachers, child care workers, social workers, and psychologists. Working with large numbers of displaced and dependent children who were left homeless by the war, the educateur became a transdisciplinary professional who could attend to the total needs of individuals, using the knowledge and skills of a number of disciplines.

The idea of the educateur was brought to North America by Jeannine Guindon, who referred to the "re-education" process of delinquent youth in France. She established a "psychoeducateur" undergraduate program at the University of Montreal. Nicolas Hobbs and others brought these ideas to the United States in the form of "Project Re-Ed" in 1956. This new approach to educating children and youth with emotional and behavioral problems was built upon two fundamental concepts: the educateur and the team model.

Several universities in the United States have developed programs to prepare educateurs to work in both human service and educational settings. The acceptance of this role in the United States, however, has not been as widespread as in Europe. A major factor contributing to this trend are federal and state mandates for services to children in prescribed categories of disabilities with requirements that these children be served by professionals licensed in specialized roles.

The educateur is a professional who is well prepared to serve as a member of teams in which all relevant information regarding a child is brought together and used in developing a holistic plan and coordinated services. The educateur is by training and philosophy able to transcend the traditional barriers separating education, child care, social work, recreation, psychology, and even the health fields. This new professional is able to work directly with children, youth, and families in schools, residential programs, and community settings. In short, the educateur is a highly trained generalist who is able to integrate the knowledge and skills of various specialties in the direct care of children and youth.

A transdisciplinary profession may be required by society in its effort to respond more effectively to drug and alcohol abuse, violence, gangs, teenage pregnancy, and homelessness among young people. These complex problems and their solutions clearly cross discipline lines, and no one discipline or profession has the answers. As the year 2000 approaches, a team approach will be required to solve these societal problems. If, and when, a holistic approach to these serious problems is chosen, the educateur, the transdisciplinary professional, will be prepared and ready to serve as a vital member of the team.

REFERENCES

Barnes, F. H. (1980). The child care worker: A conceptual approach. In Denholm, C., Ferguson, R., and Pence, A. *Professional child and youth care: The Canadian perspective* (pp. 153–174). Vancouver: University of British Columbia Press.

Brendtro, L. (1980). Bridging teaching and treatment: The American educateur. *Journal of teacher education, 31*(5), 23–26.

Brendtro, L., Ness, A., & Nicolaou, A. (1983). Peer group treatment: Its use and misuse. In L. K. Brendtro and A. E. Ness (Eds.), *Re-educating troubled youth: Environments for teaching and treatment* (pp. 203–254). New York: Aldine.

Brendtro, L., & Ness, A. (1983). *Re-educating troubled youth: Environments for teaching and treatment.* New York: Aldine.

Carbone, P. (1980). Liberal education and teacher preparation. *Journal of Teacher Education, 31*(3), 13–17.

Comer, J. P. (1980). *School power: Implications of an intervention project.* New York: Free Press.

Gabor, P. (1987). Community-based child care. In C. Denholm, R. Ferguson, & A. Pence (Eds.), *Professional child and youth care: The Canadian perspective* (pp. 155–174). Vancouver: University of British Columbia Press.

Garner, H. (1982). *Teamwork in programs for children and youth.* Springfield, IL: Thomas.

Garner, H. (1994). Multidisciplinary versus interdisciplinary teamwork. In H. Garner & F. Orelove (Eds.), *Teamwork in human services: Models and applications across the lifespan.* Boston, MA: Butterworth-Heineman.

Ginger, S. (1990). The concept of specialized educateur: A holistic approach. In M. Mitchell, C. Tobin, J. Johncox, & R. Rocco (Eds.), *Proceedings of the XII World Congress* (pp. 147–153). Albion, MI.: Starr Commonwealth Institute Press.

Guindon, J. (1973). The reeducational process. *International Journal of Mental Health. 11*(1), 15–26.

Hobbs, N. (1965). How the Re-Ed plan developed. In N. J. Long, W. C. Morse, & R. G. Newman (Eds.), *Conflict in the classroom: The education of emotionally disturbed children* (pp. 286–294). Belmont, CA: Wadsworth.

Hood, T. (1983). The educateur: A model for today. *Residential Group Care,* Spring/Summer, 14–16.

Kaplan, G. (Ed.). (1961). *Prevention of mental disorders in children,* New York: Basic Books.

Lewis, S. (1990). Children of all nations. In M. Mitchell, C. Tobin, J. Johncox, & R. Rocco (Eds.), *Proceedings of the XII World Congress* (pp. 147–153). Albion, MI: Starr Commonwealth Institute Press.

Linton, T. (1971). The educateur model: A theoretical monograph. *Journal of Special Education, 5*(2), 155–191.

Mitchell, M., & Nicolaou, A. (1988). The educateur: A specialized generalist. *Caring, 4*(3), 24–26.

Morse, W., Bruno, F., & Morgan, S. (1971). *Training teachers for the emotionally disturbed.* Ann Arbor: University of Michigan, School of Education.

Nicolaou, A., & Brendtro, L. (1983). Curriculum for caring: Service learning with behaviorally disordered students. Monograph in *Behavioral Disorders,* Summer, 108–115.

Nicolaou, A., & McCauley, K. (1991). Training the American educateur: An interagency approach. *Child and Youth Care Forum, 20*(4), 275–290.

Redl, F., & Wineman, D. (1952). *Controls from within.* New York: Free Press.

Tessier, B. (1974). The psycho-educative model in action: A description of the Boscoville and St. Helene Re-Education Center. Montreal: Unpublished.

Swap, S. (1991). Ecological theory and practice. In J. L. Paul & B. C. Epanchin (Eds.), *Educating emotionally disturbed children and youth* (pp. 243–272). New York: Macmillan.

Vorrath, H. & Brendtro, L. (1985) *Positive peer culture.* (2d ed.) Chicago: Aldine.

▶ 5

Youth Empowerment and Teamwork

Larry Brendtro   Joan Bacon

INTRODUCTION

The most potent decision a leader makes is to decide who shares in making decisions. The democratic principle is that all citizens have a voice in determining their destiny. Those deprived of power are oppressed, observes Paulo Friere, even when ruled by benevolent authority. The history of Western culture is a saga about who is to rule and who must submit. Serfs obeyed nobles and subjects obeyed kings. The victor owned the conquered, and wives were the chattel of husbands. In time, women and other slaves broke free from their bondage. Now, only children remain powerless, for they are but "future citizens."

As Raychaba (1990) suggests, children and adolescents have historically been marginal members of the dominant culture, deprived of significant voice in matters affecting them. He summarizes Freire's vision of empowerment pedagogy as including these key elements:

- *Dialogue and collaboration* between young persons and those who work with them
- *Involvement in decision making* so that young persons can alter their personal landscapes
- *The provision of options and real choice,* which requires mutual exchange and learning

In contrast, "disempowerment" is a form of dehumanization in which adults engage in monologue instead of dialogue and fail to offer youth any semblance of involvement in decision making and authentic choice (Freire, 1985).

Courage for Discouraged Youth

Alienation between children and adults in modern society has reached crisis proportions, and large numbers of youth are at risk physically, emotionally, educationally, and spiritually. In an earlier work we presented a "reclaiming" model of education that drew from the rich heritage of youthwork pioneers, from Native American philosophies of child care, and from emerging youth development research (Brendtro, Brokenleg, & Van Bockern, 1990). These proposals represent a paradigm shift from traditional obedience approaches that focus on the control of deviance.

Table 5-1 contrasts the patriarchal model that has long governed child rearing in Western civilization with the empowerment model; the first controls and silences youth, while the second encourages and empowers them.

To be empowered is to experience belonging, mastery, independence, and generosity. The development of courageous youth entails the cultivation of the human qualities of attachment, achievement, autonomy, and altruism.

TABLE 5-1 • **Patriarchal versus Empowerment Models of Education and Child Care**

	The Patriarchal Model	
	Egoistic INDIVIDUALISM	
Discipline for OBEDIENCE	DISCOURAGED youth	Factory school ALIENATION
	Achievement as WINNING	
	The Empowerment Model	
	Altruistic GENEROSITY	
Discipline for INDEPENDENCE	COURAGEOUS youth	Communities of BELONGING
	Achievement as MASTERY	

Traditional patriarchal approaches are driven by contrary values. The large, anonymous factory school fuels a sense of alienation. Competitive education is a zero-sum game enthroning "winners" and ensuring an abundance of losers. *Obedient responsibility* is an oxymoron. Finally, young people desperately need a purpose for living beyond the narcissistic pursuit of self-centered pleasures.

Historical Roots of Youth Empowerment

Horace Mann declared that the purpose of schools in a democracy was to provide an "apprenticeship in responsibility." Mann was far ahead of his time, for the dominant model of education worldwide was still the authoritarian pedagogue. By the beginning of the twentieth century other calls for youth empowerment were heard. Schools are major institutions for "scholastic slavery," argued Maria Montesorri, for children must submit in passive silence like mounted butterflies pinned to their desks. John Dewey objected to treating children as "future" citizens because it devalued their present role. Schools should be structured as democratic communities where students are active participants in the educational process.

Despite the efforts of progressive educators like Dewey, schools were pushed to conform to the "factory model" of operation, a paradigm that persists today. In the factory school the procedures, materials, and methods used in schools are rigid and standardized as schools become impersonal bureaucracies modeled after nineteenth-century theories of "scientific management." While many children have been amazingly resilient in factory schools, others were like "round pegs in square holes." These children were routinely bent and distorted to force them to conform. Those who would not were discarded.

Janusz Korczak of Poland, sometimes called "the Karl Marx of Children," declared that the child was the ultimate underdog in Western society. He argued that just as we failed to see the woman, peasant, or poor as oppressed in earlier times, so we remain blind to the inferior status of children. Perennially small and inexperienced, children are forever vulnerable to being domineered by patriarchal adults. Korczak said children must be treated with all the respect due "citizens in embryo." In the 1920s he transformed schools and institutions into "pedocracies" where children became full partners in decision making. His children's court was cited by Lawrence Kohlberg as the prototype of the just community school (Brendtro & Hinders, 1990).

In the same era, reformers extended ideas of empowerment to troubled youth as well. With great enthusiasm their democratic ideal of self-determination was used to transform children's homes and facilities for wayward youth. The United States gave citizenship to wayward youth as they held elected offices in their Junior Republics, Boys' Towns, and Little Commonwealths. In 1916 Karl Wilker of Germany revolutionized Berlin's most infamous youth prison. After serious discussions about the meaning of responsibility, staff and inmates sawed off the prison bars and christened their new school as "Lindenhof." By 1928 Cora Liepman of the Weimar Republic could write an international history of self-governance models for delinquents.

But democracy was a fragile flower, and each of these noble experiments was overwhelmed by reactionary forces. Wilker was galloping too far ahead of his time, and he was fired for trying to plant such alien "American" democratic ideas in German soil. Later he would be imprisoned by Hitler, then banished to South Africa where he resumed his lonely struggle as a teacher of black children. Reflecting on his lost dream, Wilker recounted in *Lindenhof* (1921): "It would have been the empire of the young, it would have been their republic. But, for Germany this remains a dream!" (p. 24). And elsewhere as well.

Silencing the Voice of Youth

In spite of the rich tradition of youth empowerment among educational thinkers the voice of youth is seldom heard in contemporary youth programs, where adults are preoccupied with management and control. Why must the child be only an object of our deliberations and not a participating subject? To make any person an object is to dehumanize and disempower. Korczak argued that most adults look down on the thinking of children, as if it were somehow inferior in quality to that of adults. He strongly disagreed, arguing that one has to stretch rather than stoop to comprehend the ideas presented by young people.

In her study of school dropouts at a large urban school, Michelle Fine (1991) shows how students have been systematically silenced and excluded from significant input in their own education. She suggests that now, since business is advocating participation of employees in decision making, student participation in schools is more in vogue, albeit more often with "advanced" classes than with "remedial." Yet, even if students are encouraged to express their views, this is typically followed by the authorized teacher version of truth. As one youth exclaimed, "Why do they ask for our opinion when they are going to tell us that their way is the right way? May as well not answer" (p. 45). Even adults who believe they are involving youth may be silencing them.

The literature on teamwork cautions against unequal partnerships where professionals overwhelm parents. This problem of asymmetrical power also plagues collaboration attempts with youth. As Fine (1991) notes, it is easier to achieve equality of *access* than of *outcome*. Those once locked out can be brought in, but inclusion in an oppressive system will not automatically be empowering. To authoritarian adults, youth involvement may be just another invitation to intimidation:

> One alternative school for troubled youth invites students to attend meetings of the interdisciplinary teams involved in developing treatment plans. The student is then boxed into signing a written contract of behavioral expectations with provisions crafted in advance to achieve the adults' desired control outcomes.
>
> A New England school board has a policy of including students in "hearings" involving discipline. A girl who was suspended for disruptive behavior was angrily scolded by board members. Had they been willing to

listen, they would have found that her acting out was triggered by having been raped. Her lawyer subsequently filed a suit against the school board.

Shared problem solving cannot occur in a climate of condemnation. Conflicts involving students, teachers, and parents become contests over who owns the problem. Typically parents are most likely to blame the youth, then the school, and last of all themselves. In contrast, school personnel usually attribute problems first to the student, then to parents, and finally to the school. This defensive posture is exaggerated by excluding students from deliberations: The absent youth becomes the easiest target for blame.

Some adults are afraid of youthful opinions. When the Canadian government was holding hearings on juvenile prostitution in Ottawa, child prostitutes offered to testify. Several officials refused to listen to these children, rationalizing that this might be "destructive." The keen and frank criticisms of young people threaten the secure biases of authoritarian adults. A cartoon in an education journal shows a pompous teacher telling his pupils, "I expect you all to be independent, innovative, critical thinkers who will do exactly as I say." Jonathon Kozol argues that one of the "pious lies" that schools teach children is not to criticize if they can't offer a better solution. Why not? Perhaps the best contribution youth can make is to strip the tinsel from our fancy failing systems.

Someone's Missing

While the term *empowerment* frequently appears in literature about teamwork, it usually refers to professionals empowering one another through the sharing of power, information, or resources. In many cases, parents are also included on the team and perhaps even "empowered" to participate. Unfortunately, the person who is missing, who most often has no voice among the empowered, is the child! In a leading book about teaming, Morsink, Thomas, and Correa (1991) omit children from the model of collaboration. No less than 18 empowered adults, ranging from the principal and the parent to the adaptive physical educator and the dietician, are poised like armed starships encircling an intruding alien, ready to strike. An artist's rendition of this "student/client centered" model indicates only adult team membership, while the child is the team target.

From the time of P.L. 94-142, parental involvement in teaming was mandated and student participation was encouraged "when appropriate." But the professional literature is largely silent about the topic of students as team members. An ERIC computer search from 1982 to June of 1991 yielded 340 articles on IEPs but less than 10 articles about student involvement in the IEP process.

The student is also missing from most textbook descriptions of the IEP process. While works on learning disabilities or mainstreaming may discuss student empowerment, this is seldom in the context of IEP meetings:

- Reynolds and Birch (1988) stress the importance of teaching self-management skills, giving children choices, and encouraging self-advocacy by persons with disabilities. However, the chapter "Teaching and Teamwork" does not include the child on the team or at the IEP meeting.

- Smith's (1991) textbook discusses motivation, assertiveness training, and the importance of understanding the child's thought processes. But, once again, there was is discussion of involving children in the real-life decision making of the team.

- The Gearharts (1989) criticize assessment teams for not gaining student perceptions about learning problems. They also lament that many adults with learning disabilities do not understand their disabilities. However, their account of the IEP process fails to mention student involvement.

We are forced to conclude that children are seldom seen or heard at team meetings. As Van Reusen and Bos (1990) report "[s]tudent participation in this conference, even at the secondary level, is for the most part either nonexistent or passive" (p. 30). While teams are expressly designed for special-needs students, Peters (1990) aptly captures the irony in her article "Someone's Missing: The Student as an Overlooked Participant in the IEP Process."

What Do Youth Have to Say?

Anna Freud once said that if you don't understand something, perhaps you could ask the children. The co-editors of a new interdisciplinary journal on the problems of youth (Brendtro & Long, 1992) made a philosophical commitment to begin each issue with "Voices of Children and Youth." Before attending to one another, adults would first have to encounter the thoughts and feelings of children. Perhaps little minds don't have answers to big questions that stump adults, but without the perceptual correction of the youth perspective, adults are locked in narrow assumptions.

Youth with problems are often seen as immature and irresponsible, and professionals seldom involve them in planning services they are to receive. Gabor and Greene (1991) provide rich data supporting the participation of youth in educational and treatment planning. They examined in depth the views of 36 youth in out-of-home placement in western Canada. Of particular interest was whether young people believe they can influence the development of plans that affect their future. Their research showed that youth and professionals held widely divergent perceptions about a wide range of important issues.

Not one of the 36 young people indicated that he or she had been involved in designing the case plan; by contrast, the great majority of parents and child care professionals had participated in planning meetings. While it seems likely that there must have been some adults who tried to involve youth in decision making, the youth responses conveyed feelings of helplessness in the face of adults who controlled their lives. A typical response came from a young person who was expecting to be released from residential placement: "I was supposed to go home but a meeting took place between my social worker, staff, and my parents, and I didn't get to go home."

Gabor and Greene found that nearly half of the young people had not been provided meaningful information about their out-of-home placement prior to their arrival. Not surprisingly, a majority of youth reported their initial reaction to placement was dislike, and this negativism increased over the course of placement. Young people who are not involved in planning their futures will have difficulty in developing responsibility, a frequently stated goal of care. There is limited commitment when plans are not well understood and are externally imposed.

Gabor and Greene suggest that the absence of direct dialogue heightens the discrepancy in viewpoint between adults and youth. For example, youth gauged their like or dislike for a program on the basis of positive relationships with adults and peers, good food and activities, and the absence of unreasonable rules or restrictions. Professionals attuned to lofty educational and treatment goals seemed unaware that young people most wanted to live in harmony, comfort, and dignity.

Considering the stated "family focus" of most agencies, it is disquieting to note the discordant views about family relationships. Almost all young people, even those whose families were in conflict, found it highly enjoyable to spend time in family visits: This contact seemed to give them a sense of belonging and identity. However, professionals often saw family visits as treatment fodder demonstrating the wisdom of the case plan, particularly for skeptical youth. For example, common professional goals for visits were to recognize family dysfunction so they would understand why they had been removed from the home. Not a single child in the study shared these pessimistic goals.

Gabor and Greene call for a new spirit of authentic participation of youth in the planning process. Such involvement allows adults to clarify the plan and its rationale with the youth. Should the youth disagree, the voice of dissent should not be silenced; rather, professionals should be advocates who ensure that the young person has the opportunity to express views, even when the professional may not agree. Without such co-planning, feelings of powerlessness and dependence will fester, while self-confidence and responsible independence will fail to develop.

> Young people have their own views and opinions about their situation and about the services they are receiving. They will share these views if given encouragement and the opportunity. If the services provided to young people are to be of real assistance to them, those closest to them . . . must ensure that young people are provided the opportunity to express their views and that, when they do, someone is listening! (Gabor & Greene, 1991, p. 18)

ROADBLOCKS TO STUDENT PARTICIPATION IN TEAMS

Practical experiences in educational and child care agencies provides abundant evidence of the pervasiveness of barriers that prevent access of young people to responsible team participation. As in other cases of prejudice, the subjugated are "kept in their place" by stereotypes and rationalizations that justify patriarchal authority. Among these myths and misconceptions are the following:

1. *Youth would not want to participate in team meetings anyway. They should not be forced to attend.*

Certainly, compelling a student to collaborate with teams is not desirable. However, one might wonder just why a young person would decline a valid invitation to participate in such important matters. Some youth who try to avoid participation have had bad previous experiences with team meetings. For others, meeting avoidance is rooted in the expectation that nobody really cares what they think, and powerful adults will remain in control of what happens to them (Adelman et al., 1990). With youth who have been "burned" before, adults will have to take time and effort to rebuild the trust needed to overcome their reluctance to participate.

Adults might well put themselves in the shoes of children who are aware that people are talking about them. Reflect back on situations in which you were asked to "wait outside a few minutes" while persons in another room made important decisions about your tenure, salary, medical treatment, or professional advancement. Even the most secure adult feels anxious, frustrated, and powerless. Schultz (1985) tells of a psychiatrist who confronted a teacher about the absence of a student at a conference about the child's behavior: "Doesn't he know we are talking about him? If you were in that position, wouldn't you rather be on this side of the door?" (p. 5).

"Which side of the door" the youth is on during the team meeting is a litmus test of the team's beliefs about youth empowerment. Adults who assume youth do not want to attend may also tend to see them as untrustworthy, irresponsible, and immature. These expectations, often self-fulfilling, strongly lean toward the viewpoints held in the patriarchal model—that adults know best, and the appropriate role for youth is silence. An empowerment model ensures that youth are on the same side of the door as other team members. As Adelman and colleagues suggest, ". . . there is an increasing body of research suggesting that many youngsters, even preteenagers and those with psychoeducational problems, are capable of participating competently in decision-making forums" (p. 171). If we do not bar the door, youth will enter.

2. *Children would not understand what's happening at the meeting anyway.*

Many adults have the same problem. Parents may not fathom the fine points of the team meeting: the procedures, the vocabulary, how the systems of a school or agency work, or what role they have in the meeting. The result is that parents tend to be passive participants or, like youth who have meeting aversions, simply avoid them altogether. Professionals are often just as confused when drowned in jargon or hypertechnical vocabulary. When "insiders" use language as an instrument of power and domination, others are robbed of their right to understand and participate in important decisions.

We have attended meetings in which the occupational therapist used words like "upper right extremity" (right arm), "lower maxillary process" (jaw and throat area), and "masticate" (chew). Special educators have their own doozies: acronyms such as IEP, LRE, LD, and WRAT. Counselors, speech therapists, psychologists, and other professionals are all nimble with Newspeak, intoning pompous terms not comprehensible to outsiders. In accounting there is a concept called "grandparent's rule." If a CPA cannot give a report so that a reasonably intelligent grandparent can understand it, one should suspect something is fishy.

3. *It isn't necessary for children to attend the meeting. Parents or other adults can tell them about it later.*

Those locked out of a meeting run a great risk of misunderstanding what happened in their absence. Sometimes students receive almost no information about discussions held at meetings. In other cases the "designated messenger adult" brings a tale so cursive or distorted that the child cannot possibly comprehend what has transpired (Shea & Bauer, 1991).

Second-hand information often stresses what the child has done wrong. Receiving only negative feedback after a team meeting discourages children and compounds the feeling that adults do not appreciate the child's efforts or feelings. Such miscommunications exacerbate conflicts between the child, the parents, and other team members (Shea & Bauer, 1991). Many youngsters who are the subjects of team meetings have experienced chronic negative evaluations from adult authorities. Incomplete and negative reports only serve to alienate them further.

Even the most problematic child needs to receive adult affection and affirmation. Team meetings can be one vehicle for confirming the child's importance—after all, this roomful of adults are all meeting for him or her. To cut off children from positive evaluative information that offsets negatives is to rob them of hope and courage.

4. *Adults are experienced and know what is best for the child. Really, what could a child add?*

Teams exist largely because we have discovered that purely "expert" decisions made by narrowly trained specialists have little utility in real-life settings. Part of the strength of the team concept is in the idea of synergy—that two or more heads are better than one in solving complex problems. Teaming ensures that different perspectives about a child are heard and can complement each other, resulting in better decisions. By including parents and practitioners who work with the child along with "experts," teaming is more likely to result in practical plans that can be carried out by those on the front line of the child's life space.

The child has much to add, even on a team made up of the best experts, the most caring parents, and the most skilled practitioners. The child's perspective is unique because it is the only one fully grounded in the daily life, struggles, and dreams of a developing human being. Children can tell us of their interests, goals, fears, hopes, and even what they want to learn. A resource room teacher in Wisconsin told us of her pride when one of her eighth-grade "behavior disordered" students explained to his IEP team that he should not be placed in the same mainstream class with several of his friends. He wanted to succeed in the class and realized that progress would be jeopardized by the presence of these particular buddies. We have heard students explain why a certain teacher harmonized with their learning style, or why they found it easiest to trust a particular counselor.

Iano (1990) challenges educators to become involved in transformational collaboration with students. The task is "to diagnose their students' particular situations in such a way that the bases for the alienation, discouragement, and distortion become clear enough to indicate possible roads back" (p. 465).

6. *Having the child participate in the meeting will take too much time away from "doing the business" of the meeting.*

Regardless of who participates, there is seldom enough time for effective teaming. Schools simply have not been structured in ways that accommodate these processes. However, the extra time it may take to include a child in the decision-making process will pay big dividends.

Democratic processes are slower than snap authoritarian decision making. Gaining a group consensus is more cumbersome than top-down patriarchal management. However, any advantage of boss management is lost when it comes time to implement decisions. People are notoriously reluctant to support a plan in which they had no input. But when the team has ownership and understands the decision, the commitment to action has been built.

Adults often forget this basic principle of participatory decision making. We "team" without the child's participation, attempt to plan and carry out treatments or instructional activities without considering the child's priorities or interests, and then blame the child for being resistant or passive. While excluding the child may streamline meetings, it impedes implementation.

Decisions made by teams should be in harmony with the child's own preferences and interests (Turnbull & Turnbull, 1991), and these cannot be understood if the child is not present to explain them. The business of the meeting is not to fill in forms to meet the requirements of an agency, but to understand and meet a child's needs.

7. *Students might become resistant, disruptive, or manipulative and would upset the meeting.*

Shea and Bauer (1991) found that some parents were reluctant to have their children present at conferences. They were afraid that the child might disclose private family information, that the child's presence might inhibit them or other team members from speaking openly, or that the meeting might be too stressful for the child. Other parents may fear that the child will show the same kinds of negative behaviors that required a meeting in the first place.

Professionals also may be concerned that the child might say or do something embarrassing. The child's opinions and actions are less predictable than those of most adults and may not be couched in terms and behaviors that are socially appropriate. Adults might look foolish or inadequate if they can't "control" the child during the meeting. Certainly no one likes to be put on the spot, especially in front of important peers. But should children be silenced to help adults save face?

Adults must become courageous enough to risk being uncomfortable or embarrassed. It was, after all, a child who announced in the middle of an otherwise dignified and formal processional, "The Emperor has no clothes!" Children whose needs are not being addressed certainly can tell us that our interdisciplinary dance has no clothes. The candor of children can save us all from polite little lies that mask the impotence of our interventions.

8. *Children need to be protected from information that might be damaging to their self-esteem.*

Our society doesn't do a very good job of protecting our children from violence, poverty, infant mortality, drugs, pornography, and a host of other evils. Indeed, many children who are the subjects of team meetings already have first-hand knowledge of these social problems. Well-meaning adults may want to protect them from yet another burden—the burden of a psycho-educational label—or from hearing the "bad news" that their performance or behavior is not up to expectations. But Bill Mitchell (1988), a professional who has a mobility impairment himself, cautions against such overprotection, suggesting that those who care most about the person with disability sometimes shelter them from the very experiences that would teach them to take control of their lives.

Children are realists concerning their own performance and behavior. Very young children are capable of making comparisons between themselves and others. Schools send all sorts of messages about winners and losers, including report cards, tests graded on the curve, creative writing corrected with red ink, and lock-step curricula. Children are aware of labels given to them by their peers that are much more potent than the ones we use in meetings, many so colorful they couldn't be repeated here. All of this "bad news" is also discouraging to children.

Children and youth need reliable, factual information about their abilities and their disabilities. Unfortunately, we have not done a very good job of giving them accurate information. Recent literature on helping students with disabilities bridge the gap between school and adult life tells us that many students do not understand their disabilities (Sachs, Iliff, & Donnelly, 1987; Ness & Price, 1990). Yet, such understanding is vital to students' academic and psychological growth and can be provided to students as early as in the elementary grades (Heyman, 1990).

When we provide children information and empower them in the decision-making process, we place them in an excellent position to improve their self-esteem. Beane (1991) insists that we stop viewing self-esteem as a namby-pamby, soft, individualistic quality. Instead, he sees self-esteem as cast in the crucible of interactions with the environment. It cannot be separated from themes like democracy, human dignity, and respect for others. These concepts form the foundation of empowerment theory.

"Self-esteem" is a psychological synonym for courage. Bednar, Wells, and

Peterson (1989) view self-esteem as a natural consequence of either coping with or avoiding things we fear. Team meetings can provide a natural and supportive environment for students to face, understand, and begin to resolve their problems, gaining courage in the process. Keeping children out of team meetings may serve to enable undesirable behaviors such as avoidance, denial of responsibility, and learned helplessness, all of which further undermine self-esteem and contribute to discouragement.

THE SEARCH FOR A SHARED VISION

As mandates for collaboration are institutionalized, professionals have created the cultural ritual of team meetings. Analyzing this process in the IEP of special education, Skrtic (1991) concludes that there is much confusion of the letter and the spirit of the law. Three competing models for decision making can be found in the professional culture of special education:

1. "Machine bureaucracy," where participants are preoccupied with regulations and legal compliance
2. "Professional bureaucracy," where decisions proceed according to standardized professional procedures
3. "Adhocracy," defined as the search for a shared vision through joint problem solving by staff, parents, and student

Unfortunately, true adhocracy is very rare. The more common situation is for professionals with technical expertise to keep control of the process, permitting token input from parents and virtually none from students. Harkins (1991) studied the school careers of three behavior-disordered students, Tim, Pete, and Jenny. Board policy in their large midwestern school district was unusual in that student attendance in IEP meetings was mandated. However, neither parents nor students were equal partners, and decision making was bureaucratic and deficit oriented:

> Case presentations almost always began with the history of the handicapping condition. This ritual also included careful control of information by presenter(s). Almost without exception, IEPs and case study evaluation documents were available to special education personnel, and almost never to the student, parents, and private experts. . . . Professional decision makers almost always sat at one end of a long, tribunal-like conference table. Parents and students experienced this context and the decision-making procedures as alienating and objectifying. By contrast, professionals defined a "Good PST conference" as one that was well controlled. (Harkins, 1991, p. 249)

Harkins concludes that bureaucratized process is a kind of pseudocollaboration that cannot produce a "shared vision" by participants. Furthermore, the "deficit orientation," that is, focusing mainly on what is wrong and pathological, may be procedurally legal but destructive. Years of exposure to the negative grind away at the self-esteem of parents and students. Tim, Pete, and Jenny, as they course through elementary, middle, and senior high school special education, come to view themselves as "damaged" and "defective." Their parents alternately battle the school, grudgingly comply, or view themselves as failures.

Ideally the IEP should be a learning experience for all. Harkins found that it often became "essentially a cold war agreement in which the protocol of the multidisciplinary staff conference arena was employed to resolve conflict" (p. 104). In the triangular relationships of professional, parent, and student the school's goal was to enlist parental support in a "united front" against the young person. The battle metaphor continues, as the child becomes the common enemy to be conquered.

A true adhocracy with shared vision requires moving beyond strained relationships and formalized communications. When teams can focus on strengths and goals, then problems and deficits can be put into proper perspective. One such IEP conference with Jenny approached this ideal. Prior to the meeting, Jenny requested that her history of past school failures and psychiatric hospitalizations not be reviewed, as was the normal practice. Staff interpreted this as Jenny's positive attempt to make a break with the past. The new starting point for the conference became a celebration of the fact that Jenny had made it through a year without psychiatric hospitalization. Concerns that Jenny expressed about having been inappropriately placed in a mainstream algebra course (which she failed) were taken seriously, and options for adjustments were developed. The team was able to share with Jenny their perceptions about her tendency to exaggerate the significance of her failures, and this criticism was accepted in a new climate of trust. Recalling that conference, Jenny exclaimed: "I've never seen my mom beam before. My parents were so satisfied that they took me to MacDonald's" (p. 241). What might have been another battleground became an adhocracy of shared vision.

EMPOWERED YOUTH IN ACTION

There are now abundant models of successful youth participation, and research supports the efficacy of these programs in transforming the culture of schools and youth organizations. For example:

- The National Peer Helpers Association operated a large network of supportive services initiated by peers in schools, churches, and community settings. Youth have been successfully involved in dropout prevention, suicide awareness, conflict resolution, and gang-related interventions (Varenhorst, 1984).
- Youth who have been passive recipients of services from mental health or social service professionals become cotherapists, helping to solve their own problems

and those of peers. Even with serious difficulties, such as alcoholism, sexual abuse and violent offenses, the best change agents may be young people who have been there (Vorrath & Brendtro, 1985; Brendtro & Wasmund, 1989).

Courageous schools are also pioneering the uncharted waters of youth involvement in educational planning conferences. In the field of learning disabilities, Van Reusen and Bos have developed methods of including adolescents with learning disabilities in school-based IEP conferences by teaching them various participation strategies. I-PLAN (Van Reusen & Bos, 1990) uses from one to two weeks of daily, 45-minute sessions to teach adolescents how to inventory their strengths, weaknesses, goals, and interests and how to use the inventories at IEP meetings.

In California, Male (1991) developed worksheets for children and parents to help them prepare for Student Study Team meetings. These forms help children identify favorite activities, interests, personal strengths, changes they would like to see in school or in particular classes, and future goals. The parent form contains questions about discipline techniques, expectations for the child, concerns, and what the parent particularly enjoys about the child.

Peters (1990) has also developed a model for youth participation in team meetings. She reviewed studies on self-efficacy, self-monitoring, resistance, and student contributions as they related to greater involvement in the IEP process. Her model includes strategies to improve student involvement in the entire IEP process, with special emphasis on the IEP conference itself.

Gillespie and Turnbull (1983) offer practical suggestions for helping children understand team meetings. Children must be allowed enough time to share information, even if another meeting is needed. They should be encouraged to preview written reports with an adult, discuss goals, and relate lessons and assignments back to these goals. Treating students with respect requires jargon-free communication, talking with students rather than about them, and inviting their input as helpful and valuable. The goal is to empower students to "make decisions and take responsibility concerning their needs, and more important, their futures" (Van Reusen, 1990, p. 32).

Canadian youth whose problems have brought them in contact with the child welfare system now have their own advocacy organization staffed by former youth in care: The National Youth in Care Network (NYICN) is involved in a wide range of efforts to improve services to children with special needs. Brian Raychaba, one of the early leaders of this network, describes what can happen when youth who have long been silenced are finally empowered to voice their concerns:

> In 1987, a delegation of NYICN members, all survivors of child sexual abuse, presented before a special committee of the Canadian Senate, voicing their concerns and opinions on proposed legislation dealing with testimony and evidence issues relating to child sexual abuse.
>
> "You are the only group of this kind we have heard from and will likely

hear from," commented one committee member. "You have served the cause well for yourselves and for others who will suffer this problem."
A number of the recommendations put forward by the youth delegation were translated into legislation. This was advocacy at work, young people in care affecting change for themselves and others like them; this was empowerment! (Raychaba, 1990, p. 35)

"Youth in care" are regular participants at meetings of many Canadian professional groups, serving on panels and in workshops, providing that unique perspective that can only come from direct experience. Raychaba (1990) shares these reflections from a group of 30 Canadian youth who had been recipients of services from the child welfare system:

It is vitally important that those treating us recognize that *we must be party to our own healing*. In our opinion, the treatment system at the present time is not child or young person focused. . . . Choice is crucial. We know what helps and what doesn't. We must have some say in the design, implementation, and evaluation of particular treatment programs. (p. 30)

SUMMARY AND CONCLUSIONS

Part I of this book introduces the models and benefits of teamwork. No matter what model is used—interagency, multidisciplinary, interdisciplinary, or transdisciplinary—good teamwork should be undergirded by empowerment values. Empowerment must not be reserved for already powerful administrators, professionals, and adults. We learned from once silenced voices of youth that if healing is to begin and intervention is to make any difference, adults on teams must go beyond polite, perfunctory listening. If the ultimate benefit of teamwork is to improve the decision-making process and thereby enhance the effectiveness of treatment or education plans, those traditionally excluded—children and youth facing challenging difficulties—must have a voice. We must invite them into our circles of collaboration and listen to them with openness and respect.

Professional teams develop over time and move through distinct stages (joining, storming, norming, and performing). Likewise, young persons develop over time and move through stages. At each developmental stage they are destined to assume increasing freedom and responsibility. As team development unfolds and procedures become institutionalized, team members must avoid ensnarement in the old traps of patriarchy, bureaucracy, and factory efficiency. To exclude youth from the team process—to treat them only as future citizens with no say in their present lives—is paternalistic. To ignore their individual voices is bureaucratic and ultimately inefficient. Teams, whatever their stage of development, must remain open adhocracies that hear, understand, and build upon the developmental stages of young or less skilled participants.

Youth, as embryonic citizens, must be provided opportunities to become competent team members and thereby create their own destinies. They need invitations to articulate their goals, commit to the plans, experience the collaborative climate, and receive support for and recognition of their contributions. When teams truly "co-labor" with youth as entitled members, the door of teaming swings open, letting out the stale myths of manipulation, control, and exclusion and allowing in the fresh vision of empowerment.

REFERENCES

Adelman, H., MacDonald, V., Nelson, P., Smith, D., & Taylor, L. (1990). Motivational readiness and the participation of children with learning and behavior problems in psychoeducational decision making. *Journal of Learning Disabilities, 23*(3), 171–176.

Beane, J. (1991). Sorting out the self-esteem controversy. *Educational Leadership, 49*(1), 25–30.

Bednar, R., Wells, M., & Peterson, S. (1989). *Self-esteem: Paradoxes and innovations in clinical theory and practice.* Washington, DC: American Psychological Association.

Brendtro, L., Brokenleg, M., & Van Bockern, S. (1990). *Reclaiming youth at risk.* Bloomington, IN: National Educational Service.

Brendtro, L., & Hinders, D. (1990). A saga of Janusz Korczak, the king of children. *Harvard Educational Review, 60*(2), 237–246.

Brendtro, L., & Long, N. (1993). *The journal of emotional and behavioral problems.* Bloomington, IN: National Educational Service.

Brendtro, L., & Wasmund, W. (1989). The peer culture model. In R. Lyman & S. Prentice-Dunn (Eds.), *Residential and inpatient treatment of children and adolescents.* New York: Plenum Press.

Fine, M. (1991). *Framing dropouts: Notes on the politics of an urban public high school.* Albany: State University of New York Press.

Freire, P. (1985). *The politics of education.* South Hadley, MA: Bergin and Garvey.

Gabor, P., & Greene, I. (1991). Views from the inside: Young people's perceptions of residential services. *Journal of Child and Youth Care Work, 7,* 6–19.

Gearhart, B., & Gearhart, C. (1989). *Learning disabilities: Educational strategies* (5th ed.). Columbus, OH: Merrill.

Gillespie, E., & Turnbull, A. (1983). It's my IEP: Involving students in the planning process. *Teaching Exceptional Children, 16*(1), 26–29.

Harkins, S. (1991). The IEP as a lived experience: Portraits of students in behavior disorder programs. Doctoral dissertation, National College of Education, National-Louis University, Chicago.

Heyman, W. (1990). The self-perception of a learning disability and its relationship to academic self-concept and self-esteem. *Journal of Learning Disabilities, 23*(8), 472–475.

Iano, R. (1990). Special education teachers: Technicians or educators. *Journal of Learning Disabilities, 23*(8), 462–465.

Liepmann, C. M. (1928) *Die Selbstverwaltung der Gefangenen.* In M. Liepmann (Ed.), Hamburgishe Schriftn zur gesamten Strafrechstswessenschaft (vol. 12). Mannheim/Berlin/Leipzig.

Male, M. (1991). Effective team participation. *Preventing School Failure, 35*(4), 29–35.

Mitchell, B. (1988). Who chooses? *Transition Summary, 5,* 4. National Information Center for Children and Youth with Handicaps.

Morsink, C., Thomas, C., & Correa, V. (1991). *Interactive teaming: Consultation and collaboration in special programs.* New York: Macmillan.

Ness, J., & Price, L. (1990). Meeting the psychosocial needs of adolescents and adults with LD. *Intervention in School and Clinic, 26*(1), 16–21.

Peters, M. (1990). Someone's missing: The student as an overlooked participant in the IEP process. *Preventing School Failure, 34*(4), 32–36.

Raychaba, B. (1990). Empowerment. In F. Kool (Ed.), *The power to change lies within the families.* Rijswijk, Netherlands: Ministry of Welfare, Health and Culture.

Reynolds, M., & Birch, J. (1988). *Adaptive mainstreaming* (3d ed.). White Plains, NY: Longman.

Turnbull, A., & Turnbull, R. (1991). *Families, professionals, & exceptionalities: A special partnership (2d ed.).* Columbus, OH: Merrill.

Turnbull, A., & Turnbull, R. (1991). Including all children. *Children today,* 20, 2, p. 3–5.

Sachs, J., Iliff, V., & Donnelly, R. (1987). Oh, ok, I'm LD! *Journal of Learning Disabilities, 20*(2), 92–93.

Schultz, J. (1985). The parent/professional conflict. In H. R. Turnbull & A. Turnbull (Eds.) *Parents speak out: Then and now* (2d ed.). Columbus, OH: Merrill.

Shea, T., & Bauer, A. (1991). *Parents and teachers of children with exceptionalities: A handbook for collaboration* (2d ed.). Needham Heights, MA: Allyn & Bacon.

Skrtic, T. M. (1991). *Behind special education: A critical analysis of professional culture and school organization.* Denver, CO: Love.

Smith, C. (1991). *Learning disabilities: The interaction of learner, task and setting.* Needham Heights, MA: Allyn & Bacon.

Van Reusen, A., & Bos, C. (1990). I-PLAN: Helping students communicate in planning conferences. *Teaching Exceptional Children, 22*(4), 30–32.

Varenhorst, B. (1984). Peer counseling: Past promises, current status and future directions. In *Handbook of counseling psychology* (pp. 716–751). New York: Wiley.

Vorrath, H., & Brendtro, L. (1985). *Positive peer culture* (2d ed.). New York: Aldine-De-Gruyter.

Wilker, K. (1921). *Der Lindenhof: Werden und Wollen von Karl Wilker.* Heilbronn am Neckar: Lichtkampf-Verlag Hanns Alternann.

▶ 6

Planning for Change

Rochelle Haimes

INTRODUCTION

Imagine this scene:

> *Anywhere, USA. The Central Children's Home staff are gathered for a meeting with the Executive Director. She has just returned from a seminar on "Teamwork." And she has decided that this model of organization will cure all the problems that have been prevalent in the Home's program— the competition between departments, the turf protection, the lack of coordinated planning for the children in residence. She plans to meet next month with the Board of Directors and announce the newly organized programs. A revised organizational chart of the agency is presented to the staff, with current staff grouped into teams. Just before the meeting, she informed the recreation staff that they would be assigned to teams and that two supervisory positions would be eliminated. A memo attached to the new organizational chart gives dates and times of three training sessions to further orient staff to the new model. The director ends the meeting with these words, "Now we are teams. Let the practice begin!"*

Now, imagine this scene:

> *Anywhere, USA. Central High's basketball team huddles before the game. The bleachers are filled with cheering friends and families. The coach ends the pep talk with these words; "We've been working for a year. We've practiced night and day. You've each been selected for your individual talents and for your ability to be part of this team. We can win this game if we remember that we are more together than we are as separate players. And, if we lose, let us lose gracefully and as a team. Now, go out there and play ball!*

Somewhat exaggerated examples of teamwork? Informal review of human service organizations indicates that too often change is introduced without adequate planning and preparation, as in the first example. This chapter will address how achieving interdisciplinary teamwork in schools, residential child care, and other settings is often an elusive reality in the absence of careful planning for change. Residential child care programs will provide the primary examples in this chapter, but the concepts are applicable to other settings and facilities.

What motivates the urge to change from a departmental to a team model in human service organizations? Some possible factors are:

- The quick fix: We want the benefits of change, and we want them quickly because the children are rioting and the staff is rapidly exiting.
- The *Newsweek* approach: We read about a new method in the magazine last night; let's try it in the classroom/cottage tomorrow.
- Gridlock: The staff are spending too much time defending their departmental turfs and less time on the needs of the children; the children are too often the pawns and put in the middle while departments are competing.
- The end of the book is the best: The benefits of teamwork are more exciting to learn about than the process of change from the old system to the new one.

Without substantial planning, and in the absence of an environment conducive to teamwork, teams start functioning from an inadequate base. Quite often, when the teams do not perform, it is believed that the *model* failed. In many of these cases the problem was that the environment was not ready for change. The organizational structure, administrative leadership, and training level of staff did not provide the essential basis for teamwork to *succeed*.

PLANNING FOR THE TRANSITION TO TEAMWORK

Organizations that decide to implement the team model, or that are considering this approach, must *plan* for transition. In most human service agencies this means changing from a departmental structure. Staff will be faced with different expectations for performance and communication. Many of the "old rules" will no longer apply. It is not uncommon for subtle and overt resistance to occur as the former structure is replaced.

Residential group care when organized departmentally usually assigns contact with public schools to the child's social worker. The team model will assign service delivery to a group of staff, each with some different responsibilities, but with less rigid and inviolate boundaries. It was not surprising that, for the first few months after the team model was introduced at one children's home, Team A's social worker was the only team member to contact community schools attended by the children in her cottage. In theory, any member of the team could have had some contact with the school or responded to inquiries. The old role definitions continued even under a new model. (Example from anecdotal information from staff of the Adolescent Center at Barium Springs Home for Children, NC.)

It is critical to keep in mind that reorganization is a *process*. Change will not just happen; it will need to evolve through planning. If the process is grounded in careful planning, continual evaluation, and modification as needed, the team model can emerge as an effective vehicle for service delivery. (These factors are further discussed in Chapter 7, "The Process of Reorganization.")

The assumption in this chapter is that teamwork is more than a value system or a philosophy of working together more effectively. It is the *result* of an informed and supportive governing body, administrative vision and leadership, an organizational structure that supports teamwork, trained personnel, and resources that support team functioning.

Administrative Leadership

Planned change does not happen in a vacuum, nor does it emerge without administrative leadership from the "top" of the organization. The Chief Executive Officer (CEO) needs to initiate the process and articulate the vision. The CEO may delegate much of the actual work to others, but this is the position that must educate the board members and must identify those in the organization who will have primary responsibility *and* authority for planning and implementing change. This education and identification will enable other positions to work within an environment that supports a changed model of delivering services. If not, those same people will spend too much energy convincing the CEO that change is needed and too little energy on the very tough work ahead.

Attitudes and Values

An organization's value system is critical. Attitudes that can support (or interfere with) the team model include: (1) flexibility to consider different approaches and interventions with clients, (2) respect for change and ability to plan for change, and (3) decentralized and delegated authority evident in present programming and organizational life. Administrative attitudes that are conducive to planned change will include: (1) having realistic expectations, (2) having no expectations of a "finished product" without adequate preparation, (3) seeing the need to evaluate progress regularly, and (4) determining needed refinements so that resources and interventions can be planned accordingly.

ASSESSING ORGANIZATIONAL READINESS

The process begins with a careful assessment of the organization to determine what level of "readiness" exists before the team model is implemented. Several factors need to be examined to determine if they will support or interfere with effective teamwork.

Assessment

A careful, candid, and thorough assessment of the organization as it currently operates will determine readiness and may indicate areas that need attention in planning for a transition to teamwork. Central to this assessment is identifying variables and factors that *support* the team model. This assessment also includes factors that may be *barriers* to reorganizing. The general questions addressed are: What is in place? What needs to be in place? What resources will be necessary to prepare the environment for the team model? This activity will set the stage for thinking about change and will begin to create an environment conducive to that successful change.

Variables That Support Reorganization

Each of the variables discussed in the following subsections can be a support or barrier to reorganization of service delivery. Successful planning to implement the team model will expect that each of these variables be in place to some significant extent from the start.

Endorsement of the Governing Body. The governing body cannot be the last to know! In most organizations this group is not responsible for implementing day-to-day programming. It is, however, responsible for defining the mission of the organization, the general philosophy, and the basic values.

The team model brings a distinct philosophy and value system to service delivery. Significant responsibilities and authority are delegated to direct service staff, who are both organized into teams and responsible for most of the service delivery to clients. Supervisors and departments are no longer the focal point of the agency's organizational chart. Therefore, it is crucial that the governing body understand the theory of teamwork so that its members can endorse the adoption of this model. This will provide the background for regular progress reports on the transition within the organization. Moreover, the endorsement by the board will lend credibility and provide support as the staff become involved in program change.

An effective way to begin is for the CEO to appoint a planning committee with representation from the board, the CEO, key administrative staff, and representatives from direct service personnel. This committee begins systematically to collect information and to bring this information periodically to the board and to the general staff. An evaluation of how services are currently organized can be a starting point. It is important that this assessment include candid appraisals of how the present organizational structure supports or impedes delivering services to clients. Client satisfaction surveys, data on client services outcomes, and information from referral sources are some sources of information. The committee can next explore the alternative team-work model by reviewing information in the professional literature and by visiting one or two agencies that have successfully implemented the team model. This committee would present findings to the full board with some plan for transition to the team model. An informed board can then give the necessary endorsement to begin changing the service delivery system.

There are varied opinions on the use of a consultant at this point of the change process. This writer's point of view supports a consultant as a *facilitator* as opposed to a "supreme authority." There is an adage that warns that "local saints perform no miracles." The consultant can provide information to the board without having a vested interest and can enable the group to participate in the change process. The consultant who goes beyond this role and does too much of the actual work for the board and staff unintentionally will limit the board and staff involvement and thus their responsibility for and ownership of the outcomes.

Administrative Vision. Oren Harari (1991) has defined the essence of leadership as "creating change, even when colleagues within the organization don't quite see the need for it. . . . Effective leaders challenge the status quo, and they do it regularly" (p. 63). This certainly typifies the role of the administrator who has been flexible and looked at alternative models of service delivery. If teamwork has been embraced in theory, the commitment needs to extend to the *process,* beginning with enabling the governing body to endorse the work, from assessment of the organization to implementation of the model. The commitment will include planning for change, challenging staff to learn other ways of working, providing consistent support, and involving others in the process.

Depending on the size and structure of an organization, the CEO may or may not be the primary change agent. In small organizations the CEO may have direct involvement in planning and implementing the change. In all cases this is *the* position that sees the need and challenges others to become involved in the process. The majority of the work of implementation may then be delegated to others by the director of the children's home or the principal of the school. The CEO then has continuing responsibilities that are crucial to the process of reorganization: (1) supporting and consulting to the staff directly responsible for implementing the change to teamwork, (2) advocating for and assisting in acquiring the necessary resources, and (3) reporting and interpreting to the governing body.

PREPARING THE ENVIRONMENT AND STAFF FOR CHANGE

Capable administrators know that understanding how people respond to change is critical in preparing the environment to accept change. To most people, thinking about change is unsettling; the known, no matter how unpleasant or dysfunctional, is more secure than the unknown. Also, it is not unusual that perceiving change as a threat is directly proportional to how involved one is in the process. Those with little understanding of the background of change and with less responsibility for the outcomes are the most apprehensive. Therefore, administrative leadership needs to help staff experience change as a process of moving from one way of working to another.

Moore and Gergen (1989) describe four stages of staff response to change:

1. *Shock:* Change is seen as a threat and the ability to hear and understand is limited. Staff need some time to understand the need for proposed changes, what their role will be, what will *not* change, and an opportunity to express concerns. This is *not* a time to expect people to become involved in planning.

2. *Defensive Retreat:* There is a tendency to invest energy in maintaining usual ways of doing things. Some anxiety or anger can encourage a refusal to let go of the past. At this stage, staff need help in identifying what will *not* change and what makes them most uncomfortable. Introducing clear expectations as well as more information about changes in roles is helpful at this point.

3. *Acknowledgement:* As staff are enabled to let go, they can begin to see more value in what is coming. The sense of sadness may be gradually replaced by some excitement about the future and how they can participate. Energy can begin to refocus on some of the future tasks. Staff can be involved more effectively in planning at this stage. Taking risks can be encouraged by emphasizing that everyone is learning from the process.

4. *Adaptation:* Most staff are ready to take on new roles and establish new routines and work methods. Plans can be more fully implemented at this stage. Those few staff who are less able to move ahead will be easier to identify. Some may be "stuck" in the earlier stages (as opposed to being genuinely resistant to change). With some additional time, some can move to the acknowledgment stage. However, some may be unable to participate in the new organization.

Administrative leadership that understands human response to change will allow time for staff to go through these stages and to be better prepared to participate in teamwork.

Fullan (1991) offered additional perspectives on the change process. He emphasizes that implementation results from several dynamic factors that eventually must combine to support re-learning and produce change. Staff need to become active participants, to feel both pressure and support for a change, to learn new techniques as well as supporting beliefs, and to gradually acquire ownership for the new model. Chapter 7 gives further attention to the importance of ownership.

The administrator will appreciate not only the complexity of change but also the many variables that must come together to eventually implement change. Chapter 7 continues this theme and offers additional insights into the process.

Personnel

Leadership. The position responsible for the day-to-day operation of the team model is perhaps the most crucial factor to consider. Programs that have operated successfully in a departmental model have usually had directors who function well in a hierarchical model. Direction of a team model requires different talents and skills. Garner (1982) identified three major categories of administrative responsibilities: (1) establishing a basic structure for the team model, (2) assigning specific responsibilities and authority to the teams, and (3) monitoring and supporting team functioning. The program director who can be successful in carrying out these responsibilities would have these abilities: (1) comfort with decentralization, (2) ability to delegate authority and to assign clear expectations for teams, (3) ability to establish the team model structure, and (4) ability to enable staff to function as teams by providing training and consulting. The importance of this position is also considered in the next chapter and in Part III.

As the Executive Director considers the leadership personnel variable, he or she most probably considers the current program manager or some other staff member who has shown potential or interest in program management. Perlmutter's (1990) discussion of human service administration would urge the executive to first identify what leadership the teamwork model needs (versus who is available) and to evaluate candidates against those factors. The alternative may be to recruit new leadership with talents more suited to the team model and its success.

Direct Practice Staff. Many staff who have worked effectively within a departmental structure can transfer to and succeed in a team model. However, some staff may not have the values and potential to develop the needed skills. As with the program Director, it is critical to develop a profile of qualities needed in staff who will be able to function as part of an interdisciplinary team. This profile will also be useful in assessing current personnel and their ability to transition into another model of service delivery.

Some of the skills needed to work well as a team member are: (1) ability to identify with an interdisciplinary team, versus a department of like positions; (2) ability to manage job responsibilities without hierarchical supervision; (3) some work experience with other disciplines in co-planning and coordinating services for clients; (4) some demonstrated ability to problem solve as part of a work group; (5) above-average communication skills; and (6) some ability to share responsibility for successes as well as for failures.

Additional tools that assist the administrator in assessing staff ability to be part of a team are revised job descriptions. These would be revised to include team responsibilities. Training that prepares staff to function as a team would be planned as both orientation to the new model and as ongoing once the transition has occurred.

It is not uncommon for some staff not to be able to work as effectively in a team model, even after adequate training and sufficient practice time. They were initially employed for another model of organization and may have skills appropriate to departmental functioning and behavior. This situation presents a particular challenge to the program director, who may be faced with long-term staff unable to be productive as team members. Several programs that have continued with tenured staff in order to avoid replacing them have threatened the advance of the teams. The preferred stance is for the team model to direct the recruiting profile, versus allowing the skills of current staff to determine how far the model can succeed.

Brendtro and Ness (1983) concur on the issue that some staff who have succeeded in a hierarchical model will have difficulty as part of a team where responsibility is shared with others. They believe, however, that most staff transitioning to teamwork are motivated by believing (and experiencing) that teams will have genuine authority. This is a crucial point for the program administrator to understand as staff are oriented to the team model. Examples of where teams *will* have responsibility and decision-making authority can serve to engage staff's interest and understanding of the new model.

There is more detailed focus on team personnel in Chapter 9. The authors consider both the general qualifications of direct practice staff that can best function in the team model and some direction for recruiting and training.

Program Structure

Written Documents.   Policies, procedures, practice standards, job descriptions, and related written materials form the structure of service delivery programs. One of the most obvious variables needing change is the written material that provides structure and reflects the program. To the extent that policies and practices continue to reflect the former program design, the team model will lack written reinforcers. Examination of written documents will clearly show where the concepts and standards of teamwork need to be added. As these documents change and refinements continue, the team structure becomes institutionalized as a more permanent cornerstone of the program (Krueger, 1987).

Job descriptions have been previously mentioned as an example of a key written document that needs to include team responsibilities as well as those specific to the role, for example, social worker, or counselor. The organizational chart of the agency can visually reflect the change from departmental to teamwork structure; additionally, this document visually reinforces how staff are organized to deliver services. The organizational chart of Residential Services from Barium Springs Home for Children (Figure 6-1) illustrates this point.

Physical Plant.   The physical organization for programs organized departmentally will not automatically support teamwork. This variable is often overlooked in planning for the transition to teams. Teams need to have physical proximity for their members just as departments are often housed together. In residential group care settings, teams housed in cottages together usually function more effectively than if any members are

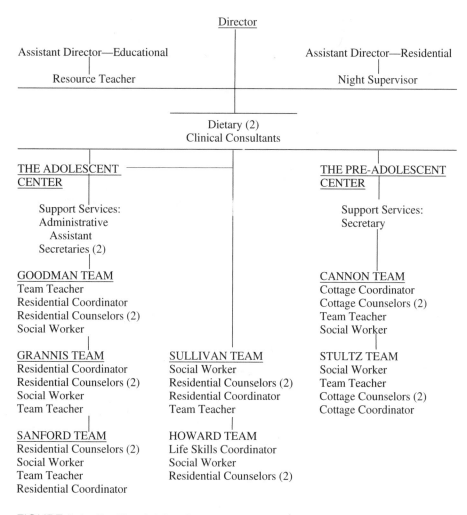

FIGURE 6-1 **Residential Services**

separately housed. Although it may involve some planning and cost, it is important to
identify modifications that will be needed in the physical plant.

Financial Resources

This variable is one of the more difficult to evaluate when initial planning for teams
begins. There is a great deal of focus on reorganizing human resources from departments to teams. At the same time, attention to reallocation and differential use of
resources can either support or hinder team development.

Salaries and staff development funds are two common factors to assess. The experience of one residential program showed that no additional monies were needed for salaries; instead, the monies that had been budgeted were used to equalize salaries for child care workers, social workers, and teachers. Instead of each department having different salaries, with child care workers in the lower range, salaries for all staff were determined by education and experience. In another facility, all money allocated for the annual staff development budget was divided equally among the four teams. Also, each team was the recipient of training dollars and decided what their training needs were.

The program administrator can creatively allocate financial resources in other ways to support team functioning. He or she can delegate responsibility for some appropriate budget line items directly to the teams instead of centrally overseeing all operating monies. Some typical line items would include food, cottage and/or classroom supplies, and activity/recreation.

SUMMARY AND CONCLUSIONS

Back at the Central Children's Home:

The Executive Director is meeting with the staff to review planning for the transition to the team model. The director first reports that the board continues to support the transition plan and has received full information regarding the phasing out of departments. In fact, a special meeting of the board will occur next week and the focus will be on planning for teamwork. At this point the Executive Director asks the Program Director to give the final report of the Planning Committee. This committee has included representation from the board and staff from administration and direct service. They have evaluated benefits and constraints of the traditional departmental model and have explored teamwork as an alternative way of organizing services. They have looked at the many variables in the agency that will support or hinder the transition to teams. Their suggestions for activity that will support the transition to teams have been implemented in many areas; some initial training on teamwork has been completed, and more is scheduled. Most of the staff are feeling optimistic about being part of a team; a few are unsure about their ability to work in the "new" way. The committee then distributes the finalized job descriptions, which a subgroup of the staff developed. Staff assignments to teams will be on the agenda for the next meeting. Let the practice begin!

This chapter echoes a common theme that appears throughout this volume: that implementing teamwork in human service organizations is challenging and not without complications. Proponents of this model are usually the first to acknowledge that, although the model has the *potential* for more effective service delivery, putting the structure in place takes effort, patience, and time. Organizational change does not occur quickly, nor do anticipated results occur magically. This has been the experience of practitioners in schools, residential programs, and other services that use a team model of organization.

Both of the chapters in Part II stress the importance of *planning* for the transition from a departmental, hierarchical model to a teamwork model. A core belief is that change cannot occur without the endorsement of the governing body, focused and effective administrative leadership, and attitudes and values that support a different way of working with clients. Articulating the vision is critical at all stages of the process, from the beginning stages of reorganization and through each step of the process that leads to implementing a changed program.

The process of assessing organizational readiness takes into account a variety of factors that have the potential to support or impede change to the teamwork model. Taking a careful look at each of the variables that support reorganization is necessary work for the program administrator who gives leadership to changing the structure of the agency. This process is an important prerequisite for the team model to succeed.

REFERENCES

Brendtro, L., & Ness, A. (1983). *Re-educating troubled youth.* New York: Aldine.

Fullan, M. (1991). *The new meaning of educational change.* New York: Teachers College Press.

Garner, H. (1982). *Teamwork in programs for children and youth.* Springfield, IL: Thomas.

Harari, O. (1991). The essence of leadership. *Management Review, 7,* 63.

Krueger, M. (1987). Making the team approach work in residential group care. *Child Welfare, 66,* 447–457.

Moore, M., & Gergen, P. (1989). *Managing risk taking during organizational change.* King of Prussia, PA: Organizational Design and Development.

Perlmutter, F. (1990). *Changing hats: From social work practice to administration.* Washington, DC: NASW Press.

▶ 7

The Process of Reorganization

Steven A. Roy

GETTING STARTED

Change looks so easy when we read about it. Writers of reform do an injustice when they present an easy, step-by-step process toward implementing change. Change is not easy! Getting started is also not easy and has its own set of complications. When an organization needs to reorganize for teamwork, who is responsible for initiating the change? The team model values and uses participation in decision making by those who are affected by and carry out decisions. However, it is important to distinguish change initiation from change participation. It is the author's experience that major organizational restructuring must be supported by those who have the authority and responsibility for the total organization. Participation in the change process is for all to partake in, but it is the chief executive who needs to get the ball rolling. (This chief executive officer may be a president, school superintendent, principal, or director.) Thus, this chapter focuses on the process of reorganization with a focus on the role of the chief executive. The chapter attempts to provide a clear prescription of steps the leader of an organization needs to take in initiating and managing change.

Planning and Preparation

Reorganization into a team model is a serious endeavor. It should not be taken lightly by those who will act as "change agents" within or outside the organization. The most critical ingredients in getting the organization on the right path are planning and preparation prior to actual implementation of the team model. The author of the previous chapter presented a plan for change that focuses on the issue of transition and the required preparation necessary for a smooth changeover from a departmentalized model to a model for teamwork. The following sections of this chapter continue this discussion from a reorganization perspective.

When one is contemplating adopting a teamwork model, it is important to follow four basic strategies. The following are considered fundamental prerequisites to the planning and preparation process:

1. Assess change readiness within your organization (see Chapter 6).
2. Develop a clear vision of what the change will be, the reasons behind the change, and the benefits to be realized.
3. Articulate the values of the organization (Kanter, 1991).
4. Use research to support your plan (Glickman, 1991).

Assessing Readiness for Change

Is your organization ready for change? Is the timing right? These two questions are extremely important in the reorganization process. Change is difficult for people. There are many reasons why change may be looked upon with suspicion by those who will experience the process. Each organization will have its own major areas of suspicion and concern. It is important for an organization to assess its own unique situation and develop some ways of reducing or eliminating resistance to change. Following are some of the reasons why people resist change:

- New goals are not accepted.
- People fear the unknown.
- People fear failure in the new situation.
- People like the current situation and arrangement.
- Reasons for change are not communicated well enough.
- People do not like or trust the individual or group initiating the change.
- New goals are unimportant to people.
- The changing environment is seen as an opportunity to oppose management.
- People fear loss of status, rights, and privileges.
- People resist change because it's change.

Although this list does not exhaust the potential reasons why people may resist change, it does point out the importance of being aware of the need to assess the situation and prepare for ways of reducing or eliminating the resistance. Some practical ways that have been successful are:

- Involve interested parties in contributing to the planning of change.
- Design flexibility into change. Make change in phases, where possible, to allow for the completion of initial efforts and the development of new behaviors.

- Have open sessions where those involved can express their feelings about the change and raise concerns for consideration.
- Do not leave openings for a return to the status quo. To do so is to encourage resistance.
- Design change to minimize the effects on the rights, benefits, and privileges of the people affected by the change.

Developing a Clear Vision

Besides assessing change readiness, individuals involved in reorganization must also be sure they develop a clear vision of what the change will achieve. In the prior chapter, administrative visioning was discussed. This *vision* requires that goals and objectives be established, as well as the reasons behind change and the benefits for the future. It is important to be open and honest in developing a shared vision. Do not deny that negative aspects of change exist, for all change has potential negative effects. No system or structure is perfect, and, thus, the vision for the future should include an awareness of what may be lost in the process of change.

The values of the organization should be articulated at this stage. As indicated in Chapter 6, the organization's attitudes and values are a critical factor. Reorganization should flow from the mission statement of the organization. It should include the beliefs and values of the organiaztion as well as those of the employees. This is an essential step in the process of reorganization because it allows the organization to build on its traditions, strengths, and values.

Using Research to Support the Plan

What is the place of research literature when preparing and planning the reorganization process? Literature is not only a way to learn about others' experience, but also a way to find necessary support for your organization's reorganization plan. In other words, do your homework. Studying the experiences of other organizations will help to avoid potential pitfalls of poor planning and preparation. Much has been written about the process of teamwork. A review of the literature is one way of ensuring that your organization is well prepared for its upcoming reorganization into a teamwork model.

One must not forget the value of relying on others for help. Some organizations make considerable use of consultants as well as colleagues to help organize the process. This is part of good planning and preparation. Visiting other facilities that have gone through the reorganization process is another way of ensuring that the organization has covered all possibilities. Do not be afraid to include as many staff members as possible. Involve interested parties in these facility visitations. This helps those who will be affected by the change to imagine how they might benefit.

Table 7-1 presents a reorganization planning model that can be used by an organization. Planning and preparation are the most essential part of reorganization. They should not be taken lightly.

TABLE 7 • **Reorganization Planning Model**

DESIGN THE PROGRAM AND TEAM MODEL
ACCORDING TO THE MISSION STATEMENT
AND CORE BELIEFS

ARTICULATE THE VALUES OF THE
ORGANIZATION

ASSESS CHANGE READINESS WITHIN THE
ORGANIZATION

DEVELOP A CLEAR VISION OF CHANGE, REASONS
FOR CHANGE AND THE BENEFITS OF CHANGE

USE RESEARCH TO SUPPORT REORGANIZATION

SOLICIT FEEDBACK FROM TEAMS

IMPLEMENT THE PROGRAM WITHIN MISSION
STATEMENT

OBSERVE AND MONITOR

REFINE

AN ORGANIZED PROCESS OF CHANGE

Reorganizing an organization along the teamwork model requires a process that is arranged in a way that, as a final result, permits teamwork to be the highest priority within the organization. It is important to reiterate that the basic purpose of a team model is to develop a client-centered approach to child care and education. The organization is arranged around clients and not staff. The organization becomes client-centered.

To reorganize a residential or educational program into a client-centered one is not easy. Aren't all schools and residential institutions client-centered? Unfortunately, in many cases the answer is "no"; many are centered on disciplines, departments, or specializations. What then should be included in a process that will result in an organization devoted to teamwork and client-centeredness? The following steps will be discussed in detail:

1. Explain the team model and its benefits to the Board of Directors and key administrators to gain their support.
2. Subdivide larger groups of staff (departments) and clients (campus cottages) into smaller groupings, if necessary.
3. Redefine physical space (turf).
4. Present the team model to direct service staff.
5. Present the team model to families and clients.
6. Form teams and involve them in the reorganization process.
7. Share responsibility and authority.
8. Reorganize the program budget according to the number of teams formed.
9. Provide an organizational home for every client and staff member.

Gaining Support at the Top

When reorganizing, it is essential to involve the Board of Directors early in the change process. As pointed out in Chapter 6, board members cannot be the last to know! Before making a board presentation, one should be well prepared to show the benefits of reorganization. Board members are often more concerned with financial issues than they are with day-to-day program operation. Therefore, it is important that the chief executive present to the board the financial implications of reorganization. If resistance occurs, do not be afraid to present research literature, as well as testimony from colleagues and consultants, as a way of building support for change.

If your board has a program committee, it will be important to meet with its members to discuss the general condition of the organization. It is beneficial to share with them the results of your assessment of the organization's readiness for change and your plan for reducing or eliminating the resistance. Again, the secret is *be prepared and do your homework.*

Much the same should be done with your key administrators—the heads of the departments that may be eliminated or drastically altered. It is essential that they comprehend the reasons beind the proposed changes. It is important for them to understand that you as the chief executive will also have to make significant changes—everyone will be affected. Again, it is imperative that you be able to show the benefits of change, not only for them but for the program in general.

Early in the process you will need to spend some time helping department heads see their new places of responsibility. Some will become supervisors of teams rather than supervisors of departments based on a single discipline. This interdisciplinary aspect will give them a new focus of responsibility. Allow your key administrators the opportunity to think about the changes. Do not rush the process. They will need time to digest what you are presenting. If a look of shock is the first response, do not panic, and, above all, be sensitive to their feelings. Be prepared to answer questions and concerns now or at a later time. It is essential to gain the support of your key administrators. They will be your public relations people and your cheerleaders among your line staff.

One way of gaining support for the new structure is to provide opportunities for key administrators to visit facilities where interdisciplinary teamwork is a way of life. When they observe firsthand the marvelous benefits that teamwork provides, their fears often subside and a renewed sense of confidence surfaces. Providing books and publications on teamwork and using consultants to meet with small groups of individuals who are hesitant about the restructuring are other ways of gaining the necessary support for change. In cases where key administrators are not willing to listen or even entertain the notion of change, use your other key administrators who find your ideas positive to help lessen their fears.

It is important to note that most administrators come around once they see the real benefits and realize they have a position in the new structure. Proceeding with caution is healthy when implementing change. Chief executives need to assess the mood and situation during these early steps in the process.

Forming Smaller Units

The process of reorganizing for teamwork will require that the organization be subdivided from large units into smaller, manageable groupings with two to five teams. The number of clients in each subdivision should be limited. The purpose of subdividing is to allow for better service to each client without the problems associated with large numbers. It is also important to look for noticeable signs of turf protection such as staff attaching themselves to particular residents or students and not wanting to lose relationships, staff resisting a change of physical location or administrator, or staff removing objects from their previous work site and taking them to their new locations. Do not be afraid to challenge these behaviors in a positive way. Often individuals are not aware of their actions and the effects on others. Stress the importance of client-centeredness and the benefits that subdividing can provide to those in care. Make use of administrators and other line staff by having them discuss issues with staff who are exhibiting behaviors that disrupt the transition process.

When subdividing, it is essential that the developmental levels of the students or clients be addressed. In schools and residential programs with campus schools the process may be simplified because of the natural break in age and grade level. Some residential programs have divided very large campuses into several separate communities of 50 to 60 clients. In small residential treatment centers with limited numbers of clients it may not be necessary to subdivide into units. Large middle schools have formed small communities serving 120 pupils each.

Other issues that need addressing at this time relate to staffing. The chief executive will have to assess the staffing needs created by the reorganization process. It is important to be creative when reviewing these needs to ensure that each team and subunit has all the specialists necessary to provide the program's direct services. Often present staff can be reassigned to different positions within the organization. Some staff may be asked to assume more than one role, such as recreation specialist and classroom substitute, in order to ensure that each subdivision is sufficiently staffed. In some cases, additional staff may be needed in order to be sure that each subunit has the necessary support to serve the clients assigned. New administrators may be hired from outside the organization while some are promoted from within. It is important to keep two questions in mind: "What are our present needs?" and "How can we make use of our existing resources to address these needs?"

Redefining Space

Another primary task when developing an organized process is that of redefining space. Human beings are, by nature, turf oriented. People are very conscious of their "life space." They protect it and become disturbed when it is invaded. When reorganizing, it is important that this issue be addressed. It will be necessary for staff to be assigned to "new space" and to learn to share and value that space with others. Permitting staff to wander without designating a new area of operation can devastate the change process. Subunits may be assigned new offices, classrooms, and residential space, as well as a new area for program support staff. People will be asked to move offices and classrooms in order to centralize the work spaces of team members serving the same children. Failure to redefine space will only lead to a desire to return to the status quo, which will encourage continued resistance to the reorganization process.

Presenting the Model to Direct Service Staff

When the chief executive has explained the team model and its benefits to key administrators and has developed a plan to subdivide and redefine space, it becomes necessary to involve the direct service staff in the process. It is important that everyone hear the news at the same time. This will avoid information sharing by rumor. It also shows consideration on the part of the whole organization. All key administrators should be involved in the presentation to the staff. One person should be chosen as the main presenter. This person does not necessarily have to be the chief executive of the organization, although this individual should be present. The purpose of this presentation is to inform staff of the organization's plan to reorganize into a model for teamwork. The presentation should examine patterns of organizational stress and deficiencies in the present structure, as well as the benefits of the proposed model. The presenter should use good presentation techniques, including organizational charts and other visual aids. The discussion should include the topics of subdividing the program into child-centered units and redefining space.

Time should be allotted for questions as well as initial comments and concerns from staff. *Not allowing time for questions and reactions shows a lack of preparedness and insecurity on the part of the administration.* However, one will find that there is often very little discussion at this point. Few questions are asked and little reaction is noticed. This is typical since staff will need time to process the information and think about it. They will need the opportunity to discuss it with their fellow employees. Time to reflect and think is an important part of the process and is necessary in order to establish a working relationship among staff and administration.

Each organization will have to organize its presentation to staff according to its own situation. What is vital is that employees are made aware of the proposed changes and the reasons behind them. It is important to provide times for questions from staff. Opportunities for small-group discussion, as well as larger group interaction, are essential. Having several administrators lead these gatherings can show solidarity within the organization's management. When administrators are willing to discuss the issues at hand, it exhibits a confidence and comfortableness with the organization's direction. Questions most often asked tend to concentrate on procedures and issues of daily management. Rarely do staff confront the teamwork concept. It is difficult to argue against client-centeredness and working with others.

Including Families and Clients

Families and clients should also be involved in the process of reorganization. After all, the clients and families will also benefit from an organization that holds teamwork as its highest priority. Clients and families have rich experiences coming from their involvement in the organization's life as well as their personal lives. These experiences contain valuable information that can impact the reorganization process. In addition, participation in the process of planning for change will result in their active support during the implementation phase.

The chief executive should ensure that clients and families are made aware of the organization's desire to reorganize. This can be accomplished by inviting clients and families to attend a presentation similar to the one recommended in the previous section. It is important to note that clients and families are interested in the organization and want it to be successful. Look for ways of involving clients and families by sharing information, inviting input, and participating as team members. This can be accomplished through mailings, telephone conversations, client and family committees, family visits, and team membership. Public schools that follow the team model usually have parent representatives on the planning councils that coordinate the change process.

Forming Teams

A well-organized process of reorganization into a model for teamwork obviously requires the formation of teams. The basic guideline is to organize teams around groups of clients or students. One way to accomplish this is by developing interdisciplinary teams. These teams should include personnel from each former department that served the team's clients. In organizations serving clients who are children or youth, this can be accomplished by forming teams to include educators, social workers, counselors, child and youth care workers, and so forth. These individuals make up the core team and are responsible for the care and education of a limited number of clients. They are called the *core team* because they are the individuals who have daily interactions with the clients or students. It is important to note that in some organizations, clients and parents have been asked to participate as members of the team. As strongly encouraged in Part I, inclusion of clients and parents as participating members of the team should be given strong consideration when teams are being formed. They bring a unique perspective to decisions, and their support of the change process may be critical.

Teamwork requires people to work closely together, to give and take, to be open to other opinions, to be willing to address the concerns of others, and to respect other team members. When reorganizing, it is important to match staff properly so that these teamwork requirements can be realized. This is very difficult. In larger organizations the administrator may have to work with a hundred or so individuals who will need a home within the new team model. Some staff carry emotional baggage from the past. Some have only hearsay information about others. Some have had disagreements. Some do not like others. These factors have to be considered when teams are initially organized.

In order to help lessen conflict, it is important for the chief executive to collect as much data as possible. Some data can be collected by means of a written questionnaire. This form of inquiry concentrates on people's work relationships and choices. If different age groups are to be served, staff can express their preferences for and their perceived effectiveness with those groups. Individuals are asked to list a certain number of potential team members with whom they believe they would work well. They are also asked to list those with whom they would not wish to serve on a team. This information is one factor to be used in the initial formation of teams. It is important that confidentiality be maintained in the process. It is significant to note that, even with great effort, it is impossible to satisfy the desires of all individuals. There will be some dissatisfied employees. What is important is that the chief executive take the necessary steps to ensure that initial teams get off to the best start possible by putting the needs of the children and youth first.

These newly organized teams can become part of the reorganization process. Following initial training in team decision making, teams can work with administrators in making plans for the team meeting schedules, meeting format, team handbook and team budget, as well as the organization of team responsibilities. During this time, responsibilities are redefined in order to allow the team not only the responsibility for the total program of the client but also the authority to make significant program decisions. They become the primary care givers and receive the sanctions needed to perform their responsibilities within the organization's client-centered philosophy.

Sharing Power and Control

The issue of power and control is at the heart of the client-centered philosophy. In organizations with a hierarchical structure, power and control belong to a few. Weber (1947) describes power as "the probability that one actor within a social relationship will be in a position to carry out his own will despite resistance, regardless of the basis on which this probability rests" (p. 152). In institutions that promote teamwork there needs to be more than "one actor." Teamwork requires many actors with scripts that are identical.

When reorganizing, it is necessary to be aware of the issue of power and control and its impact on the process. Reorganizing requires that power and control be decentralized from a tightly structured chain of command to one that is loosely structured, where leadership and power are shared by those who work directly with the clients. It is important to examine the power structure of your organization prior to reorganization. How is power presently shared. Who has control? When the process begins, it is important that the issue of power and control be discussed by those who presently have the authority.

It is also very important to understand that organizations that have team models are not freed from the issue of power and control. The difference lies in the matter of *shared* power and control. Another term for this is an "organization of empowerment." In an organization of empowerment, staff are truely empowered to participate in decision making, have a sense of authority and responsibility for what they do, and share the title of "expert." In residential and educational programs that practice teamwork, chief executives need to understand that shared power is not a loss of control, but an enhancing of the organization's potential to serve clients in a much better way. In fact, many chief executives have only felt "in control" when they were able to share power with those who had daily responsibilities for the clients and students.

Newly organized teams will not function if the team members are not aware of their responsibilities. It is necessary that a clear understanding be established as to which issues a team can decide and which issues are outside their circle of influence. It is essential to articulate these at an early stage in the reorganization process.

Reorganizing the Program Budget

Team decision making about the program budget is one area that should be within the teams' circle of influence. The teams should assume the responsibility for their budgets. It is important to recognize the parallel between power and control and the amount of money allocated to a team budget. Money is power. Specific dollar amounts should be determined by the administration prior to team budgeting. Some teams may need more money than others because of various reasons (such as number of clients), but great care should be taken to ensure that equity among teams is maintained. Teams should have the responsibility to budget their allocated dollars across all aspects of the program including food, classroom materials, recreation equipment, cottage appliances, clothing, staff development, and client recreation—to name a few. This puts the responsibility for fiscal management on the individuals who are directly involved with the clients. It empowers team members to become good stewards of the limited funds available within organizations serving children and youth. Tough financial decisions can be made by team members without administrative intervention. Teams are capable of making difficult choices among the many things that need to be purchased. Frugality often accompanies control of the purse strings.

It is also important to remember that soliciting the recommendations of a team, even when it is not within their authority to make the decision, is an important step in establishing a trusting and healthy working relationship among teams and administrators. Realistically, teams cannot be consulted on all aspects of the organization—nor should they be—although the rule of thumb should be to obtain their input whenever possible.

In summary, teams should have power and control over specific aspects of the program and input into other issues, when appropriate. Table 7-2 illustrates some specific functions and responsibilities a team can have within an organization.

Locating a Place for Everyone

The final step in an organized process of reorganization requires that the chief executive ensure that all employees have a place within the framework of teams. Support services staff such as psychologists, secretaries, therapists, and special educators, to name a few, should have their responsibilities defined within the new organizational structure. They will need a home within this new organizational structure. This may be difficult because there are often not enough of these individuals for each team. When this occurs, direct service personnel can be assigned to support teams or resource teams within the subunits. Their role is to assist all the teams within each subunit by providing services to the teams and to the clients in their specific field of expertise. All individuals should have a place within the new structure. Failure to complete this part of the process can result in the establishment of minidepartments within the team model. This pitfall should be avoided at all costs.

There are several other support staff who may be members of teams. In large organizations, staff involved in food services, maintenance, fund raising, and business—among others—would probably not be considered as core team members. Some of these individuals, however, can be assigned to units when the organization is initially subdivided. Since they are not team members, it is important that they understand how the organization has been reorganized. It is also essential that they understand the new roles these teams will play, as well as their new responsibilities.

TABLE 7-2 • **Team Responsibilities**

The teams have the primary responsibility to provide services to the children and their families. They need to implement administrative decisions and maintain a record of their meetings. Routine tasks include:

1. Holding team meetings at least once a week; keeping accurate minutes of the team's discussions, recommendations, and decisions by sharing these minutes with the community director.
2. Using consensus decision making; hearing everyone's opinion; using problem-solving and decision-making skills, implementing team decisions.
3. Establishing service plans; developing, implementing, evaluating, and modifying.
4. Determining daily routine and expectations for the children of the team; establishing following, evaluating, and modifying.
5. Developing daily and weekly schedule of program activities with the recreation specialist: planning, implementing, and evaluating.
6. Implementing behavior management system; maintaining consistency, evaluating, and modifying.
7. Creating weekly staff schedules; scheduling coverage and time off. Consulting with the community director for approval of time off.
8. Taking part in the budgeting process; monitoring, implementing, and making recommendations.
9. Sharing information with the team about individual children, the home, and the team; gathering and sharing all pertinent team information, evaluating the effectiveness of the team, providing support and encouragement to team members, and providing guidance and regular feedback to team members regarding the effects of their behavior on the children and on the team.
10. Communicating with the children's natural families; maintaining regular communication with the families through the team's social worker.
11. Advising the community director of student openings; communicating team needs, evaluating potential applicants, and selecting a new student from the applicants presented.
12. Communicating team membership needs to the human resources department; interviewing and recommending hiring or rejection.
13. Providing staff development training for team members in conjunction with the community director; participating in both formal and informal evaluations of team members.
14. Generating and discussing new ideas for improving the total program; serving as consultants to the CEO and the community director in evaluating proposals for change.
15. Establishing team goals; writing goals that support those of the administration, reviewing those goals at least twice a year, and working toward achievement of goals.

This will avoid potential misunderstandings between the teams and other members of the organization's staff. Although these individuals may not be core members of the teams serving the clients, it is important to build a sense of teamwork within these departments. This can be accomplished by forming teams within the departments in order to develop a philosophy of participatory management that will permeate the whole organization.

In summary, reorganization requires an organized process. This process calls for an explanation of the team model, subdivision of the organization into smaller units, a redefinition of space, formation of teams, and the establishment of shared responsibility and authority. Chief executives should design and be responsible for an organized process based on the organization's specific needs and concerns at the time of initial reorganization.

A NEW JOB FOR THE CHIEF EXECUTIVE OFFICER

What, then, becomes the job of chief executives in the team-oriented model? They become navigators. Chief executives need to be proactive by guiding the ship. They are the keepers of the mission statement, values, and beliefs. They do not retire or disappear when the organization is reorganized. Some administrators following reorganization report beginning a new life of administration, no longer fearing to answer the office telephone. The organization has changed. Teams and team members have assumed responsibility for the program. They no longer require administrative input into every decision. With this new life of administration, time becomes available to develop a strategic plan to guide the organization, to provide training and support, to observe and monitor, to build relationships with other administrators, and to recognize new opportunities for the organization. Interactions with staff now focus on the mission statement, values, and beliefs. Some CEOs now have time to write articles, to accept positions on boards, and to still be responsible for the well-being of the organization. Part of this new well-being can be in the area of finance, with the CEO becoming more deeply involved in fund raising to support the work of teams with adequate fiscal resourses. All of this can be done without becoming distant from the daily life of the organization.

Redefining Executive Authority

Chief executives need to realize that reorganization into teams will permit them to concentrate on issues of greater importance. The days of choosing toilet paper and dealing with petty conflicts and daily crises are past. Their authority will not be diminished—it will be restructured and redistributed. The responsibility and authority are given to others; they are not abdicated. Chief executives should not be frightened by the issue of power and authority. It is understandable for those in charge to feel uneasy, reluctant, and even anxious about sharing real power. The author found it helpful to generate a clear vision of his new responsibilities as well as allowing time to process and reflect on the change that was about to take place. Chief executives, as well as line staff, want to know where they stand and what is expected of them. It is helpful, therefore, to discuss with other administrators what their responsibilities will be and to permit oneself to draw strength and assurance from them. It is also important to articulate directly the benefits of change and to focus on the client-centeredness of teamwork. Chief executives are service-oriented, caring people. They are interested in the future well-being of their staff as well as the well-being and success of the organization's clients. It is also helpful to spend time with consultants, discussing the benefits of teamwork and the CEO's new role within the organization. This takes time, but it is well worth the effort.

Providing Support and Training

When reorganizing an organization into a model for teamwork, it is essential that chief executives take action to ensure that the final outcome is supported by good practice. One way of ensuring favorable results is to provide support to the teams and the individuals involved in teamwork. This becomes an important role for the chief executive. Teamwork requires more of staff. This, in turn, requires that chief executives pay close attention to the needs of the teams. Teamwork is not easy. Teams will require extra assistance during their initial involvement in the process of teamwork.

Training is one way chief executives can provide support to the teams. On cannot assume that team members know what teamwork is or how it should work. Consultants and other individuals who have been involved in the process of teamwork can be very beneficial by providing this understanding and support. Training in issues such as active listening skills, giving and receiving feedback, consensus decision making, and team leadership are important team development experiences.

Time should be given for team members to provide feedback to others within their team. Such opportunities will allow learning to take place among fellow team members. Some individuals will exhibit higher-level teamwork skills from the start. It is important that team members be allowed to share and model skills that are beneficial to the team as a whole. This modeling can be a positive learning situation within the team and will often lead to a higher level of team functioning.

Another step leading the way to a quality product is the chief executive's concern for new staff who will join teams. It is imperative that an organized training program be developed for new team members. This training period permits new team members to learn about the mission statement, core beliefs, values of the team model, team organization, team responsibilities, and team functioning. Although this idea may seem quite elementary, it is very important to the future health of the teams and the organization in general. The rule of thumb is: Do not assume that people know what teamwork is or how it works.

Guiding the Selection of Treatment Models

When teams are given authority and responsibility for programming, it is important and inevitable that the treatment models and programming be examined. In some organizations these topics have been at the center of discussion for a long time. It is imperative that the chief executive play a role in these discussions. In large organizations that have campus schools the issue may focus on the needs of children and youth at different developmental levels and the impact treatment models have on how clients can best be served.

It is possible to use a variety of techniques within an organization. Many residential and educational organizations employ an eclectic approach. Thus, within a team organization, each campus subdivision may use methods and techniques that are appropriate for the different developmental levels of the clients being served. Most agencies have a philosophy and policies related to treatment. The chief executive articulates the philosophy and policies of the organization while participating in these discussions. Teams will need initial guidance in the selection and refinement processes. The issue of programming should not be determined exclusively by teams. The needs of clients have to be at the center of the discussion. In a client-centered organization that utilizes teamwork it is important that the chief executive add this dimension and focus to the dialogue.

Observing and Monitoring

The initial monitoring of team functioning is an important job requirement of the chief executive working within an organization that has been reorganized into a model for teamwork.

When teams are functioning well, chief executives will be able to observe a specific character, appearance, and attitude within the teams. It is the same when teams are functioning poorly. Chief executives must be aware that teams will experience different stages of development during their lifetimes.

During this time of growth the chief executive should ensure that teams receive support and assistance in the areas of training, conflict resolution, clarification of rules and goals, and feedback to help develop teams that function optimally.

The chief executive can be involved in these areas in several ways:

- Do not be afraid to use your own expertise to assist with team training.
- Work with fellow administrators in facilitating conflict resolution.
- Work with the teams to help them clarify their roles and goals by providing information pertaining to the mission statement, beliefs, and values of the organization.
- Visit teams and show interest in their work.
- Provide feedback to teams, both verbally and in written form, when appropriate.
- Thank teams for their efforts, especially when they have made difficult decisions.
- Avoid dealing with individuals by referring information and questions to the proper teams.
- Allocate time and resources for team training by other professionals who specialize in this area.

FINAL PRODUCT

The final outcome of the process of reorganization from a departmental to a team model is a powerful experience for chief executives, administrators, staff, and clients. If done properly, it will have as its outcome an organizational transformation. This transformation will result in the organization's review of its past and its present and a realization that it has discovered a new future of teamwork. This new future will be one of client-centeredness, empowerment, and shared responsibility.

The final product of reorganization creates a significant increase in communication among staff. It permits the organization to coordinate its services better because individuals are not only communicating but also working together more closely. The organization notices a decrease in acting-out behaviors of clients. Clients become aware that the teams are responsible for their programs and progress. They recognize that the teams have not only responsibility but also the authority to make decisions and carry them out. This understanding on the part of clients leads to a decrease in manipulation of staff by the residents.

There are many other results of teamwork that may be enjoyed by the organization as a whole:

- Client-centeredness
- Increased communication
- Fewer behavior problems among clients or students
- Participatory decision making
- Increased accountability and shared ownership
- Program consistency
- Less manipulation of staff by clients
- Conflict reduction
- Cooperation and support
- Better coordination of services
- Decreased competition among staff
- Improved morale
- Less staff turnover
- Increased confidence in administration

As mentioned earlier in this chapter, reorganization takes time. It is not completed overnight, and the true benefits of teamwork are experienced over a period of time. As an organization follows good teamwork practices, it realizes more and more results of its labors.

Reorganization is a process. It takes planning and preparation, organization, refinement and fine-tuning, time, and, of course, patience before a final product emerges that gives pride and joy. Teamwork requires dedication on the part of chief executives, administrators, and staff in order to meet the challenge and opportunity presented them in the professions of education and child care.

SUMMARY AND CONCLUSIONS

Much has been written on the topic of teamwork and its impact on organizations. Often organizations need to restructure to realize the full benefits teamwork can provide. Part II discussed not only the process of reorganization but also ways to plan for change so teamwork can become a reality.

Reorganization requires a commitment on the part of all involved. It challenges the CEO to take the lead by developing an organized process of change. This process calls for the assistance of board members, administrators, clients, families, and direct service staff. It requires that smaller units be formed and space be redefined. Most importantly, the process mandates that teams be formed within this new structure.

When teams are established, they must be empowered to assume responsibility for significant decisions and program elements. Although CEOs often experience some anxiety when asked to share organizational power, the empowerment of the staff in functioning teams to assume real responsibility for the program has allowed some chief administrators to experience their programs being "under control" for the first time. This experience is consistent with the concepts of staff empowerment, discussed in Part I.

When an organization is restructured, the chief executive takes on the role of navigator. The CEO becomes the keeper of the mission statement, values, and beliefs of the organization. No longer is administrative input required in every decision. Time is now available to provide support and training to the teams. This can be accomplished by helping administrators facilitate conflict; working with teams to help them clarify their roles and goals; and, most importantly, taking time to visit teams to show interest in their work and to thank them for their efforts. In Part III you will discover more ways in which support and training can be accomplished by individuals who assist teams in their work.

The final outcome of the process of reorganization is a powerful experience for chief executives, administrators, staff, and clients. It creates a new future of teamwork—a future of client-centeredness, empowerment, and shared responsibility.

REFERENCES

Edmonds, R. (1979). Some schools work and more can. *Social Policy, 9*(2), 28–32.

Glickman, C. (1991). Pretending not to know what we know. *Educational Leadership, 49,* 4–10.

Kanter, R. (1991). Championing change: An interview with Bell Atlantic's CEO Raymond Smith. *Harvard Business Review, 69,* 119–130.

Weber, M. (1947). *The theory of social and economic organizations* (T. Parsons, Trans.). New York: Free Press.

► 8

Team Recruitment, Team Building, and Skill Development

Abe M. Wilkinson   Maxine M. Smith

Perhaps by now you have made the decision to move toward a team model for your organization. But many questions surrounding the mechanics of the process remain unanswered. How does one go about recruiting staff to work in a team organization? Who makes the decision to hire? What are the qualities of personnel that result in effective team membership and make a person a desirable team member? What is the administrator's and the team's role in providing orientation to new staff? How can the probationary period be used to develop team commitment and skills? What types of training are needed? What can the administrator do to help teams function effectively? How are the monitoring and evaluation of teams and individuals accomplished? The purpose of this chapter is to provide the administrator with tools to answer these questions. It reflects the authors' experience as a two-person administrative team in a residential program for youth between the ages of 10 and 17.

THE HIRING AND ORIENTATION PROCESSES

Recruiting

Prior to the screening process, the team, with the assistance of the program administrators if necessary, assesses the team's strengths and weaknesses. This allows the team to describe the type of candidate who will help to reestablish a good balance.

The review and screening of applications/résumés is an administrative responsibility. We identify those who meet the minimum qualifications as defined by the positions including relevant education or a degree, paid and volunteer experience in the field, and general life experience. Equally important, but sometimes overlooked, aspects of screening include the quality of the writing and the general form/appearance of the cover letter, résumé, and application.

Once this initial screening is completed by administrators, the paperwork for the top three to five applicants is forwarded to the teams. Teams are responsible for contacting the applicants and scheduling interviews. The team interview, with all team members having the opportunity to meet the applicant, focuses on responsibilities outlined in the job description, program philosophy, teamwork, and identifying qualities of the applicant as a potential member of the team.

The interview provides the team the opportunity to describe their work and expectations and to get to know the candidates. A team is in the best position to explain the responsibilities of a team and its individual members. What often happens, however, is that a team becomes so intent on making the applicant aware of the many aspects of working on a team that the applicant listens for an extended period of time but may not adequately share how he or she might contribute to the team/program. As important as it is to give the candidate an informed description of the team and program, it is equally important that the team listen to the candidate.

We often compare working on a team to a five-way marriage (our teams have five members). Anyone who has experienced the difficulties of maintaining a two-person relationship can identify with the increased difficulty that this image conjures up. The interview, therefore, should be approached with the same sense of importance that one would bring to a proposal of marriage!

A series of open-ended questions, normally developed by reviewing the résumé in advance of the interview, will give the team the information they need to make a good decision. The outcome will be the result of congruency between what the candidate presents on paper and what he or she presents in person. Applicants at this stage are also required to complete a questionnaire designed to identify traits that we feel are desirable to becoming a productive member of a team in this particular agency.

Identifying Desirable Traits

Several years ago our agency developed an instrument to provide a measurement of desirable characteristics and skills of potential employees (Powell, 1988). Administration of this test, completed at the time of the team interview, yields information about areas of strength, deficit areas requiring further training or supervision, and an estimate of the ability of the candidate to fit in as a member of the team.

The instrument consists of 12 problem situations typically encountered in a residential care setting. The candidate is asked to answer each using a narrative response format. Questions are designed to measure the following characteristics:

- Ability to function in stressful situations
- Capacity to work as part of a team and to function independently
- Ability to use self effectively/self-awareness
- A tolerance of one's own ambivalence
- A belief in commitment
- A systems view of family conflict and family connections
- Refusal to be rejected by child and family
- Being intrusive in a caring way
- Controlling in a caring way
- Ability to see success in progress toward goals
- Sensitivity to psychological dynamics operating in a situation
- Flexibility

Each response is then scored using varying combinations of the following criteria:

- Capacity to work as a part of a team
- Ability to use self effectively or self-awareness
- A systems view of family conflict and family connections
- Intrusion and/or control in a caring way
- Flexibility

As a result, we have a profile of how the candidate will function as a member of our agency and the team, based on characteristics that are the foundation of our program. Any agency can develop a similar assessment instrument. Norms can be established for specific programs and needs. We have found our custom-developed instrument to be a much more effective assessment tool for our program than using results obtained from instruments with national norms, such as the MMPI.

One caution that we offer is not to use the results from this type of assessment as the sole basis for a hiring decision. It is one of many factors for consideration. It is invaluable, however, in combination with information gathered through interviews and reference checks, to identify goals on which the individual needs to concentrate during the initial probationary period.

The Decision to Hire

Upon completion of the interview, the team recommends their top two choices to the administrator. This is a critical part of the screening process. We have been amazed at the lack of importance that many child care programs give to checking references. Our experience has been that when one of our employees leaves after a number of years of work to take a position in a similar organization, reference checks are not made with anyone in our agency.

We have learned through years of trial and error that it is much more effective to have one person responsible for checking all references. The advantage of having one person complete the reference calls is that he or she learns to pick up on the intent of the response versus the content of the response. Our preference is to do these checks over the telephone instead of through the mail. We developed a standard eight-question form for employment and character reference checks, with generically stated, open-ended questions. The response rate is much better and the information received is more credible, and usually more detailed.

During the reference check process, we maintain communication with the team to update them on progress, delays, or unusual feedback. Once the process is completed, unless something extraordinary has developed, we contact the team to reaffirm their selection. If any information alerts us to potential difficulties, we share this with the team and ask for additional information from the candidate or move on to the team's second choice.

About a year ago we had an applicant for a social work position who had significant academic preparation but limited practical experience. One of her academic professors whom she listed as a reference indicated that she would willingly accept assignments but not complete them. The comment was qualified with a statement reflecting personal difficulties that may have interfered with her internship. Another reference indicated similar concerns but in a different setting. These concerns were presented to the team, and they were informed that the administrators would contact the candidate for more information. The candidate was telephoned and provided us with the name of an individual to contact as a character reference. This reference assured us that the candidate had been in counseling and dealt with her personal problems. The team and administration agreed to offer her the position, outlining goals that needed attention during the initial probation. However, even with these precautionary measures, the candidate was unable to successfully complete probation.

Until recently a representative of administration was part of the interview process at the team level. We thought this was the most efficient use of our time and skills. We found, however, that it was too time-consuming, often intimidating to team members, and did not provide much additional information or insight. As a result, we decided to add an additional step of an administrative interview. The purpose of this interview is varied. It gives administrators a chance to meet and evaluate the candidate face to face and offers an opportunity to evaluate the team's ability to effectively communicate the program to the candidate. It is also an opportunity to satisfy any concerns that may have been raised when checking references. The questions that we use as a foundation are:

- Now that you have been interviewed by the team, explain the program in your own words.
- Tell us what strengths you will bring to the program.
- In what areas will you need help/training?
- We have checked your references. What do you think they have identified as greatest strengths and possible areas of concern?

The final step, of course, is to offer the position to the person, discuss a salary, and set a starting date. We have found it beneficial to wait until after the candidate begins work before notifying other candidates of the final decision.

Orientation of New Staff by Administration

We feel that it is an obligation of administration to introduce new employees to the agency and its program. During the first few days of employment we set aside one day to "indoctrinate" people to our program's philosophy, values, and established practices. The purpose is to communicate clearly the administrative expectations and standards against which all future information and experiences can be measured.

Tom Peters in *A Passion for Excellence* (Austin & Peters, 1985) discussed the concept of MBWA,—"management by wandering around." Depending on the size of the organization, many administrators may think our orientation process (and subsequent monitoring) is too time-consuming, too intrusive, too hands-on. One has to make a decision as to where time is best spent and then create the time necessary for the commitment. Our experience has been that, too often, teams and administrators want to circumvent the recruiting and orientation process in order to get someone "in place" right away. We have found that when we do that, we trade short-term discomfort for long-term agony. Inadequate recruiting and orientation usually result in inadequate employees and, consequently, inadequate teams.

Agencies can develop lists of orientation topics to be covered that are specific to their programs. Ours include:

- Agency philosophy and values
- Probationary period: time and goals
- Team process
- Proper confrontation methods
- Communication
- Documentation
- Team and individual responsibilities
- Team rotation schedules
- Scheduled meetings for programs and disciplines
- Program-specific components
- Rules/discipline for staff and residents
- Consistency
- Job descriptions
- Evaluation process
- Benefits

Many of these areas will be covered in other sections of this chapter or in other chapters of this book.

Orientation of New Staff by Teams

The second phase of orientation is coordinated by the team and typically lasts two weeks. It is vital for administration to empower the teams to complete this part of the training successfully. While there is a program manual in place to define the boundaries of the program, the teams and their members are the real "training manual" for new staff.

Originally teams were expected to provide orientation to their new staff at the exclusion of other teams. More recently we have found it advantageous to the entire program to include tenured and experienced staff from other teams as part of this process. Not only does it provide a broader base of knowledge to new staff and enhance consistency throughout the program; it is a distinction to those who are chosen to assist in the training (Austin and Peters, 1985).

A minimum time of two weeks devoted to orientation should be respected and required regardless of the individual's previous experience and education. We have discovered that there is no educational preparation or relevant experience that quite prepares someone to work as a member of a team. Training, naturally, will continue throughout the probationary period and optimally throughout employment.

Probationary Period

We recommend a probationary period of ninety days for new employees. During this period, the newly hired staff can be observed in action by the team and administrators. The team and administrators can also be observed in action by the newly hired staff. It is when all parties can determine if the "fit" is a good one and if a longer commitment can be made. The probationary period is a time that a decision to terminate the employment can be made by either party without negative repercussions. A square peg does not fit well in a round hole. It is much easier to "cut your losses" at this point than to try to lay a paper trail to terminate someone's employment once they have been removed from probation.

THE TRAINING PROCESS

Training for New Staff

In reality, training actually begins when program information is shared during the interviews. There the candidate obtains a basic knowledge of philosophy, values, and expectations. During the interviews and reference check process we make note of areas of concern on which the candidate will need to focus attention and receive future training. The combination of information sharing and noting attention areas provides a road map for training during and beyond the initial orientation.

Internally, training continues with the administrative orientation and the introduction to the program practices of the teams and their members. This would normally last for two weeks, but it can be extended depending on the needs of the individual and the team.

As previously noted, we also include tenured, experienced members from teams other than the hiring team to be part of the training process. This provides recognition to the selected individuals or teams for the quality of their work and also enhances program consistency. The selection of individuals and teams is based on their particular skills in relation to the needs of the new employee. For example, we recently hired several new staff for a cottage that had a reputation for being unstructured and at times chaotic. It seemed a good time to include well-structured teams, as part of the orientation training, to try to break the cycle of having such a team solely responsible for training its own. We asked the teams providing the training to focus on scheduling, behavior management, and role modeling since these were the hiring team's weakest areas. In general, this practice accomplishes its purpose.

Training for Tenured Staff

Periodically (we suggest twice a year) an assessment should be completed by administrators with input from all teams and support staff about the staff's training needs. Prior to a general staff meeting, teams and support staff are asked to identify and prioritize their top three needs for training. At the meeting the staff members list their perceived training needs on a chart. After discussion, consensus is reached on those topics that are most important and on the number of training events to be held during the year. This process empowers staff to directly affect the direction of the training for the coming year. It is an excellent opportunity for administrators to look at the needs of the agency as a whole as well as the specific needs of individual teams.

Additionally, teams can request training at any time during the year to gain or refine needed skills. Administrators also have a mandate to direct teams toward needed training experiences based on their knowledge of how the teams are functioning. For example, one team recently recognized difficulties in effectively communicating with one another. The addition of two new team members had changed the dynamics of the five-person team as well as the process through which the team shared information. Even though we had covered this topic with the previous team members, the "new" team felt a review would be beneficial. In essence, this would give them help in the areas they needed assistance with as well as provide an opportunity to evaluate progress that had been made since the last training. In this instance we chose to intervene as requested, with positive results.

As a two-person administrative team we have varied academic backgrounds and extensive training experiences that allow each of us to provide formal training to our teams on a team-by-team basis. Also, we continually train on an informal basis both by providing guidance and direction and by serving as role models for the teams. In many agencies it can be difficult for staff to accept a "local prophet." In our particular situation we have established our credibility with our staff through our actions within the agency and continued training at state, regional, and national conferences.

From time to time it is in everyone's best interest to have a fresh assessment of the skill levels of the individual teams and their ability to function as teams. An external consultant can be used to meet with teams prior to the development of a training plan to identify their needs. For instance, one team may have a need for increasing their communication skills, another for developing better conflict-resolution skills, and another for building skills in behavior management. Training can then be designed to address those needs specifically. In most cases the value of having this perspective should serve to confirm what the administrator has already identified as areas needing attention.

Recently we found that a cooperative training effort with a similar program, located within a two-hour drive, produced multiple positive effects. It allowed staff an opportunity to meet and interact with staff from another program and to "compare and contrast." Training costs were shared. Reduced costs allowed for more and varied training to be offered targeting the specific needs of the staff. Finally, training can be offered on multiple days, thus alleviating the stress that coverage problems often present.

Other Training Opportunities

For non–agency-sponsored training, information concerning all relevant events is posted on a training board. These can be as inclusive as seminars on grammar to institutes that "train the trainer" in working with sexual offenders. Individuals are encouraged to attend based on needs identified in their evaluations. This is accomplished by providing paid time and financial assistance to participate.

Not all training needs of employees will be met through the specific training discussed so far. Often agency and employee needs can best be met through enrollment in formal education courses. Many agencies overlook the benefits gained from this and fail to plan their training budgets to support these endeavors. We have a long history of encouraging this for our staff and have derived substantial returns on our investments of time and money.

Administrative pride can be taken in developing an intelligent, skilled, trained staff. Individual pride in accomplishments can be reinforced by encouraging staff to share their expertise with others at the agency, state, and national levels. Again, this requires advanced planning of time and money. This is probably one of the best public relations tools that your agency can develop.

ESTABLISHING THE CONTEXT FOR TEAMS TO FUNCTION

With a system of checks and balances in place our teams have a wide range in which to function. They have weighted input regarding admissions, discharges, personnel, and cottage procedures. Although it is sometimes a difficult concept for our teams to accept, it is ultimately the administrators who are responsible for the success or failure of the program. It is necessary, therefore, that we reserve the right to override a team recommendation or decision.

While rarely needed, it is important for administrators to clearly define the differences between team decisions and team recommendations. This may vary from program to program. However, it is important to accept responsibility, as administrators, for program decisions regardless of whether they are made at the team level or the administrative level. Teams tend to make decisions and recommendations from their own perspective and based on how the outcome will affect their team. Administrators, on the other hand, are responsible for the programwide effects.

It is imperative, therefore, to create an environment in which all staff can accept the driving forces behind the organization. Athos and Pascale (1981) describe the "Seven S's" needed to manage effectively in the right environment. We have slightly modified them to accommodate the nonprofit model in which we work.

The first three are known as "hard S's" and must be present in any successful organization.

1. *Strategy* is the plan of action needed in order to reach the defined goals of the program. This needs to be developed cooperatively between administrators and teams. Teams are more likely to accept and implement a strategy in which they have had significant input.

2. *Structure* is a definition of how the organization is designed. For example, what reports are generated centrally and what reports are generated by the team? How are training responsibilities shared between administration and teams? When are personnel issues managed by the team or by administrators with input from the team? Does the organizational chart support the actual practice of the program and support achievement of the program goals? Structure is determined based on whether an organization is centralized or decentralized. In a centralized organization the structure would be determined by the hierarchical head, such as the CEO or president. The program administrator would be responsible for determining the structure in a decentralized organization.

3. *Systems* are the procedural reports and routine processes such as scheduled meetings, the sharing of information, the resolution of conflict. Assurance should be given that meetings are held because they are necessary and not because they are "on the schedule." Information is power and is often used to control. Administrators and teams must recognize that all relevant information must be shared if the program and the team are to survive, thrive, and meet strategic goals.

The final four are called "soft S's." They act as the lubricant for the mechanics of strategy, structure, and systems.

4. *Staff* focuses on the contributions of the individual to the whole. It means that the individual must be indoctrinated into a "team" way of thinking and acting, where the whole is greater than its parts, and performance is greater than seniority.

5. *Style* reflects the need of administrators and teams to role model expectations, to set the tone for the cultural climate, and to share the "war stories." It is an administrative responsibility to know when to manage more or less intrusively, to intervene to build competence, and ultimately to develop extraordinary qualities in ordinary people.

6. *Skills* are those abilities identified as necessary to perform as a member of a team, as well as those needed to perform discipline-specific tasks. These skills can be measured through the development of a questionnaire, as previously discussed, as well as through the interview process and the careful check of references and qualifications. A well-written job description will be the foundation for helping administrators and teams match the skills of the applicant to the skills needed for the position.

7. *Superordinate goals* are the guiding concepts and shared values of the people who put the program into effect and make it successful. Some programs allow 10-minutes of meeting time for an individual, team, or administrator to reiterate the mutually shared goals of the program.

Once the "Seven *S*'s" are defined for an organization, there are four principles—fairness, freedom, commitment, and discretion—that can assist in keeping the organization bound together (Austin & Peters, 1985).

Fairness, although seldom defined, can be expected by administrators and teams alike. We acknowledge that the world is not "fair." In fact, some of our teams, in dealing with the residents, refer to this as the "*F*" word. But we also recognize that a sincere effort to achieve fairness in a team model preserves good feelings and avoids destructive dissension. Keep in mind that "fair" does not always mean the same or equal. Different people/teams need different things at different times. Administrators need to adapt their styles to match the level of maturation of the individual and/or team.

Freedom means allowing, helping, and encouraging each other to grow in knowledge, skill, scope of responsibility, and range of activity. Implicit in the ability to grow is the necessity to experience failure. This means that administrators and teams will sometimes make wrong choices. It also means that one can profit from the experience and use it to make better decisions the next time.

Commitment is the power behind the desire to succeed. No one can legislate commitment. All commitments are self-commitments. Beginning with orientation, administrators make it clear to new staff that the probationary period of employment should be used to examine themselves and the program. At the end of probation, staff will be asked to make a commitment not only to remain employed, but to carry out the mission and the goals of the agency. We have found that it is necessary for everyone in the organization to reexamine their commitment formally on an annual basis. An annual evaluation provides a good mechanism for doing this. In working with staff, our experience has been that informal examination of one's commitment occurs more frequently. As in any good relationship, frequently renewing commitment is a good idea.

Discretion should be taken in dealing with appropriate team members when an action has the potential of inflicting serious harm on the reputation, success, or survival of the agency. We are all on the same ship. Boring holes below the water line will sink the ship. Teams (and administrators), as we said, should have the opportunity to fail and to grow. But too many failures and too little growth cannot be tolerated for long without affecting the services delivered by the agency.

MONITORING TEAM AND INDIVIDUAL PERFORMANCE

In business, and increasingly in human services, this section could be titled "Quality Assurance" or "Quality Control." It is, in essence, our way of ensuring that a certain level of quality is maintained. Monitoring produces the information needed for identifying team-building and skill development needs. We found that it is impossible to keep watch over everything, but it is also not necessary. The cockpit of an airplane has hundreds of gauges that provide myriads of information. Once the airplane is off the ground, however, only a handful are needed to make sure that the correct course is being taken. This is also true of an agency. Once the program is in place, only a few key monitors are needed to keep you aware of everything that is going on.

Monitoring Instruments and Opportunities

- *Team Agendas:* These include basic information such as administrative input/requests, information sharing, application/admission status, discharge planning, staff performance, cottage business, resident performance, weekly planning, level requests/reviews, and any other cottage business. The agendas are turned in a day before the team meeting, are reviewed and initialed by the administrator(s), and are returned to the teams. With the review, administrators can decide which team meetings to attend and which issues need addressing.
- *Team Minutes:* These are completed during the team meeting by the designated recorder and are turned back in to administration. The minutes are expanded versions of the team agendas and let us know how topics on the agendas have been addressed. The minutes should be brief and to the point, stating the problem, the discussion, and the resolution. Do not expect or encourage a novel.
- *Team Meetings:* The decision to attend team meetings is based on the review of the team agendas and other monitoring devices. The team, also, can request an administrator to attend. The role of the administrator at the team meeting can be to mediate, redirect, listen, brainstorm, assist in problem solving, provide a new perspective, and/or reinforce established policy and practice. Occasionally the administrator may simply attend the meeting to monitor the way the team

members interact with one another or the effectiveness of their team meeting methods.

- *Discipline Meetings:* Each of the disciplines (education, child care, and social work) on our campus meet on a weekly or bimonthly basis. The purpose of these meetings is to problem solve and strengthen skills by sharing experiences. They are not intended to be gripe sessions, nor do they supplant the team as the primary source of support. The disciplines each have different demands placed upon them; therefore, the focus of the meeting will be different for each group.
- *Family Service Meetings:* These meetings are held every two weeks, with a minimum of an hour devoted to each team by an administrator. The time is used to focus on admissions, discharges, and current residents in care. It is an opportune time, with most team members present, to discuss changes that need to be made regarding staff behaviors and interventions.
- *Incident Reports:* Serious incidents are recorded on a standard form and turned in for administrative review. These reports provide valuable information about how the staff intervened and ask, from staff's perspective, how things could have been handled differently. One section of the report allows for administrative comments and is another way of giving feedback to teams. These reports are coded and entered into a computer for future reference as to patterns, trends, and so on.
- *Reviews:* Each resident is tracked on paper beginning with a comprehensive assessment, continuing with treatment plan reviews, and ending with a discharge summary. All these documents are reviewed by an administrator. The teams have the option of obtaining administrative input even before the reviews are typed. Again, this provides the opportunity for administrators to re-educate and reinforce previously stated expectations, as well as monitor the delivery of services in the program.
- *On-Call:* Although this is a shared administrative responsibility, one person assumes primary duties. On-call is designed to provide immediate emergency interventions. It does not take responsibility away from the team to deal with a crisis. Rather, it provides the chance for administration to model and/or supervise appropriate interventions.
- *MBWA:* "Management by wandering around" (Austin & Peters, 1985) is the most informal and nonstructured part of monitoring and the most valuable tool for gauging the pulse of the program. By observation an administrator can see the condition of the cottage, whether residents have been doing their chores, if needed maintenance has been completed, how staff supervision of campus work programs is being provided, or the atmosphere created by a teacher in the classroom.

Final Decisions

Although we have mentioned this before, it is important to reiterate at this point the need for a clear distinction between team recommendations and administrative decisions. If the information identified in this section is gathered accurately, when administrative decisions become necessary they are reached expediently and with validity.

As an example, let us consider a pending unplanned discharge. If what we have recommended is in place, this is one way the process might work. The team would identify the resident on the team agenda as in need of discharge planning. The administrator would already have discussed the case in a family service meeting with the team. By having observed in the classroom and the cottage, the administrator would have seen the types of behaviors described by the team as being routinely exhibited. Incident reports would have left a "paper trail" documenting those behaviors. In discipline meetings, staff might have asked for direction on how to handle the behaviors. In the end, although formally unplanned, little disagreement remains between staff and administration about the course of action needed.

EVALUATING THE PERFORMANCE OF TEAMS AND INDIVIDUALS

Staff performance evaluations are conducted at the end of the first 90 days of employment. Goals for the first year of employment are established and reviewed every three months by the staff person, the team(s), and the administrator(s).

Annual employment evaluations are completed around the anniversary date of the staff person's initial employment. Goals established at this time are also reviewed on a quarterly basis.

There are many ways to evaluate the performance of individuals and teams—we have tried most of them! But by trial and error we have determined that what best serves our program is a combination of approaches that evaluates both the individual and the team.

Our process of evaluating team members is conducted in the following order:

1. On the weekly team agenda the team lists the name of the person to be evaluated (preferably two weeks prior to the evaluation).
2. Each team member privately evaluates the individual's performance and the team's performance prior to the actual evaluation using a standard form (included below). The team member being evaluated will also complete an evaluation.
3. Administration completes an evaluation of the individual's performance and the team's performance and attends the team meeting at which the evaluation will be completed.
4. All scores are shared at the team meeting. Ratings from the team and administration are weighted equally in determining a final score.
5. The evaluations are turned in to the administrator for compilation. The team's evaluation counts for one-half the evaluation; administrative input counts for the

other half. Goals are established by the team member being evaluated with assistance from the administrator, if needed.

6. A final draft is completed, signed by the team member, and placed in the individual's personnel file. A copy is provided to the team member.

The evaluation form itself (Table 8-1) is divided into two sections, a team section and a discipline specific section. The team section begins the evaluation, underscoring the importance of the team, and evaluates the team as a whole, not the individual's contribution to team functioning. The second section of the evaluation, not included here, would deal with the areas that are specific to the discipline of the team member being evaluated, i.e., counselor, social worker, teacher.

As you will note on the evaluation form, we use a 4-point scale, with 4 being the highest. If we were grading on percentages, a 3 would equal 100 percent. We are very stingy with giving a score of 4, feeling it is for performance truly above and beyond the call of duty.

If administration has monitored well and the teams have an accurate self-perception, there should be no more than a 0.5 discrepancy between the team and administrative scores. Until expectations have been defined and well established, administrators can expect not only resistance but vocal rebellion and a discrepancy in scores far exceeding 0.5. In our program it took about a year for all the components to achieve this level of consistency.

This one tool provides enough information to do the following: gauge administration's perception of the team, gauge the team's perception of itself, show discrepancies between the two, and identify areas for training that address specific deficiencies.

HELPFUL INTERVENTIONS BY ADMINISTRATORS

We need to state our basic belief regarding interventions before we begin to describe the different types: Knowing when *not to* intervene is as important as knowing when to intervene.

Teams consist of people who are at different levels of maturation. Similarly, teams are at different levels of development. This means that administrators must be flexible in their responses to team and individual staff needs.

Blanchard (1985) describes situational leadership with the following categories:

- *Delegating:* Low supportive and low directive behavior. This would apply to a mature individual/team capable of functioning "on-target" with little or no intervention.
- *Supportive:* High supportive and low directive behavior. These people/teams have good skills but lack the confidence they need to put them into practice.

TABLE 8-1 • Form Used for Evaluation

Staff Evaluation Form

The following scale is to be used in the completion of this evaluation:

4—Exceeds Job Requirement
3—Meets Job Requirement
2—Needs Improvement
1—Unacceptable

Please write the appropriate number in the space to the left of the job requirement. Additional documentation (i.e., examples) needs to be provided for all areas receiving a rating of a 1 or a 4 and may be attached to this evaluation.

_____ 1.1 To meet at least once per week and to keep accurate minutes of the team's discussions and decisions; to share these minutes with program administration.

_____ 1.2 To assess the needs of the individuals, custodians, and cottage group served by the team; to set priorities for those needs in order to plan the team's program.

_____ 1.3 To develop written plans that specify the needs, the long-term goals, short-term objectives, and the strategies to be employed for the individual, custodians, and cottage group.

_____ 1.4 To promote and maintain the connection of each resident to his/her family/custodian and/or significant other(s) through telephone and mail contacts and flexible arrangements for family time as outlined in the treatment plan.

_____ 1.5 To promote the coordination of services with other agencies and institutions who are working with the same resident and family/custodian.

_____ 1.6 To coordinate the implementation of the team's strategies, interventions, and activities, including their timing and their sequence.

_____ 1.7 To establish a structure and routine that provide clear and reasonable expectations and consequences that are consistently applied and logically related to behaviors.

_____ 1.8 To assist in the development of problem-solving, decision making, and relationship-building skills through the use of group and individual counseling, role play, and other appropriate methods.

_____ 1.9 To act as a role model for the residents in care and provide guidance to the custodian/family to accomplish the tasks outlined in the job description.

_____ 1.10 To use preventative intervention techniques when needed to prevent injury (self or others) and major damage to property.

_____ 1.11 To provide support, encouragement, and guidance to the team's members.

_____ 1.12 To provide regular feedback to team members regarding the effects of their behavior on the residents, custodians, and team members.

_____ 1.13 To participate in the periodic formal evaluation of each team member's performance.

_____ 1.14 To participate in the evaluation, selection, and training of new team members.

_____ 1.15 To coordinate with other team members to ensure that individual responsibilities are being met.

_____ 1.16 To evaluate the effectiveness of the team's program and services and to modify these services according to need.

_____ 1.17 To allocate the team's program budget.

_____ 1.18 To generate and discuss new ideas for improving the total program of the agency.

_____ 1.19 To serve as a consultant to the program administrator in evaluating proposals for change.

_____ 1.20 To keep the team and the program administration informed of resident, custodian, and cottage issues.

_____ 1.21 To assist in scheduling the work of all team members, including time off and the arrangement of alternate supervision and services for the resident.

_____ 1.22 To share equally with other team members in the rotation of coverage during the absence of a team member.

Form based on concepts adapted from Garner (1982).

Administrative support and encouragement are used to help them along the road to maturity.

- *Coaching:* High directive and high supportive behavior. Innate skills are usually present but administration needs to function as a very active coach in helping them perform their duties.
- *Directing:* High directive and low supportive behavior. Just tell them what to do! This may be a new employee/team that simply needs direction, or it could be a problem employee/team with whom other approaches have failed. It is not the way a good administrator would normally function, but it is appropriate.

Any type of effective leadership, from parenting to running a major corporation, involves a few basic steps. We found these most concisely developed by Austin and Peters (1985). These steps can be implemented in any order and used on a continual basis to upgrade skills, experience, and education:

1. *Educate:* Used when goals, roles, or conditions change. The tone is positive and supportive, with the outcome focused on acquiring new skills.
2. *Sponsor:* Used when an individual/team can make a special contribution. The tone is positive and enthusiastic, providing a showcase for outstanding skills. Creativity is rewarded.
3. *Coach:* Used for special encouragement before or after a "first" to make simple, brief corrections. The tone is encouraging and enthusiastic while providing explanation and preparation. The outcome will be defined by enhanced confidence, skills, and better performance.
4. *Counsel:* Used when problems damage performance, after educating and coaching have been exhausted. The emphasis is on problem solving using positive and structured two-way discussion. The goal is to have the employee/team "turn around," enhance their sense of ownership and accountability, and display a renewed commitment.
5. *Confront:* Used when persistent performance problems are not resolved; the individual/team is unable to meet expectations despite education and counseling. The tone is positive and supportive but firm, with an emphasis on the need to make a decision and a time at which a decision will be made. The outcome may be reassignment, restructuring of the current position, curtailment of responsibilities, or dismissal.

A number of personnel actions can be taken in conjunction with this five-step intervention process, ranging from an oral warning to termination of employment. With the exception of termination, all other personnel action needs to be designed to provide feedback to the individual/team to support improvement in job performance. By doing this, administrators can discipline and re-educate without becoming punitive.

Let us illustrate the above concepts by sharing three recent situations in which they were applied.

Team I

This team required a directing approach from administration. The team had a difficult time accomplishing anything without being told what to do. During the team meetings attended by administrators, it became obvious that there was one member who was extremely dysfunctional, to the point of intentionally creating and maintaining chaos in the rest of the team.

The role of the administrators was to meet with the dysfunctional individual in order to re-educate him to his role on the team and the administrative expectations of him, first verbally and then in writing. After each meeting the individual was given the opportunity to put these suggestions into practice with the team. With the passage of a short period of time and no noticeable changes, the administrators brought the individual back in to be coached and counseled. Finally the individual was placed on probation by administration (with the agreement of the team), and specific goals were identified as needing to be achieved within a 60-day period. The role of the team was to assist in monitoring his progress toward the goals. This was reviewed at the end of 30 days and again at the end of 60 days. In this case, because no progress was made, the individual was dismissed.

Team II

This team required a supportive approach from administration. All the team members had been through extensive training on team development. They knew what skills were needed to be an effective team but were unable to put them into practice. Because of the increased level of maturity of this team, and their recognition of a problem that needed addressing, they were able to request administrative intervention.

The role of the administrators was to assist the team in identifying barriers that prevented them from putting their skills into practice. In this case, creative interventions like role playing were useful as well as fun. In an informal setting the team was coached into making simple corrections, and the process was wrapped up quickly.

Team III

This team required a role from administration that was highly directive and highly supportive (coaching). Over a period of time the administrators tried numerous approaches with this team, all with limited impact. The team continued to be a revolving door for staff and residents alike.

As a last resort, and with the four people who were left, the administrators called each team member in separately. The administrators focused on the strengths that each brought to the team as well as what each person needed to change. All were charged with accepting the problem as their own. Each team member was then responsible for sharing this feedback and discussing ideas for change at the next team meeting. The administrators were present at the team meeting to facilitate discussion, brainstorming, problem solving, and resolution.

Three of these four team members are still on the team. The team strengthened its ability to move quickly from a problem to a solution. This became increasingly uncomfortable to one member, who later resigned. The team has since hired two new members and seems to have profited from the experience because they are all functioning at a much higher level and are working collectively toward being an effective team.

As a final comment, we strongly advocate "stirring things up" occasionally. Examples include showing up unannounced at a team meeting, observing unexpectedly in a classroom, or providing special refreshments at a staff meeting. Controlled unpredictability creates a healthy tension where everyone performs at a higher level.

WHEN ALL ELSE FAILS: TERMINATION OF EMPLOYMENT

As discussed previously, administrators have a variety of monitors that allow them to evaluate the level at which a team is functioning. These monitors also provide information regarding the job performance of individual team members. Information gathered through these monitors is the basis for initiating a number of personnel actions up to and including termination.

The decision to recommend termination should not be a surprise to the team member or to the administrator(s) if these monitors are being used. A recommendation to terminate employment normally will have been preceded by a series of progressive disciplinary actions aimed at correcting poor job performance. Unfortunately, there is no guarantee that these corrective measures will have eliminated the unwanted job behaviors.

Under the best of circumstances the team member will recognize that he or she has made a poor selection in choosing the job and will resign to seek employment elsewhere. At the other extreme the team member may simply fail to see the mismatch between his or her skills and the requirements of the position. In these instances it becomes necessary for the team or the administrator to recommend termination. Garner (1988) outlines some of the steps to consider during this process.

When the team is at the point of making a recommendation for a termination of employment, the discussion is best conducted during a team meeting with all team members present. The administrator should be invited to be part of this discussion. This allows the administrator to listen to the concerns of the team and interject any perceptions of his or her own. It also provides an opportunity for the administrator to ensure that the team has fulfilled its responsibilities in providing supervision to the team member and that all possibilities for continued employment have been exhausted.

A new team in the early stages of development may be reluctant to recommend the termination of a fellow team member. They may have empathy for the person being fired or feel guilty about making a recommendation; they may fear that they will be the next ones to be fired; or they may not want to take responsibility for the recommendation, holding to a shared belief that termination is the sole responsibility of the administrator.

Even in mature teams there is a reluctance to "give up" on a team member. We are, after all, working in a profession where there is an emphasis on helping others. Large quantities of time and energy have probably been invested in the team and its members. Recommending termination can be perceived by the team as an admission of failure.

When either of these scenarios occurs, the administrator must take the initiative to recommend termination to the team. The administrator should first meet with the team member individually and discuss the possibility of dismissal. A team meeting needs to be scheduled as quickly as possible, with all team members present. The administrator, during the team meeting, can review the corrective efforts that have been taken to salvage the employment of the team member. The administrator can solicit team input, gathering any information that might provide options other than termination, such as continuation of a probation period. If no new information is provided, the administrator then sets the termination date and discusses with the team how and when to present the decision to the residents.

The termination of employment of a team member is a disturbing and uncomfortable event, even when it is in the best interests of all involved. In an attempt to expedite the healing process, the administrator should immediately engage the team in preparing for the recruitment and selection of a new team member.

A STYLE OF ADMINISTRATIVE LEADERSHIP PROMOTING TEAMWORK

Until this point we have discussed the mechanics of recruiting and building and maintaining skilled teams. We think that it is equally important to discuss briefly how the administrator's *style* supports and empowers this process.

The tendency of most administrators has traditionally been to favor the strategic or hard side of leadership over the personal or soft side. There is a myth that one cannot exist in harmony with the other, that proficiency in one damages the success of the other. In reality, in order to be an effective administrator of a team model, there needs to be a blend of both.

Darrell Sifford (1991), a syndicated columnist, wrote of a conversation with Peter Kostenbaum, a corporate consultant. Kostenbaum emphasized four components of soft-side leadership, which we feel need special attention.

- *Loyalty:* A sense of commitment, keeping promises, being reliable, serving others, feeling that you belong. What is important is to create an organization in which loyalty not only exists but makes sense.

- *Courage*: A decision you make to prepare you to tolerate anxiety. It is a benchmark of quality leadership. This may mean, if you are a middle manager, to challenge the CEO. If you are a CEO, it may mean to challenge the Board of Directors. It means having the courage to create an environment in which the teams feel comfortable in challenging the administration.
- *Creativity:* To create thinking that is not linear, logical, step-by-step. It taps into the unconscious to make connections, find solutions in colorful, new ways that are not predictable. It means throwing out the old paradigms and creating new ones.
- *Maturity,* To grow up, to be realistic and candid. It means you can honor commitments, that you don't fall apart when you are frustrated. You take responsibility for your life and you don't expect others to take care of you.

Leadership cannot be taught, but it can be learned. The role of the leader, then, is to learn and to create surroundings in which others want to learn, to create surroundings where we all believe we are, indeed, on the same side.

SUMMARY AND CONCLUSIONS

The team model allows teams and administrators to work together in team recruitment, team building, and skill development. The process of recruiting and hiring involves the administrator advertising for and screening applicants. Qualified applicants are interviewed by the teams, and the teams make a recommendation to the administrator to hire the person or not. Teams are able to assess whether an applicant has the necessary skills and personal qualities to work effectively as a team member. The process of the teams' helping to select their new members increases their commitment to the individual and to their success. Once the person is hired, the orientation of the new employee is also a shared responsibility between the administration and the team.

Staff training is an important aspect of the team model. In addition to enhancing professional skills in one's respective discipline, new and experienced staff need to learn how to work together on a team. For example, team members need to learn how to communicate effectively with one another, how to participate in consensus decision making, and how to give and receive feedback during team meetings. Teams also can play an important role in identifying specific training needs that are discipline-specific or generic to all team members.

Successful organizations create a supportive context within which teams can function. Positive environments for teams include clearly defined strategy, structure, and systems. Lubricants to these foundations are staff, style, skills, and superordinate goals. As teams and administrators work together in pursuit of the organization's goals, it is important to define clearly those decisions that teams make and those that administrators make, using the team's recommendations or input.

The administrator has important roles to play in monitoring and evaluating both team and individual performance. Systems are established to ensure that both teams and administrators communicate all relevant information regarding the quality of services provided by the team to clients and students and the functioning of the team itself. Individual performance is evaluated through a process that involves and integrates self, team, and administrative evaluation. Under the team model, feedback is highly valued and is viewed as a basis for both professional and personal growth. As noted in the chapters in Part I, teamwork requires high levels of trust. Thus, teams are best able to participate in a shared evaluation process when they are in the higher stages of team development.

Highly functioning teams are able to provide helpful feedback to team members, which provides the basis for growth and the development of skills. Even with this support and feedback, however, some team members may have difficulty performing at the required levels of effectiveness. When this occurs, intensive training and supervision are necessary. In some cases, probation and termination may be appropriate personnel actions. Again, teams and administrators have important roles to play to ensure that the needs of the individual staff member, the team, and the program are respected.

The leadership of teams requires an administrative style that emphasizes loyalty, courage, creativity, and maturity. The administrator in the team model works to create an environment in which teams feel empowered to take responsibility for many aspects of the organization that previously were reserved to administration. The leader of such an organization must have self confidence and trust in others. In such an organization, administrators and teams are working together toward the same goals.

REFERENCES

Athos, A. G., & Pascale, R. T. (1981). *The art of Japanese management.* New York: Warner Books.

Austin, N., & Peters, T. (1985). *A passion for excellence.* New York: Random House.

Blanchard, K. (1985). *Situational leadership II.* Escondido, CA: Blanchard Training & Development.

Garner, H. G. (1982). *Teamwork in programs for children and youth.* Springfield, IL: Thomas.

Garner, H. G. (1988). *Helping others through teamwork: A handbook for professionals.* Washington, DC: Child Welfare League of America.

Powell, J. (1988). *The E.G.G. test: A pre-employment tool for screening.* Unpublished manuscript.

Sifford, D. (1991, February). Business needs to look at the human side, not just the hard facts. *Charlotte Observer,* p. E2.

▶ 9

Administrative Styles and Teamwork

Martin L. Mitchell   Christine A. Ameen

THE CONCEPT OF THE IDEAL TEAM

Within peer group settings, providing clients with the highest-quality and most responsive treatment is the ultimate goal. The nature of the client's needs dictates that the professionals providing the immediate, direct service be empowered to make whatever decisions necessary, as quickly as possible, with little direction from program administrators. Within this context it is critical to the success of the interventions that the team providing the care is operating at peak performance. Peak performance is what an *ideal team* exemplifies; maintaining that performance depends on three fundamental elements—structure, process, and skill—the organization has for building teams.

Teamwork Structure

The first element for successful team building is structure. Organizations must structurally encourage team building by making the practice of teamwork a high priority. Brendtro and Mitchell (1983) suggest the following guidelines for operationalizing teamwork structure:

1. Teamwork must be the highest administrative priority, with other objectives playing a secondary role.
2. Teams must be organized around discrete groups of clients. Any staff who have regular, direct contact with clients should be included on the team.

3. The total number of adults serving a group of clients should be minimized, to the extent possible, to allow for maximized primary group relationships.
4. The delivery of service should be reconceptualized as smaller, self-contained units of service, such that the size of the team is from 5 to 10 members.
5. The membership of the team should reflect an interdisciplinary approach, with a diversity of staff backgrounds.
6. The team must become the organizational unit with responsibility for and authority to implement the program. The primary loyalty is to the group of clients being served, rather than to a department.
7. Power and authority must be invested in all team members, and each team should report to only one higher authority within the organization.
8. Teams must be expected to assume as much responsibility as possible, even for duties previously assumed to be administrative.
9. A structure for team meetings must be in place that allows for teams to meet weekly for at least two hours. The responsibility for chairing and recording the meetings should be shared among all members.
10. The channels of communication between the team and the administration must be direct and be used on a regular basis, with the administrator providing input to the team, rather than directing team decisions.
11. Staff development must be an ongoing process within the team, whereby there is constructive and supportive critique and development of clinical and team-work skills.
12. The organizational structure must allow for staff to participate in the management of the program.

Teamwork Process

The second element for successful team building is process. Process is the actual functioning of the team, in terms of how each member contributes to team communication, decision making, conflict resolution, and relationship building. Process, in essence, makes possible the teamwork skills that allow the staff to function as a unit.

Teamwork process consists of two major ingredients. The first is the interpersonal process. Lafferty, Weber, and Pond (1978) suggest there are three skills necessary for successful interpersonal relationships: listening, supporting, and differing. The act of listening is more than hearing what is said. Effective listening requires that we:

1. *Anticipate where the discussion is going;*
2. *Objectively weigh the evidence being offered;*
3. *Periodically review and summarize what has been said;*
4. *Pay attention to nonverbal as well as verbal behavior. (Lafferty, Weber, & Pond, 1978, p. 22)*

Along with listening, it is critical to take a supportive stance when working closely with others. Effective supporters do the following:

1. *Assume the other person has useful ideas, information and points of view;*
2. *Feed back to the other person the elements in the discussion which they find useful;*
3. *Continue to build the discussion on those useful elements. (Lafferty, Weber, & Pond, 1978, p. 25)*

Of course, the team that has a diversity of talent and skill will inevitably find itself in situations where there are differing opinions about issues. The ability to differ productively is very important in these situations. Effective differers do the following:

1. *Actively listen;*
2. *Actively support;*
3. *State differences of opinion as their own (ownership) concern and not the other person's problem;*
4. *Specify and clarify the differences. (Lafferty, Weber, & Pond, 1978, p. 26)*

The second component central to the teamwork process is consensus decision making. Maier (1973) suggests that effective decision making is dependent upon the quality of the decision as well as the acceptance of the decision. Logically, a high-quality decision that is not accepted will not be fully implemented. A poor decision could potentially be accepted, in which case the outcome is simply a poor decision. The effective decision is one that is high quality and well accepted. Within the context of teamwork, consensus decision making, we believe, will result in the most effective decisions. Lafferty, Weber, and Pond (1978) offer the following guidelines for effective consensus:

1. *Teams must always strive for the best answers. Teams must think in terms of cause and effect, while trying to identify actual problems, not just symptoms and solutions;*
2. *Teams must assume problems are solvable and avoid win-lose situations. Discussions don't have to reach the point of stalemate;*
3. *Teams should engage everyone in the discussion and decision-making process. Disagreements should be seen as enhancing the process and the quality of the final decisions. The very best alternatives must be sought;*
4. *When making decisions which affect others, teams need to empathize with how those others may react to the decision, by "walking a mile in their shoes";*
5. *Teams should avoid conflict-reducing techniques, such as majority vote, averaging, coin-flipping, or bargaining. Conflict should be viewed as a productive part of the process;*

6. *Teams need to be alert to their human needs and work in ways to reduce tension and formality and to resolve differences. However, camaraderie, harmony, and good fellowship should never substitute for sound decisions;*
7. *Teams need to be sensitive to being time-effective and cost-effective in their process. (Lafferty, Weber, & Pond, 1978, p. 19)*

Together, structure and process provide the organizational foundation upon which teamwork is built. The environment that supports both elements abundantly has the potential for producing the ideal team. Climates with less structure and process produce less than highly functioning teams, as demonstrated on the grid in Figure 9-1, where 10 shows the highest amount and 1 the lowest.

When structure and process do not provide organizational support for the teams, teamwork for all practical purposes is nonexistent *(no team functioning)*. Organizations that have traditional hierarchical structures and operate on a departmental basis reflect this type of climate. In situations where staff know the process of how to work together but are not supported by the organization in terms of structure, the result is *Frustrated Team Functioning.* This can occur in any organization where staff want to work together but organizational barriers prevent them from doing so. Something as basic as a lack of time to meet and make decisions becomes a major source of frustration.

Poor Team Functioning is a result of lack of teamwork process by staff in a

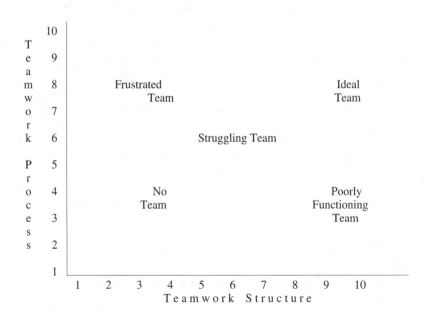

FIGURE 9-1 **The Mitchell–Ameen Teamwork Grid**

climate where the organization does provide the structure to support the team. This is often the case in organizations that make a commitment to teamwork and are just beginning to implement the structure. Staff do not yet possess the teamwork process skills, simply due to lack of training and experience.

Ideal Team Functioning develops where the organization supports the team by its structure and the staff know and practice the process of teamwork. With time and concerted effort, it is possible to move from Poor Team Functioning to High Team Functioning, by providing training and feedback to staff. In many organizations that are new to the concept of teamwork, this is often the pattern.

Clinical Skill

While structure and process are absolutes within the organizational climate, there is a third requirement for successful team development: individual team members' clinical skill. Clinical skill is defined not only in terms of whether or not team members have the clinical skills for the role, but to what extent they have the basic characteristics that make them compatible with the teamwork environment. Those traits are:

- A need for independence
- The willingness to assume responsibility
- A high tolerance for ambiguity
- An interest in the team's goals

When clincal skill is factored into the organizational equation, how successful a team is will reflect not only how the team functions, but how the team performs. Combining structure, process, and clinical skill as factors produces eight possible outcomes for what type of team will result, as shown in Figure 9-2 (*H* stands for high; *L* = low).

The goal for any organization committed to teamwork is to provide optimum structure and process to teams of highly clinically skilled staff. This combination results in what we refer to as the *peak performers*. Any variation of any of the three key elements will produce levels of team functioning that are significantly different than that of the Peak Performers.

Promising Performers result from two circumstances. Where there is low teamwork structure but the staff have high clinical skill and are capable of teamwork process, performance will be fairly high. The only barrier to peak performance here is the organization's lack of commitment to teamwork structure. Performance is promising in situations where the structure and process of teamwork are high but clinical skills are lacking. This situation arises in teamwork settings where new, less experienced staff are hired. With experience and training focused on clinical skill development, there is no reason why these Promising Performers can't become Peak Performers.

Marginal Performers exist in two situations. Where the structure for teamwork

	Structure	Process	Skill
Peak Performers	H	H	H
Promising Performers	L	H	H
	H	H	L
Marginal Performers	L	L	H
	H	H	L
Limited Performers	L	L	H
	H	L	L
Nonperformers	L	L	L

FIGURE 9-2   **The Mitchell–Ameen Team Performance Index**

is high and the team is clinically skilled, performance will be lacking if the team cannot manage issues using teamwork process. In this instance, decision making, conflict resolution, and communication are severely hampered by the team's inability to function as a team. Marginal performance will also result when the staff possess the teamwork process skills but lack everything else; that is, there is no structure and they lack clinical skill. In essence, they know how to make decisions and solve problems but lack the structure for working together. They also lack in clinical "know-how," so the decisions they make will be clinically invalid.

The circumstance where all that exists is clinical skill will result in *Limited Performers*. The treatment provided will lack quality because of limits imposed when structure and process do not exist. The benefits of generating many ideas, solving problems together, and communicating well that are so necessary for making good decisions will not be realized, thus severely limiting the potential of the staff's performance. Limited performance also comes about in those situations where the structure for teamwork is strong but the process is lacking and the staff have poor clinical skills. Staff simply don't know how to make decisions or what the content of those decisions should be.

Nonperformers result in settings where none of the three key elements is evident. Staff lack basic clinical skills and the teamwork environment is virtually nonexistent without structure and process.

It is important for program managers to be able to identify where their various treatment teams are on the performance index. As team performance varies on the index, we believe the leadership style that managers use must also vary. To respond to the varying levels, it is necessary for managers to practice situational leadership.

THE CONCEPT OF SITUATIONAL LEADERSHIP

In their best-selling book, *Leadership and the One Minute Manager,* Blanchard, Zigarmi, and Zigarmi (1985) offer this definition of leadership style: "Leadership style is how you behave when you are trying to influence the performance of someone else" (p. 46). They believe that leadership behavior is a combination of two distinct behaviors:

- *Directive Behavior:* Involves telling people what to do, how to do it, where to do it, and when to do it, and then closely supervising their performance.
- *Supportive Behavior:* Involves listening to people, providing support and encouragement for their efforts, and then facilitating their involvement in problem-solving and decision-making. (p. 46)

Blanchard, Zigarmi, and Zigarmi (1985) believe that the combination of these two basic behaviors results in four basic leadership styles: Directing, Coaching, Supporting, and Delegating. A grid explaining these four styles is shown in Figure 9-3.

Within this model the *Directing* style provides structure, control, and supervision and is appropriate for staff who have limited skill but a high commitment to their work. The *Coaching* style is aimed at staff who have some skill but are lacking in commitment. For these staff the leader provides directive as well as supportive behavior. For staff who have skill but lack in confidence and motivation, Blanchard, Zigarmi, and Zigarmi (1985) argue that the *Supporting* style is most appropriate, whereby leaders use a combination of praising, listening, and facilitating with staff. The *Delegating* style is reserved for staff who have skill and commitment, to whom daily decision making can be delegated.

When utilizing the teamwork approach, the behavior we try to influence occurs at two levels: individual staff performance and individual team performance. Leadership styles thus need to affect behavior at these two levels. We have applied the One Minute Manager model (Blanchard, Zigarmi, & Zigarmi, 1985) to teamwork by looking for how the styles of leadership should vary, based upon the level of team functioning, as shown in Figure 9-4.

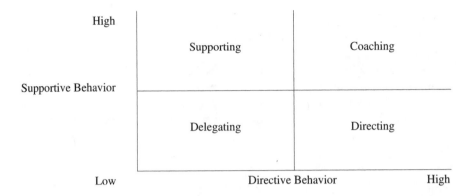

FIGURE 9-3 **Leadership Styles as a Function of Behavior**

It should be noted that some of the variation in performance is a result of whether or not the structure for teamwork has been put in place. Clearly, the lack of structure is an administrative decision, and the problems created by that lack of structure are, likewise, an administrative issue. In this circumstance a leadership style can only compensate to a limited extent for the organization's unwillingness to provide structure for the teamwork process.

The Peak Performers, who are highly functioning and very skilled, will respond best to a Delegating style. This team needs no direction and is very competent with regard to carrying out its clinical responsibilities. The teamwork structure and process are highly evident, making it unnecessary to do anything other than "give them the ball and let them run with it."

For the situation where teamwork is highly evident but the staff lack in clinical skill, the Directing style is best suited. Here the leader gives the team very clear clinical direction and exercises control over clinical decisions, while allowing the team to use its teamwork skills to implement those decisions.

For teams where structure is evident but the process of teamwork is not fully evolved, the style depends upon the level of clinical skill. The Coaching style is indicated for the team with the requisite clinical skill. This team does not need direction for clinical decisions but needs support and direction for the teamwork process. For the poorly functioning team with low clinical skill the Directing style is required, to supervise both clinical decisions and the teamwork process.

Where the organizational structure for teamwork is lacking, the leader needs to adopt the Directing style of leadership, in all cases but one. If staff have the teamwork process skills but lack clinically, the Directing style is indicated. If staff lack the teamwork process skills, the Directing style is required, whether they possess clinical skills or not. However, for those cases where the teamwork process is present and the staff are highly competent, the Supportive style of leadership will be effective, in spite of the lack of organizational commitment to teamwork structure.

	Structure	Process	Skill	
Peak Performers	H	H	H	Delegating
Promising Performers	L	H	H	Supporting
	H	H	L	Directing
Marginal Performers	H	L	H	Coaching
	L	H	L	Directing
Limited Performers	L	L	H	Directing
	H	L	L	Directing
Nonperformers	L	L	L	Directing

FIGURE 9-4   **The Mitchell–Ameen Leadership Style Index**

MONITORING TEAM FUNCTIONING

Utilizing the situational leadership model as proposed here requires managers to be able to monitor how well teams function. Logically, this implies that managers need to be able to monitor teamwork structure, teamwork process, and staff clinical skills.

Monitoring the Structure for Teamwork

For organizations that commit themselves to teamwork structure the monitoring of this element of the approach is straightforward. The following questions need to be answered:

1. Are team meetings being held regularly?
2. Are all team members attending the meetings?
3. Do the meetings have agendas and are those agendas followed?

4. Is there adequate coverage of staff responsibilities to allow teams to work together?

5. Do the teams feel supported by their administrators?

Answering the first four questions can be accomplished by simply reviewing the minutes of the team meetings. The fifth question requires a different type of information, as assessment of the perceptions that teams have about administrative support. A survey evaluation technique, described later in this chapter, makes it possible to complete this assessment.

Monitoring the Process for Teamwork

Assessing how well teams are practicing the processes of teamwork requires that we understand the following issues:

- The nature of the communication within the team
- The quality of decision making and problem solving done by the team
- How the team resolves conflicts
- The level of teamwork and support felt within the team

Ongoing supervision, staff development, and team development provide feedback about these process issues. Survey evaluation techniques can provide another source of information for assessing the extent to which teams use teamwork process in their roles.

Monitoring Clinical Skill

The third key element in successful teams is the level of clinical skill each team member possesses. Certainly, the recruitment and hiring practices of any organization include close scrutiny of clinical skill. However, each professional applies those skills in a specific setting with varying levels of success. Further, every professional needs to constantly be honing his or her clinical skills to meet the ever changing needs of the clients. The monitoring of those skills, then, is a critical element to which managers need to give attention.

The performance review process and individual professional development process that each organization uses are the traditional methods for assessing clinical skill. We would propose that there are two other indicators of clinical skill: how effective treatment is in terms of impact on the client and what impact clients believe treatment is having. Assessing the impact of treatment requires the use of program evaluation techniques (see Ameen, 1990; Mitchell & Ameen, 1989; Ameen & Tobin, 1989; Ameen, Nielsen, & Coughlin, 1989; Ameen & Mitchell, 1988). Assessing client perceptions about treatment requires the use of survey evaluation techniques, one of which is described below.

The Mitchell–Ameen Treatment Environment Surveys. In the early 1970s The Starr Commonwealth, a large child care agency in Michigan, implemented fully the philosophy of teamwork as the primary method for delivering treatment services to youth and families. Almost immediately the agency began to search for ways to monitor the teamwork process, as a mechanism for giving feedback about how to improve the process. Believing very strongly that feedback needed to come from both staff and clients, the agency decided to develop its own monitoring device, using survey evaluation techniques to ask direct questions about teamwork. During the late 1970s and early 1980s, surveys were used to assess both staff and youth perceptions about the teamwork climate in which treatment occurred.

In 1983, under the direction of Dr. Martin Mitchell, the agency's Vice-President of Program and Dr. Christine Ameen, its Director of Program Evaluation and Planning, new versions were developed and piloted to meet the technical requirements of reliability and validity. A description of the historical development of these instruments is discussed in Ameen and Mitchell (1992). These versions, now known as the Mitchell–Ameen Treatment Environment Surveys, provide a mechanism for monitoring the three elements of structure, process, and clinical skill.

The Staff Version contains questions that assess the teams' perceptions about teamwork structure and process. The items have been organized into scales:

Teamwork Structure

- *Organizational Goals:* Perceptions about how well the administrative team communicates the goals and strategies of the organization to the staff
- *Recognition:* Extent to which staff feel recognized by their administrators for performance
- *Conflict Resolution:* Perceptions about how well the administrative team helps teams that are experiencing conflict
- *Personnel Development:* Extent to which staff feel that performance reviews, performance standards, and feedback from administrators is helpful and valued
- *Communication:* Extent to which staff see administrators as open to feedback and willing to listen, and see themselves as comfortable in expressing their opinions
- *Administrative Support:* Extent to which staff feel that administrators understand their roles, provide quality supervision, and make decisions that support staff
- *Basis of Influence:* Extent to which staff are influenced by administrators because of personal credibility rather than position power
- *Administrative Style:* Perceptions about how aware the administrators are of staff opinions and feelings and the extent to which those are taken into account when decisions are made
- *Job Satisfaction:* Perceptions about how satisfied staff are with their roles, salaries, working conditions, and opportunities for advancement

Teamwork Process

- *Team Communication:* Perceptions about the quality of both written and verbal communication

- *Team Support:* Extent to which team members feel supported, trusted, and respected by other team members
- *Team Conflict Resolution:* Perceptions about how well the team manages and solves conflict
- *Decision Making/Problem Solving:* Perceptions about the quality and timeliness of making decisions and the extent to which all team members are involved in decision making
- *Teamwork:* Extent to which team members work together, are influenced by each other, and encourage each other to work as a team
- *Team Meeting Effectiveness:* Perceptions about how well the team manages all facets of team meetings
- *Youth Treatment Effectiveness:* Extent to which the team sees itself as effective with youth
- *Family Treatment Effectiveness:* Extent to which the team sees itself as effective with families

The Youth Version contains questions that assess perceptions about the group with which the youth associates in treatment and about the team responsible for the treatment of that group. Taken all together, these items reflect what the clients feel about the quality of treatment being provided and, as such, can be construed as one of the indicators of clinical skill. The questions are organized into the following scales:

Group Scale Items

- *Group Relationships:* Level of trust and care within the group and the willingness to discuss personal problems
- *Physical Intimidation:* Extent to which group members see physical intimidation occurring within the group
- *Counterculture:* Extent to which group sees itself as hiding problems, using getbacks, and using phony group processes
- *Group Effectiveness:* Extent to which youth feel being in the program and the group will help them, and that group members have the ability and willingness to help
- *Group Meeting:* Perceptions about how important and how helpful the group meeting process is

Team Scale Items

- *Staff Climate:* Perceptions about care, respect, and level of encouragement shown by staff to the group
- *Coercion:* Extent to which the group sees staff as fair, trusting of the group, and willing to allow the group to make decisions
- *Staff Effectiveness:* Extent to which the group sees staff as capable and the program as effective in preparing them to return to their communities

- *Communication with Staff:* Perceptions about how much staff listen, understand the group, and support decisions made by the group
- *Intimidation:* Extent to which youth feel threatened by or protected by staff
- *Family Effectiveness:* Perceptions about how effective staff are in caring about families and working on family issues.

Many of the ingredients in teamwork structure, process, and clinical skill are addressed by these instruments, thereby providing a reliable, objective method for assessing how well youth and staff believe these key elements are being implemented.

Using the Mitchell–Ameen Treatment Environment Surveys. The successful use of these surveys, or any other evaluation technique, is dependent upon the organizational view of change and improvement. This view must include an openness to feedback, a tolerance for critique, and a willingness to make change and improve. This view must be supported by top management, program administrators, and line staff.

These surveys may be used once or twice a year to gather feedback from youth and staff about the implementation of teamwork and the quality of treatment. The results go directly back to the teams and administrators who manage treatment. It is these staff who decide how to respond to the results. Rather than staff being directed about how to respond, program administrators facilitate how individual teams use the information. Those teams need to put the results into the context of all the other information they have about their team and their group.

In some cases the results from the surveys confirm perceptions that staff already had about a specific issue within their group or team. In other cases the results may challenge the team's perceptions, thereby providing a forum for the team to have a full and frank discussion about the issues. This same process of using results occurs at the administrative level as well, where program managers look for differences, compare results to their own perceptions, and critically challenge themselves and their teams.

The Mitchell–Ameen Treatment Environment Surveys are just one mechanism for monitoring the key elements in the development of the teamwork methodology. Although some work remains in norming these surveys and using them in a broad range of agencies, the development of the surveys does suggest that it is possible to devise ways to obtain direct, reliable, objective feedback from both staff and youth about how well the teamwork methodology is being implemented. Tools like these provide important information to administrators about teamwork structure, process, and clinical skill.

SUMMARY AND CONCLUSIONS

The education and child care fields have a great deal to offer to human services, business, and industry about the critical role that teamwork plays in the conduct of work. Implementing teamwork will have several powerful results. Team members will be empowered to make decisions—decisions that they now fully support because they participated in the process. The decisions themselves will be better ones because they arose out of a process that looked at all perspectives and valued all opinions. Of course, it follows that implementation will also be improved, because everyone who has responsibility for the work now understands how his or her work relates to the common goals toward which all are working.

Realizing these benefits will require a commitment to establishing a structure and culture for teamwork. Monitoring teamwork structure and process and supporting the professional skill development of staff are also key functions. These commitments and functions will require a shift in the mindset of those charged with the responsibility of managing people. The management style is now driven by what teams need, rather than what managers need. This style demands that administrators intimately understand what teamwork means, can diagnose what teams need to be successful, and are then flexible enough to provide only what the situation requires. The experiences shared elsewhere in this book have shown this shift in leadership style is possible to achieve and can result in successful teamwork.

REFERENCES

Ameen, C. A. (1990, February). Use of joint committee standards: Benefits gained and lessons learned. *Evaluation Practice, 11* (1).

Ameen, C. A., & Lindsley Tobin, C. (1989). Preparing an agency for program evaluation. *The Child and Youth Care Administrator, 2*(1).

Ameen, C. A., & Mitchell, M. L. (1988). How do you know when your programs are working. *Journal of Child Care,* Spring, special issue.

Ameen, C. A., & Mitchell, M. L. (1992). The Mitchell–Ameen treatment environment surveys: The user's manual. Albion, MI: Privately published.

Ameen, C. A., Nielsen, J., & Coughlin, D. (1989). Program evaluation: A tool for program development and management. *Caring, 5*(4).

Blanchard, K., Zigarmi, P., & Zigarmi, D. (1985). *Leadership and the one minute manager.* New York: Morrow.

Brendtro, L. K., & Mitchell, M. L. (1983). The organizational ethos: From tension to teamwork. In L. K. Brendtro, & A. E. Ness, *Re-educating troubled youth.* New York: Aldine.

Hersey, P., & Blanchard, K. H. (1977). *Management of organizational behavior.* Englewood Cliffs, NJ: Prentice-Hall.

Lafferty, J. C., Weber, T., & Pond, A. W. (1978). *The desert survival: Problem II.* Plymouth, MI: Human Synergistics.

Maier, N. R. F. (1973). *Psychology in industrial organizations.* Boston: Houghton-Mifflin.

Mitchell, M. L., & Ameen, C. A. (1989). *Program evaluation: A blueprint for program excellence. In E. A. Balcerak (Ed.), Group care of children: Transitions toward the year 2000.* Washington, DC: *Child Welfare League of America.*

▶ 10

Moving Toward Teamwork in Early Intervention: Adapting Models to Meet Program Needs

Corinne Welt Garland

DEVELOPMENTAL AND LEGISLATIVE FOUNDATIONS FOR TEAMWORK

Early intervention for infants and toddlers with disabilities and for their families cannot be discussed as a single service or program. Rather, early intervention has come to mean a system of services provided by an array of agencies and disciplines working toward common goals in a coordinated, collaborative way. Three factors have contributed to the widespread acceptance of a team approach, not simply as best practice but as a requirement for providing early intervention services.

First, there has been growing acknowledgment of the fact that the problems of very young children with disabilities are so complex that no one agency or discipline can provide all the needed services (Holm & McCartin, 1978). Second, the interrelatedness of development during infancy (Golin & Duncanis, 1981) provides a theoretical rationale for using integrated and holistic strategies to assess childrens' needs and to deliver early intervention services. Finally, widespread professional acceptance of the two aforementioned concepts has influenced recent legislation to such an extent that a team approach to early intervention currently holds the weight of public policy and law. This chapter includes a discussion of the principles underlying the team approach to early intervention, of varied models for team interaction that have been used, and of the ways in which new legislation has influenced the continuing effort to identify and apply successful strategies for team interaction.

When the complex nature of disabilities and the overlapping and interactive effects of a disability on a young child's development (Antoniadis & Videlock, 1991) are considered together with the remarkable extent to which development in the very young child is integrated across developmental domains, the need for a team approach becomes apparent. Many early interventionists acknowledge the need for a holistic approach to child development that contrasts sharply with assessment and intervention strategies that are based on a hypothetical differentiation of development by domain that does not correspond with infant development (Foley, 1990; Golin & Duncanis, 1981). During infancy, more than during any other period of life, developmental systems are integrated and closely interdependent (Gibbs & Teti, 1990).

When P.L. 99-457, the Education of the Handicapped Act Amendments, was passed in 1986, early intervention advocates were nearly unaminous in their conviction "that a team approach was necessary and that families were essential members of the team" (McGonigel & Garland, 1988, p. 10). That conviction is reflected in law.

The regulations for P.L. 99-457 and for its successor, P.L. 101-476, the Individuals with Disabilities Education Act (IDEA), passed in October 1990, reflect the need of very young children and their families for services that are provided by professionals representing a variety of disciplines and agencies. IDEA defines early intervention services as including, but not being limited to, assistive technology; audiology; nursing services; nutrition services; psychological services; respite; social work; special instruction; vision services; transportation; physical, occupational, and speech therapy; individual and group training, counseling and support for families; and medical services for diagnostic and evaluation purposes.

This landmark legislation goes beyond defining early intervention as a set of multiple and comprehensive services. IDEA gives the weight of law to what professionals have long come to view as best practice—that is, the need for early intervention services to be comprehensive, coordinated, multidisciplinary, and interagency. In fact, the law requires specific mechanisms for teamwork both at the statewide systems planning level and at the service delivery level.

State Interagency Coordinating Councils

The governor of each state applying for grant funds under Part H of IDEA is required to designate one agency as "lead agency" and to appoint an interagency coordinating council, or ICC, to ensure that statewide systems of early intervention are interagency, coordinated, and collaborative. The council advises and assists the lead agency in developing policies and procedures to facilitate both funding and delivery of services in a coordinated way, building on services already in place in each state while filling gaps in the statewide service delivery system.

Team Assessment, IFSP, and Service Coordination

At the local, or service delivery level, and law requires teamwork in the delivery of three specific services: assessment, development of an Individualized Family Service Plan (IFSP), and service coordination. These services must be offered at no cost to eligible children and families.

Infants and toddlers who are referred for early intervention services must receive an evaluation/assessment by a "multidisciplinary" team. In the context of IDEA, the term *multidisciplinary* does not specify a model for team interaction, but rather means that the assessment must be conducted by persons representing at least two disciplines, working together with the parents. The purpose of the evaluation/assessment is to determine whether or not a child is eligible for early intervention services under Part H of IDEA as well as to provide information about the child's developmental strengths and needs and, if the family desires, about the family's concerns, resources, and priorities related to enhancing the development of the child.

Parent membership on the assessment team is required by Part H, and early intervention professionals have been searching for strategies that encourage family participation in assessment and service planning. However, those who are supportive of the current movement toward a family-centered approach to early intervention (Shelton, Jeppson, & Johnson, 1987) suggest that professionals should be less concerned with finding a place for families on the early intervention team and should instead ask "how early intervention professionals can become part of the family's team, on which the family already functions as team captain and decision-maker" (McGonigel & Garland, 1988, p. 20).

On family-centered teams, parents will have a wide range of decision-making options about assessment (Child Development Resources, 1992) including:

- Where and when the assessment should be held
- Whose expertise is needed on the team
- What other people the family would like to have present for support
- What questions about the child's development should be answered by the team
- What role the parents will play during the assessment process
- What toys will be most likely to elicit child behaviors that the team wants to see
- What information the family chooses to share and in what format
- With whom assessment results will be shared

The information gathered by the team during assessment forms the basis for the development of the Individualized Family Service Plan, or IFSP. The IFSP is a written statement of the outcomes to be achieved for the child and family, the strategies to be used, and the services to be provided. The IFSP is, however, more than just a plan. It is a written commitment from the early intervention system to help each family reach the aspirations they have for their child and for themselves. "The IFSP is a promise to children and families—a promise that their strengths will be recognized and built on, that their beliefs and values will be respected, that their choices will be honored, and that their hopes and aspirations will be encouraged" (McGonigel, Kaufmann, & Johnson, 1991, p. 1).

The law is clear that not only is the family a member of the IFSP team, but that the family's priorities are paramount in determining the contents of the IFSP. This requirement makes the IFSP process far more important than the resulting document and challenges practitioners to find new ways of working together with families. As teams move toward increasing the extent of family participation and decision making, families involved in IFSP planning will have a range of options, similar to those previously listed, from which to choose. They will choose when and where to hold the IFSP meeting, who will attend, what information will be shared, and how and with whom it will be shared, and they will choose their own role in the process. Most importantly, families will make decisions about their concerns, resources, and priorities; about the outcomes they desire for themselves and for their children; and about what they need from the early intervention system in order to see that those outcomes are attained.

To assist the family in IFSP planning and using early intervention services, IDEA requires that a service coordinator be provided for the family of each eligible infant or toddler. The service coordination provision of IDEA stems from the recognition that gaining access to and using the services of the wide array of professionals and agencies that make up the early intervention system can be a daunting, even an overwhelming, task for families. If public schools and public health, social, and human service agencies and private providers were accustomed to pooling their resources on behalf of individual children and families, if services were easy to find and use, if professionals were accustomed to working with one another and with families as part of a team, the service coordination provision of IDEA would be superfluous. Unfortunately, since this seems not to be the case, a service coordinator is assigned to serve as the link, or bridge, between the family and the formal service system, to help in planning services and to ensure that planned services are delivered in a coordinated, collaborative way. "Because fragmented services have too often been accepted as the norm, a revolutionary change" may be necessary to achieve the goal of integrating services for handicapped children (MacQueen, 1984, p. 128).

For children whose disabilities are multiple and complex and for families who express a wide array of service needs, service coordination will involve bringing together the resources of professionals from a variety of disciplines who work under the administrative structure of a variety of agencies. "Facilitating collaboration among such a diverse group can be a difficult task" (Zipper, Weil, & Rounds, 1991, p. 83).

THREE TEAM MODELS: MULTIDISCIPLINARY, INTERDISCIPLINARY, AND TRANSDISCIPLINARY

Although early intervention programs have a long history of experimenting with structures for team interaction, successful strategies have been elusive. The terms *multidisciplinary, interdisciplinary,* and *transdisciplinary* have been used to describe the models for team organization and interaction that have most frequently been used to deliver services from multiple disciplines and agencies to young children with special needs.

The Multidisciplinary Team

The multidisciplinary team is a collection of specialists, typically within a single agency, who each work separately with the same child and family. Depending on the organizational setting in which services are provided, one discipline may be designated as "gatekeeper" (Foley, 1990). The gatekeeper has the prerogative of determining which other disciplines are invited to be involved in the assessment and care of the child. In the health care environment the physician typically is gatekeeper; in schools the special education director or school psychologist invites the participation of others such as the speech or physical therapist, the school social worker, or nurse.

On the multidisciplinary team, the team members each conduct a separate assessment, planning and providing their services separately and with little coordination (Briggs, 1991; McCollum & Hughes, 1988). When lengthy, complex, and technical diagnostic procedures are needed, the multidisciplinary approach is frequently chosen. The multidisciplinary team is strengthened by the team's access to a variety of specialists with a breadth of expertise. However, each professional is primarily concerned with his or her own clinical issues, and the multidisciplinary team lacks a strategy for pooling that expertise to reach the best collective judgment.

The multidisciplinary process "of piecing information together rather than coordinating information to form a unified, coherent picture" (McCollum & Hughes, 1988, p. 132) is at odds with both the integrated nature of infant development and with the concept of teamwork. The fact that people representing varied disciplines are involved with the same child and family does not make that group a team, nor does it guarantee that a child's needs are met across developmental domains. The multidisciplinary approach stands in contrast to the notion of teamwork as a group commitment to reaching common goals through a "transactional process" in which the results of the collective efforts of the group are qualitatively superior to those that could have been achieved "by any of the individuals working alone or alone in summation" (Brill, 1976, p. 23). The multidisciplinary approach has been compared by Peterson (1987) to the parallel play of young children, that is, "side by side, but separate" (p. 484). Families have all too often been excluded by multidisciplinary team members from the assessment and planning process and left to reassemble the pieces of fragmented, duplicative, or conflicting service plans (Orlando, 1981).

The Interdisciplinary Team

In response to the problems of the multidisciplinary team, some early intervention teams moved toward an interdisciplinary approach, recognizing that working together would lead to more effective decisions. Like the multidisciplinary team, the interdisciplinary team is strengthened by its access to the expertise of a wide variety of professionals. Although members of interdisciplinary teams conduct separate, discipline-specific assessments, their responsibility for collaboration is expanded. The interdisciplinary team has a formal structure that encourages members to share information and that enhances their capacity for decision making (Fewell, 1983; Peterson, 1987). Interdisciplinary team members typically come together to share the results of their specialized evaluations and, to some extent, to reach consensus in developing treatment plans. The family is involved in both assessment and program planning. Foley, nonetheless, regards the interdisciplinary process as less than ideal.

Each clinician comes . . . with a puzzle piece gleaned from individual assessment, and efforts are made to assemble a configuration that makes sense out of the patient's problem. Because each piece is forged from separate samples of behavior, using different methods rising from varying theoretical assumptions, identification of unifying themes is often difficult. Clinicians frequently remain wedded to individual causal hypothesis and, lacking a common vision, language, or blueprint, the team . . . frequently ends up in fragmentation. (Foley, 1990, p. 273)

On the interdisciplinary team, some problems fall between team members' responsibilities, leaving gaps in interdisciplinary assessment reports and service plans. Parents, although included at interdisciplinary team meetings, may not be viewed by others as having valuable information to share (Nash, 1990; Brinkeroff & Vincent, 1986), while other team members, perhaps accustomed to the role of gatekeeper, may expect that they will have more weight in decision making than other members of the team and may let turf issues interfere with team interaction (Fewell, 1983; Linder, 1983).

Although interdisciplinary team members may plan collaboratively and meet to share results or to update plans, services are typically delivered separately by each specialist. In the public school setting the speech therapist on an interdisciplinary team may remove a child from the classroom or visit the classroom to work individually with a child in a quiet corner. For the child served in natural or inclusive placements, several specialists may visit the home or child care center at separate times, each working with the child individually and each providing separate directions to the parent or care giver for continuing work toward discipline-specific goals.

The speech therapist says, "Do half an hour of therapy after dinner." The physical therapist says, "Do 30 minutes of therapy in your spare time." What spare time? . . . I had to choose between being my child's . . . therapist and being his mother. And I chose being his mother." (Shelton, Jeppson, & Johnson, 1987, p. 33)

The Transdisciplinary Team

The evolution of the team approach has been characterized by an increase in the extent to which team members interact with one another and the extent to which families are included as members of those teams. Building on the strengths of the earlier models—the presence of many disciplines, the pooling of assessment information, and the effort to plan services collaboratively—the National Collaborative Infant Project increased team interaction through a model of team organization that has come to be known as *transdisciplinary*. Members of the transdisciplinary team share knowledge, skills, and responsibilities across traditional disciplinary boundaries (United Cerebral Palsy, 1976) in assessment and service planning. One member from among the team is primarily responsible, together with the family, for carrying out the team's plan with support from colleague specialists. The transdisciplinary process, assessment, and program planning are described in detail in Chapter 3.

In developing the IFSP, the transdisciplinary team moves away from setting goals within discrete developmental domains. Outcomes, based on family concerns, resources, and priorities that have been arrived at with the benefit of information shared by other team members, are functional for the child in his or her natural setting and frequently involve the development of skills across developmental domains. A multidisciplinary or interdisciplinary team working with 2-year-old Shawniqua and her family may have developed an IFSP containing the following goals within developmental domains that are either specified or implicit:

- *Gross Motor:* Shawniqua will be able to maintain sitting balance for several minutes.
- *Fine Motor:* Shawniqua will use her fingers and hands to rake and grasp toys.
- *Language and Communication:* Shawniqua will point to or name the toys she wants to play with.
- *Social:* Shawniqua will engage in turn-taking games with other children.
- *Cognition:* Shawniqua will be able to follow simple directions such as "show me" or "give me."

A transdisciplinary team is more likely to have looked at an outcome that reflects the integration of those same skills in the daily-life activities of Shawniqua and her family. The outcome, stated in Shawniqua's family's own words, might be: "Shawniqua will be able to play with the neighbor's children in the sandbox in our backyard." The outcome is based on the integration of several skills in order to help Shawniqua grow in ways that are functional priorities for her family. By integrating programming across developmental domains, the team increases Shawniqua's opportunities for learning in the context of her daily routine.

The input and skills of parents and neighbors, of physical, occupational, and speech therapists, of early childhood special educators, and perhaps of other team members will be needed in order to develop appropriate strategies to reach this transdisciplinary team goal. In contrast with the multiple service providers who implement the plans of multidisciplinary and interdisciplinary teams, transdisciplinary team members will not necessarily work directly with Shawniqua and her family. Rather, one person, or primary service provider, will be chosen from the team to work with Shawniqua and her family, seeking support from colleagues on the team, to reach this and other goals specified in her IFSP. Shawniqua's primary service provider may need the help of a physical therapist for adaptive seating in the sandbox, of a speech and language specialist to help choose an augmentative communication device, or of other specialists depending on the nature and extent of Shawniqua's disability.

There are three instances in which services should be provided directly, through role support, by other transdisciplinary team members. If an intervention technique is so specialized that regulations or law limits its performance to a specific discipline, if a technique is so new that it hasn't been sufficiently mastered by the specialist so that it can be taught to the primary provider, or if the primary provider has not yet mastered the new skill, that intervention technique should be provided directly by the appropriate colleague on the transdisciplinary team.

Therapists have been concerned that program administrators will, in difficult times, reduce or eliminate highly specialized personnel, justifying those decisions by a misuse of the transdisciplinary model. The term *transdisciplinary* is not an accurate descriptor unless a child's team includes all of the disciplines needed to provide comprehensive services and unless all team members "share responsibility and accountability for meeting the needs of the child and family" (Woodruff & McGonigel, 1988, p. 178).

Participation on a transdisciplinary team requires a high degree of team interaction. Team members must be competent and secure enough in their own disciplines to enjoy the teaching and learning that occurs when releasing some roles and skills while acquiring new ones. While asking a great deal of its members, the transdisciplinary team offers a continuous process of professional development and an integrated, unintrusive approach to child development and family support.

Teams in Transition

The terms *multidisciplinary, interdisciplinary,* and *transdisciplinary* have all been used to describe the organization and structure of teams, the roles of their members, and their processes for interaction. In reality, it is rare that an early intervention team can be precisely described by any of those terms. Particularly since the passage of P.L. 99-457 in 1986, early intervention teams have been in a state of transition, working toward increasing the extent to which their teams are interagency, interdisciplinary, and inclusive of families and increasing the extent of interaction among team members. As teams have worked to comply with the law by increasing family participation and team interaction, traditionally drawn distinctions among the multidisciplinary, interdisciplinary, and transdisciplinary models have, to some extent, been blurred. As a result, those terms have lost some of their usefulness as descriptors of early intervention teamwork. McCollum and Hughes (1988), in their survey of early intervention team staffing patterns, found that within a single program, different staffing patterns and team models "were not necessarily consistent" (p. 136) across the three functions of assessment, program planning, and delivery of early intervention services. Although they attribute this variance to availability of staff, several other factors seem to influence team organization and function.

Early intervention teams working toward increasing team interaction are affected and limited not only by availability of staff, but also by the level of training in and commitment to teamwork on the part of their members, by the stability of the team and the extent of turnover among members, and by administrative commitment to provide time for team interaction and to develop policies that support teamwork.

As teams continue to change in response to legislation and emerging views of best practice, it is likely that a team's methodology may not be fully consistent with any one model, but rather may be in a dynamic state of movement along a continuum that leads toward increased interaction with families and other members of the team. Three early intervention teams that have been established for some time and that are recognized for the quality of their early intervention services currently draw their practices from several different models of team interaction. Consistent with the findings of McCollum and Hughes (1988), these teams use combinations and variations of models across the three program functions of assessment, IFSP development, and service delivery. Each team has chosen strategies that are consistent with their program's current resources while helping them move toward a more family-centered, interagency, team approach.

THREE EARLY INTERVENTION TEAMS

Project DEBT Early Childhood Intervention (Lubbock, Texas)

Project DEBT ECI, in Lubbock, Texas, is located in the administrative office of the public schools that operate the program. DEBT ECI serves children birth to age 3 who have a medical diagnosis of a disability, who are developmentally delayed, or who show documented atypical behavior. The program receives funds from multiple sources including the school district, the state lead agency for Part H (Texas Early Childhood Intervention Agency), federal Chapter I funds, and community nonprofit partnerships. DEBT ECI serves 275 children, who vary in the nature and extent of their disabilities or delays.

Project DEBT's staff is made up of 36 to 38 professionals including teachers; speech, occupational, and physical therapists; nurses; dietitian; social worker; and educational diagnostician. The staff is sometimes supplemented by contracts for services, particularly for therapies with private providers and with a local medical school.

According to program director Gloria Galey, "Each team starts with the family" (personal communication, June 18, 1993) and is made up of the disciplines that appear to be needed based on information gathered during intake. Child care providers, child protective service workers, and professionals from other agencies are frequently involved in assessments based on family concerns, priorities, and resources. Sometimes assessments are done at the local hospital so a physician or nurse who is involved with the child and family can participate.

Project DEBT ECI most often uses a transdisciplinary arena assessment method. One person is designated as the facilitator, while other team members gather around to observe and record behaviors across developmental domains. However, in a departure from classic transdisciplinary practice, sometimes another team member "will feel that she/he needs to handle the child or to ask the family a question" (Galey, ibid.).

As the DEBT ECI team has tried to move toward more transdisciplinary assessment, IFSP development, and service delivery, they have encountered several challenges. Physicians tend to prescribe discipline-specific therapies rather than integrated early intervention programs of family support and child development, reinforcing the medical, multidisciplinary approach. The team has found the transdisciplinary approach difficult to implement when using contracted services. Contract personnel have not helped develop the transdisciplinary philosophy and are therefore not "invested in its success," nor is their part-time association with the team sufficient "to build the bond and to establish the level of trust needed for (transdisciplinary) role release" (Galey, ibid.). DEBT ECI has planted the transdisciplinary seeds, and its staff is totally committed to obtaining the training they need to increase transdisciplinary interaction among all their team members.

The HOPE Program

The HOPE Infant-Family Support Program is operated by the San Diego County Office of Education. The HOPE team is similar in composition to the team at DEBT, including a social worker; nurse; teacher; vision and hearing specialist; and physical, occupational, and speech therapists. Parents employed by the program frequently make the initial contact with a newly referred family. In contrast to DEBT, a single source of funding (i.e., special education) supports HOPE's services, although other state agencies are responsible for serving some specific groups of children.

AT HOPE, as at DEBT, the person who has made the initial contact with the family tries, based on child and family needs, to anticipate the disciplines that will be needed for the assessment. The family is asked how they would like to participate in the assessment. Options for family participation include sharing information with other team members and carrying out activities with their child. Representatives of other agencies involved with the child might be invited to the assessment and to help develop an Individual Educational Plan or IEP. (The HOPE program, in compliance with California regulations, is not yet writing IFSPs.)

Prior to the assessment, which is most frequently done in the home, the team decides who will primarily interact with the child and the family based on what appears to be the child's primary presenting problem. As is typical of a transdisciplinary assessment, generally only one person interacts with the child and family. HOPE team members carry out their roles in an interdisciplinary way, observing and recording behaviors related to their specific disciplinary expertise. When the team has not accurately anticipated the nature of the child's disability, team members extend their responsibilities working in a more transdisciplinary way to observe behaviors across disciplinary boundaries, taking on new roles to compensate for team colleagues who may not be present.

The IEP is written following assessment as part of a single, continuous process. Although team members have observed child behavior from a discipline-specific perspective, they come together for an IEP meeting that is based on a transdisciplinary approach, pooling information, setting goals collaboratively, and writing a single assessment report based on their collective observations and conclusions. Information from other agencies and professionals is integrated into the assessment report.

California regulations influence HOPE's service delivery model. The responsibility for providing therapies belongs to the California Children's Medical Services, and public schools are prohibited from delivering those services directly. The therapists on HOPE's team provide only consultative services, working with parents and teachers in a transdisciplinary way to help them incorporate nursing and therapeutic input into the "instructional program" (McDonald, V., personal communication, June 18, 1993).

The HOPE program has been working at increasing the extent of team interaction and, particularly, the extent to which their team is family-centered in its practices. They have brought families and staff together for training in collaborative decision making and in communication. Parents participate, not only as learners, but also as resources, sharing their unique perspectives to ensure that families "have a share in the way our future is shaped" (McDonald, ibid.).

Scheduling and finding sufficient time for communication and followup have been significant barriers to team efforts. Staff have been unsure about whether or not to pay parents for their participation in staff development or in program planning work groups. "Letting go of the old and taking on the new" have been difficult (McDonald, ibid.). Like DEBT, the HOPE program cannot be neatly described as interdisciplinary or transdisciplinary, but rather as "part of an evolving process" (McDonald, ibid.) of working toward a family-centered team approach.

Child Development Resources' Infant-Parent Program

Child Development Resources (CDR) is a private not-for-profit agency in Lightfoot, Virginia. CDR's Infant-Parent Program is a contract service of the Colonial Community Services Board, the local arm of the Department of Mental Health, Mental Retardation, and Substance Abuse Services, the lead agency for Part H, and is supported by a variety of other funds including United Way, private contributions, Chapter I funds, Part H funds, and third-party insurance payments including Medicaid. Program staff are from the fields of maternal child health nursing; social work; early childhood special education; audiology; and speech, physical, and occupational therapy. A mental health clinician, pediatric orthopedist, and pediatric neurologist are consultants to the team. Parents serve on the governing board of the agency. CDR has well-developed policies and procedures that support the transdisciplinary approach.

In Virginia the interagency council concept extends to the local level, drawing together a wide range of agencies to develop the policies and procedures that will support the early intervention system for each locality. Based on child need and family preference, staff of other agencies—most frequently public health, social services, and public schools—participate as team members and may assume service coordination responsibility.

The family role on the team is one of both planner and user of services. The person who first represents the early intervention system to the family serves as a temporary service coordinator, assisting the family in understanding their rights and options and in making choices as the assessment is planned.

Although the CDR team is fully transdisciplinary in every other aspect of service delivery, the interdisciplinary structure of the team's play-based assessment allows each team member to play, in turn, with the child, unless the family or the child has a clear preference to the contrary. Using play to assess child development is consistent with the holistic view of the child that underlies the transdisciplinary approach. Because play provides opportunities for the child to acquire and integrate concepts and skills that cross developmental domains, play is an ideal strategy for reflecting the competence of the child (Bond, Creasey, & Abrams, 1990). Although team members observe behaviors across traditional disciplinary lines, they also retain more traditional interdisciplinary responsibility for their own areas of expertise.

During a post-assessment meeting, families and other team members share their assessment observations and the team develops an IFSP based on the family's concerns, priorities, and resources with the benefit of information from the other members of the team. The team has given much effort to learning to write IFSP outcomes in a transdisciplinary way, reflecting an integrated view of child development despite the more interdisciplinary assessment methodology.

In the classic transdisciplinary manner, one member of the team serves as primary service provider, responsible, together with the family, for carrying out the team's plan, with role support from colleague specialists. Services, based on child and family needs, are provided at home, at the center, and in child care settings. Consistent with the transdisciplinary approach, the primary service provider frequently serves as service coordinator as well. While combining these roles offers the family a relatively unintrusive model and the opportunity to develop a close and trusting working relationship, it can be difficult to provide services while also being responsible for objective monitoring of those services. Although an interagency mediation team that includes parents as members will soon be in place to help resolve conflicts that may arise, when team decisions respond to family priorities, disputes are rare.

Like all teams, CDR's team faces barriers to team interaction. Although the team has worked toward family-centered services, "family" all too often means "mother," and services that address the needs of other family members sometimes still fall short. The team struggles with maintaining the transdisciplinary approach despite a health care system that often reinforces a traditional multidisciplinary, clinical model. Health insurance providers that reimburse CDR for traditional therapies but not for transdisciplinary early intervention services are a strong economic disincentive for implementing what the team considers best practice. Therapists with both good pediatric training and a commitment to working within a family-centered team context are difficult to find. However, CDR is committed to the transdisciplinary approach, and time is given to team building and to keeping the team moving toward its teamwork goals.

PREPARING FOR TEAMWORK

Teams that require a high level of team interaction are most successful when team members' professional preparation has included training in teamwork. Skills in communication, group decision making, and conflict resolution (Nash, 1990; Thorp & McCollum, 1988) are necessary complements to the clinical skills of early intervention team members.

Unfortunately, preservice, inservice, and continuing education programs only recently have begun to respond to the need for an interdisciplinary focus (Bailey, Farel, et al., 1986; Burke, McLaughlin, & Valdivises. 1988). Preprofessional training in education, health care, and human services has rarely included the development of skills in teamwork. Bruder and McLean (1988) found that only 10 percent of special education preparation programs required coursework in team process. Bailey, Simeonsson, and colleagues (1990) reported that the undergraduates who were trained across eight early intervention disciplines they examined had received only 8.6 clock hours in teamwork; the average graduate student received only 11.4 clock hours in teamwork.

Hanson and Brekken (1991), describing California's Early Intervention Personnel (CEIP) project, offer a model of personnel preparation that not only addresses professional interaction and teamwork skills as training content, but that is transdisciplinary in training methodology as well:

> Training efforts must demonstrate the fact that early intervention involves a variety of services, agencies, and professional disciplines. Further, personnel preparation efforts also must reflect the transdisciplinary nature of training.

Transdisciplinary training focuses on disciplines receiving training together, sharing aspects of knowledge and practice skills, and developing a knowledge and appreciation for the approaches of one another. (p. *61*)

It takes time, commitment, and training to learn to work as part of a well-functioning team and "to move beyond traditional roles and expectations" (Briggs, 1991, p. 8). That learning process does not end with the completion of a degree program. Legislation and regulation, research and redefinition of best practice, and turnover in professional staff all contribute to the need for continuing professional development in teamwork. Nash (1990) suggests that "the norms, roles, and goals that worked for one family may not work for another" and even that "members may have to learn to think of the team as a new team whenever a new family is served" (p. 325). Systematic evaluation of a team's work by its members, along with continuing inservice training, mentorship, and supervision, are necessary supports for personnel who may have to adapt their roles and skills in response to changes in membership on their team and to emerging changes in the field of early intervention.

As new legislation and understanding of infant development have made teamwork an increasingly important part of early intervention services, training in the team process has become a critical component in the building of successful early intervention services (Bailey, Simeonsson, et al., 1990). Professionals joining early intervention teams will not only need to be prepared to work in a team context but also, in light of new legislation and emerging views of best practice, will need to be prepared for that context to be in a state of change for the foreseeable future.

SUMMARY AND CONCLUSIONS

The process of change is most likely to be successful when change is planned, gradual, and educational. As states continue to move toward full implementation of Part H of IDEA, early intervention teams are likely to remain in a prolonged period of transition. Although legislation and definition of best practice encourage teachers and other early intervention providers to cross traditional boundaries of agency and discipline and to create new partnerships with each other and with families, their progress has been predictably gradual. Despite the many obvious advantages of a team approach for both professionals and for families, teams have encountered many obstacles in their efforts to bring about fundamental changes in service delivery systems.

"Early intervention is still defining itself" (Healy, Keesee, & Smith, 1989, p. 121). As teams try to implement and cope with changing requirements, many find it necessary to retain strategies from one model of teamwork while reaching toward another. Teams are moving gradually toward their goals by adapting strategies from more than one model of team interaction, choosing those that best fit both their current resources and their priorities for the future. The administrative policies, systems for funding services, and availability of qualified personnel of public schools and of other community agencies all affect the extent to which early intervention teams are able to more toward their goals.

For teachers and other team members who are confronting the need for substantive changes in the ways they provide early intervention services, training in teamwork is an essential support. Training can ensure that early intervention team members share the vision of early intervention that is articulated in IDEA—a system that is responsive to individual family concerns and that can mobilize an array of community resources in a coordinated way to support families in addressing their priorities for themselves and for their children. Training must ensure that early intervention team members have the skills and strategies needed to make that vision a reality.

REFERENCES

Antoniadis, A., & Videlock, J. L. (1991). In search of teamwork: A transactional approach to team functioning. *Infant Toddler Intervention: The Transdisciplinary Journal, 1*(2), 157–167.

Bailey, D. B., Farel, A. M., O'Donnell, K. J., Simeonsson, R. J., & Miller, C. A. (1986). Preparing infant interventionists: Interdepartmental training in special education and maternal and child health. *Journal of the Division for Early Childhood, 11,* 66–77.

Bailey, D. B., Simeonsson, R. J., Yoder, D. E., & Huntingdon, G. S. (1990). Preparing professionals to serve infants and toddlers with handicaps and their families: An integrative analysis across eight disciplines. *Exceptional Children, 57*(1), 26–35.

Belsky, J., Garduque, L., & Hrncir (1984). *Developmental Psychology, 20,* 406–417.

Bond. L., Creasey, G. L., & Abrams, C. L. (1990). Play assessment, reflecting and promoting cognitive competence. In E. Gibbs & D. Teti (Eds.), *Interdisciplinary assessment of infants* (pp. 113–128). Baltimore, MD: Brookes.

Briggs, M. H. (1991). Team development: Decision-making for early intervention. *Infant-Toddler Intervention: The Transdisciplinary Journal, 1*(1), 1–9.

Brill, N. (1976). *Teamwork.* Philadelphia: Lippincott.

Brinkeroff, J., & Vincent, L. (1986). Increasing parental decision-making at the individual educational program meeting. *Journal of the Division for Early Childhood, 11,* 46–58.

Bruder, M. B., & McLean, M. (1988). Personnel preparation for infant interventionists. A review of federally funded projects. *Journal of the Division for Early Childhood, 12*(4), 299–305.

Burke, P. J., McLaughlin, M. J., & Valdiviseso, C. H. (1988). Preparing professionals to educate handicapped infants and young children: Some policy considerations. *Topics in Early Childhood Special Education, 8*(1), 73–80.

Child Development Resources. (1992). *Project Trans/Team.* Lightfoot, VA: Author.

Fewell, R. R. (1983). The team approach to infant education. In S. C. Garwood & R. R. Fewell (Eds.), *Educating handicapped infants: Issues in development and intervention* (pp. 299–322). Rockville, MD: Aspen Systems.

Fewell, R. R. (1986). *Play assessment scale* (5th rev.). Unpublished manuscript. University of Washington, Seattle.

Foley, Gilbert (1990). Portrait of the arena assessment. In E. Gibbs & D. Teti (Eds.), *Interdisciplinary assessment of infants* (pp. 271–286). Baltimore, MD: Brookes.

Gibbs, E., & Teti, D. (1990). Infant assessment. In E. Gibbs & D. Teti (Eds.), *Interdisciplinary assessment of infants* (pp. 3–13). Baltimore, MD: Brookes.

Golin, A. K., & Duncanis, A. J. (1981). *The interdisciplinary team.* Rockville, MD: Aspen Systems.

Hanson, M. J. & Brekken, L. J. (1991). Early intervention personnel model and standards: An interdisciplinary field-developed approach. *Infants and Young Children, 4,*(1), 61.

Harbin, G. L., & Van Horn, J. (1990). *Elements for inclusion in interagency agreements.* Carolina Policy Studies Program, Frank Porter Graham Child Development Center. Chapel Hill: University of North Carolina.

Healy, A., Keesee, P. D., & Smith, B. S. (1989). *Early services for children with special needs: Transactions for family support.* Baltimore, MD: Brookes.

Holm, V. A., & McCartin, R. E. (1978). Interdisciplinary child development team: Team issues and training in interdisciplinariness. In K. E. Allen, V. A. Holm, & R. E. Schiefelbusch (Eds.), *Early intervention: A team approach* (pp. 97–122). Baltimore, MD: University Park Press.

Linder, T. (1983). *Early childhood special education: Program development and administration.* Baltimore, MD: Brookes.

MacQueen, J. C. (1984). The integration of public services for handicapped children: Myth or reality. In E. Eklund (Ed.), *Developmental handicaps: Prevention and treatment II* (pp. 115–129). Silver Spring, MD: American Association of University Affiliated Programs.

McCollum, J. A., & Hughes, M. (1988). Staffing patterns and team models in infancy programs. In J. B. Jordan, J. J. Gallagher, P. Hutinger, & M. B. Karnes (Eds.), *Early childhood special education 0–3* (pp. 129–146). Reston, VA: Council for Exceptional Children.

McGonigel, M. J., Kaufmann, R. K., & Johnson, B. H. (Eds.). (1991). *Guidelines and recommended practices for the individualized family service plan* (2d ed). Bethesda, MD: Association for the Care of Children's Health.

McGonigel, M. J., & Garland, C. W. (1988). The IFSP and the early intervention team: Team and family issues and recommended practices. *Infants and Young Children, 1*(1), 10–21.

Nash, J. K. (1990). Public Law 99-457: Facilitating family participation on the multidisciplinary team. *Journal of Early Intervention, 14*(4), 318–326.

Orlando, C. (1981). Multidisciplinary team approaches in the assessment of handicapped preschool children. *Topics in Early Childhood Special Education, 1*(2), 23–30.

Peterson, N. (1987). *Early intervention for handicapped and at risk children: An introduction to early childhood special education.* Denver, CO: Love.

Shelton, T. L., Jeppson, E. S., & Johnson, B. H. (1987). *Family-centered care for children with special health care needs.* Washington, DC: Association for the Care of Children's Health.

Thorp, E. K., & McCollum, J. A. (1988). Defining the infancy specialization in early childhood special education. In J. B. Jordan, J. J. Gallagher, P. Hutinger, & M. B. Karnes (Eds.), *Early childhood special education 0–3* (pp. 147–162). Reston, VA: Council for Exceptional Children.

United Cerebral Palsy National Collaborative Infant Project. (1976). *Staff development hand-*

book: A resource for the transdisciplinary process. New York: United Cerebral Palsy Associations of America.

Woodruff, G., & McGonigel, M. J. (1988). Early intervention team approaches: The transdisciplinary model. In J. B. Jordan, J. J. Gallagher, P. Hutinger, & M. B. Karnes (Eds.), *Early childhood special education 0–3* (pp. 163–182). Reston, VA: Council for Exceptional Children.

Zipper, I. N., Weil, M., & Rounds, K. (1991). *Service coordination for early intervention: Parents and professionals.* Carolina Institute for Research on Infant Personnel Preparation, Frank Porter Graham Child Development Center. Chapel Hill: University of North Carolina.

RESOURCES

Trans/Team Outreach, Child Development Resources, P. O. Box 299, Lightfoot, VA 23090; (804) 565-0303. Contact: Adrienne Frank

Infant-Parent Program, Child Development Resources, P. O. Box 299, Lightfoot, VA 23090; (804) 565-0303. Contact: Cathie Allport

The HOPE Infant-Family Support Program, San Diego County Office of Education, 6401 Linda Vista Road, San Diego, CA 92111. Contact: Virginia McDonald

Project DEBT, 1628 19th Street, Lubbock, TX 79401. Contact: Gloria Galey

▶ 11

Inclusive Teams Serving Included Students: Regular and Special Education Teams Working in Integrated Settings

Michael Gamel-McCormick

INTRODUCTION

Teacher 1 I'm having trouble adapting the math lessons for Sean. We're working on addition skills and he doesn't even count.

Teacher 2 How are addition skills usually taught?

Teacher 1 We usually provide blocks, or sticks, or teddy bear counters and let the students explore by making and combining sets of the objects.

Teacher 2 Sean can select objects by color, can't he? Could that skill be used?

Teacher 1 Maybe. What if we ask the class to put together a group of five red blocks and three blue blocks?

Teacher 2 Sure. Sean could select the blue blocks and the red blocks. Another student could tell him when to stop selecting blocks. And another student could put the two sets of blocks together.

This chapter is dedicated to the memory of Anne P. McCormick, who helped to build a family team for 35 years.

Teacher 1 And Sean could be working on following a simple command. We could have one of his partners ask him to find blue blocks and red blocks.

Teacher 2 And we also want him to begin to understand when to stop doing something. So he could begin to work on that skill, too!

Teacher 1 And during the whole time Sean is working on his goals, the other students in the group will be working on gaining their addition skills!

Teacher 2 As well as learning to work together!

The above exchange is an example of two second-grade teachers working together. These two teachers traditionally would have the labels of "special education" teacher and "regular" teacher. Which teacher is which is not important because this is a team approach to inclusive education. It is not a special education or regular education approach. It is an example of *inclusive* educational planning; an example of shared goals, shared responsibilities, shared knowledge, and shared problem solving to meet the educational needs of all students.

This chapter will explore teamwork among those working to meet the needs of all students in inclusive elementary school settings. This includes staff who plan and provide services for students with and without disabilities. It includes staff who traditionally may be responsible for typically developing students (regular educators), teachers usually only responsible for students with disabilities (special educators), paraprofessionals (both regular and special education classroom aides), specialized staff (occupational, physical, and speech therapists as well as physical education, music, art, and other types of teachers), administrators, support staff (e.g., bus drivers, clerical workers), and, possibly most importantly, students' family members and the students themselves. The following pages will examine the need for teams to serve students in the most inclusive educational settings, the construction of such teams, the interaction of team members, and some guidelines for operating inclusive elementary-level education teams.

RATIONALE FOR INCLUSIVE EDUCATION

Parent I never know what to do with Sabrina when I take her out. She is always so disruptive. Sometimes in the grocery store she will tear all of the cans or boxes off of a shelf.

Teacher You sound so frustrated. What do you want to have happen?

Parent I want her to be able to be normal; to go places; to do things; to have friends. I don't want to be embarrassed by her. I want her to be part of my world.

Teacher You want her to go out and do things with you as normally as possible?

Parent Yes. I want her to be part of our family and part of our neighborhood. I sometimes think that she acts up so much when we are out because she knows she's not part of that world.

Teacher If you could, where would you want her to fit in?

Parent Church, Sunday School, other kids' birthday parties. And her sister's school. I'd love her to do to the same school her sister goes to. Everywhere, everywhere we live.

Family Preferences

The preceding exchange between a parent and a teacher illustrates the desire to have Sabrina be part of the family's everyday life. We do not know what disability Sabrina may have, how old she is, or what her intellectual skills may be. What we do know is that this parent wants to have Sabrina be part of the family and part of the ebb and flow of their family's day. This is an often-heard request of parents who have a child with a disability (Peck, Carlson, & Helmstetter, 1992; Vincent, 1992).

In studies that have asked parents what they want for their children with disabilities, the top two desires have been (1) to have their children make friends and (2) to have their children and themselves lead lives that are as normal as possible (Turnbull & Turnbull, 1990; Vincent, 1992). Parents often translate this into meaning that they wish their children to go their neighborhood schools, attend classes with neighborhood children, and have the same teachers that their children's siblings have had or will have. These desires are especially important at the elementary level. Unlike middle and high school students, who often come from many neighborhoods to attend a centralized school, elementary-level students usually attend neighborhood schools. When children with disabilities are sent to centralized schools for students with disabilities, the goal of parents for their children to interact with their neighborhood peers may not be met. Families' preferences for inclusive elementary placements for their children make a strong case for providing inclusive educational options implemented by a team of professionals and the family.

Student Outcomes

The development of the skills and abilities of both students with and without disabilities in inclusive settings is also a reason why students should be served in inclusive educational settings. Studies conducted on students with disabilities have resulted in three conclusions:

1. *No* experimentally controlled study comparing students in integrated and nonintegrated placements has found the nonintegrated placement to be superior when student social skills are measured (Strain, 1990).
2. Integrated settings are often highly beneficial for students with disabilities and

their development of cognitive, communication, play, and academic abilities (Jenkins, Odom, & Speltz, 1989; Harris, Handleman et al., 1990).
3. Only positive outcomes have occurred in children without disabilities who are in integrated settings (Strain, 1990).

Positive developmental and social outcomes for students in inclusive settings are dependent on a number of major variables. Strain (1990) lumps these variables together and calls them "quality services" (p. 294). One of the characteristics of quality services in inclusive settings is strong teams made up of educators with special and regular education expertise (Simpson & Myles, 1993). Effective teams are able to plan effective interventions and carry out those interventions efficiently. All the studies that have found inclusive placements to be beneficial to students with disabilities and their typically developing peers relied on program models where the staff were skilled at implementing specific curricular strategies; supported one another; and provided consistent, uniform instruction (Tomchek et al., 1992; Salend, 1990).

THE NEED FOR TEAMS IN INCLUSIVE EDUCATION

There are numerous reasons why elementary-age students in inclusive settings need to be served by teams of professionals. These reasons include: (1) more effective curriculum development and implementation by individual educators, (2) the knowledge and impact that families possess regarding their child, (3) legal and professional forces favoring teaming (Rainforth, York, & MacDonald, 1992), and (4) the specialization of school personnel.

Curriculum Development

One of the major reasons why elementary-age students being served in inclusive educational environments need teams is their complex and voluminous curriculum needs. These include the need for the development of sound individual education plans (IEPs), consideration of which special education strategies and techniques to use, and how to use related services (e.g., physical, occupational, and speech-language therapies). There is also the need to follow the regular education classroom curriculum and the structure of the classroom activities and lesson plans. Finally, there is the need to fit together the students' special education requirements and the regular education routines, activities, and curriculum.

To prepare, implement, and coordinate this volume of educational activity, a team is needed—a team that plans together and implements together. Only through a team approach can we hope to address all the educational needs of all students in an inclusive setting.

Family Information and Impact

While the elementary education team serving students with disabilities will have vast amounts of information at their disposal, they do not have ready access to the behavior, routines, and interactions of the student while not in school. This information is often crucial when planning and implementing educational services in an inclusive setting. By including a member of the student's family on the team, more efficient, effective, and appropriate instructional and social strategies can be developed for the student. In addition, including a family member on the team will ensure that the strategies implemented in the school setting will be carried over to the home.

Legal and Professional Forces

Further reasons that call for the use of teams to service students in inclusive elementary school settings include current legal and professional forces in the field of education. The assumption of the Education for All Handicapped Act (Public Law 94-142) was that teams would plan and implement educational programming for students with special needs (Rainforth, York, & Macdonald, 1992). The implication of the regulations for P.L. 94-142 and its amendments is that a *team* of professionals will provide the services necessary to see that students with disabilities receive integrated, coherent educational services.

Also, during the past 10 years, two professional education movements have taken hold and have begun to foster an assumption that inclusive schooling should be the de facto mode of educating all students with disabilities. These movements are the Regular Education Initiative (REI) and the inclusive schooling initiative (Braaten et al., 1988; Gersten & Woodward, 1990; Heller & Schilit, 1987; Miller, 1990). Both movements promote the inclusion of students with disabilities in environments with students without disabilities. Both the REI movement and the inclusive schooling movement call for the use of teams to serve students in inclusive placements (Miller, 1990; Rainforth, York, & Macdonald, 1992).

Specialization of School Personnel

Another major reason why teams are needed to provide services to students in inclusive elementary level settings is the increased specialization of school personnel. Today's school systems teem with specialists: curriculum specialists, learning disability specialists, at-risk specialists, evaluation specialists, behavior specialists—not to mention discipline specialists such as occupational therapists, speech-language pathologists, and social workers. Every one of these specialties is important. Each specialist brings his or her expertise to determine what strategies can be helpful to students.

However, the more specialists involved in any activity, the increased likelihood that they may end up working at cross-purposes. Specialists from various disciplines are trained in different ways and therefore often view the education of a student differently. This can be a drawback if the specialists see the student only from their own disciplines' viewpoint. When working from a single-discipline perspective, they are likely to prescribe and implement interventions that are characteristic of their own discipline. This is fine, unless the interventions conflict with the strategies suggested by another specialist.

Imagine that a 10-year-old female fifth-grader who has a communication disorder is having some behavior problems that include slamming lockers during the break between classes and screaming at fellow students. The school psychologist determines that a behavior management plan is necessary and institutes a reward system that includes ignoring the negative behavior and rewarding smooth transitions between class periods. At the same time, a regular education teacher feels that the student is trying to interact with her peers during the break period but is frustrated because her language skills are not efficient enough in the hectic environment of the hallway. The teacher decides that she will assist the student in communicating with her peers and will help the peers learn that they need to watch the student's verbal and nonverbal language carefully in order to understand what she is trying to communicate.

When the two professionals find out that they are both working on the same concern, because of their discipline orientation and their specialized training, they may view each other with suspicion and skepticism. The psychologist may regard the teacher's efforts as ruining the behavior management plan, while the teacher may regard the psychologist as cold and ignorant of the student's desire to communicate with her peers.

Both professionals' views may include valid points. However, as they have not discussed this matter with each other and have instituted different intervention plans, they are working at cross-purposes. If these specialists worked together as a team, they would share their points of view and develop a common intervention strategy that could be implemented by all the professionals who come in contact with the student. This would eliminate contradictory strategies and increase consistency among the educational, related services, and support staff serving all students.

The Case for Teams

The reasons for using teams to serve students in inclusive elementary-level educational settings are numerous. The increased specialization of school personnel requires that the clear, consistent communication that good teams develop be used to serve students. Federal special education laws and regulations also suggest that the best way to serve students with disabilities is through the use of professional teams. The complexity of curriculum development for classrooms of students with diverse abilities and educational needs also begs for the use of education teams. The information that families have regarding their child's behavior and skills will be accessible with a family representative on the team. And, most importantly, the preferences of parents to have their children with disabilities in settings that are as normal as possible but that provide quality services also favor the use of teams.

ESSENTIAL ELEMENTS OF TEAMS IN INCLUSIVE ELEMENTARY SCHOOLS

Team Leader What goals would we like to set with Terry for next year?

Physical Therapist I'd like to see him increase his trunk stability.

Speech Language Pathologist I'd like to see him identify colors and other abstract concepts.

Teacher I'd like to see him be able to do some predicting and hypothesizing in unique situations.

Terry's Father: I'd like him to be able to get around the house by himself.

Terry I want to go to art class with the other kids.

For educational personnel teaching students with and without disabilities in inclusive elementary school classrooms, four major elements are critical: team membership, team goals, members' roles, and the team's interactions.

Team Members

One of the most important elements of the team serving students in inclusive elementary-level settings is its composition. Who is a member of the team? In the case of those working in inclusive settings, a team may have two distinct subgroups: a core team and an extended, consultative team. The distinction among these team members is not one of status, power to make decisions, or knowledge of the students being served. It is primarily one of frequency of contact with the students.

The *core team* serving students in inclusive settings includes any educational staff who have frequent (usually daily) contact with the students being served. This usually includes the regular education teacher, the special education teacher, paraprofessionals, and families. It may, however, include a speech-language pathologist who provides daily language lessons in the classroom, a physical therapist who provides gross motor activities on a daily basis, or a nurse who assists some students with health-related concerns (tracheostomies and ventilators) as well as the general hygiene concerns of all students.

Whoever is included on this core team, it should be small—generally no more than five individuals. Also, core team members should work in the same school building or be available at the same site on a daily basis.

The smallness and easy access characteristics of the core team are important because of their responsibility for the daily implementation of educational strategies. Because the core team members implement the daily curricula, they must also have the flexibility to make decisions about implementation approaches based upon the events of the day and the interactions among students. Only by the team's being small and accessible to each other can these quick decisions be made. This core team might be thought of as the executive committee of a board of directors. Major decisions and changes cannot be made by the core group, but this group can make minor decisions that must take place quickly and on a daily basis.

The *consultative team* is composed of those professionals working with the students in inclusive settings on a less-than-daily basis. This portion of the team might include a school psychologist, a speech-language pathologist, an occupational or physical therapist, administrators, vision specialists, or any other educator who has responsibility for contributing to the advancement of the students being served in the inclusive setting.

The members who compose this portion of the team have invaluable skills and knowledge when it comes to serving students in inclusive settings. They may have specific knowledge about regular education classroom approaches (e.g., the teaching of subtraction skills), discipline-specific techniques (e.g., positioning or adaptive technology), the development of students (e.g., typical social-emotional needs of 13-year-olds), or strategies to foster understanding among students.

These consultative team members may also have varying levels of interaction with the students in the inclusive settings. A school psychologist may see some students only three or four times a year. A counselor or social worker may see some students weekly. A physical therapist may come into the classroom twice a week.

The core team may ask members of the consultative team for their assistance and input on daily curricula matters. If a student with cerebral palsy is having difficulty sitting in a circle on the floor during a third-grade language experience activity, the core team may ask the consultative team member who is most likely to be of assistance (in this case the physical therapist) to provide suggestions on positioning or using adaptive equipment.

Whatever their specific knowledge about serving students in inclusive settings and their frequency of contact with students, the crucial characteristics of consultative team members is that they subscribe to the goals for the inclusive setting and can contribute to the advancement of those goals.

The *whole team,* which includes all core team members and all consultative team members, is jointly responsible for establishing the goals and deciding upon the approaches to be used in the inclusive setting. Major shifts in curriculum strategies are never made by the core team. Likewise, consultative team members do not make unilateral decisions to change intervention approaches. Only the complete team can make those decisions that affect the goals, outcomes, or classroom strategies being implemented.

Goals

As with all efforts that aim to use the team approach, a team is not a team until the group decides on common goals (Garner, 1988). Team members working in inclusive elementary settings must agree on the goals for the students with whom they are working. The individual goals for students and the individual curricula paths for the classroom or school can and should be decided upon by the team. Other, more basic goals, however, are inherent in teams serving students in inclusive settings. These goals include:

1. To foster the educational development of *all* students to the best of the team's ability
2. To ensure that students being educated in inclusive settings learn about each other, learn to interact with each other, and learn how to assist each other
3. To ensure that the needs and educational development of one student are not neglected due to the needs or development of any one other student or group of students

These basic goals address the concerns and cautions that many educators and families have about inclusive schools and classrooms. Peck, Carlson, and Helmstetter (1993) state that teachers and parents alike are often concerned that including students with disabilities in regular education classrooms will "take away" from the resources devoted to students without disabilities. The assumption here is that the students without disabilities will suffer because of the inclusion of students with disabilities. When a team adopts the basic goals stated above, the team addresses those fears and concerns.

These basic goals must be agreed to by consensus of the team members. The goals may be adapted or modified to fit the team members and their outlooks, but the spirit of the goals must remain for the team to be dedicated to working with all students in inclusive settings.

Decisions about individual goals of students and the curricula methods used must be made by the team (Garner, 1988; Rainforth, York, & McDonald, 1992). Effective teams decide what educational objectives are important for each student, what strategies they will use to reach those objectives, and what role each team member will play in implementation of those strategies. These decisions are never made unilaterally. All team members have a part in deciding the objectives, the strategies, and the team members' roles in implementation.

The existence of goals mandates evaluation. A good team continually asks itself formative evaluation questions. These evaluative questions can concern the individual goals of students and the approaches being used to meet those goals or can address the basic goals previously cited. No matter what the evaluation question is, it is essential that the whole team take part in the process. In this way the team can decide if an education approach, team member role, or goal itself is no longer appropriate. The team can then go forward and make changes.

Team Roles, Functions, and Status

The team members serving students in inclusive elementary settings must have a set of common assumptions. These include: shared goals, shared responsibilities, shared tasks, shared techniques, and shared status.

As stated earlier, all team members must work from the same set of goals. These *shared goals* should be decided upon by all team members through a consensus process. The goals should address the needs of students *with* disabilities and students *without* disabilities. All team members should fully support and foster the goals for *all* students in the inclusive settings. A team member who ignores the goals of students without disabilities is not fulfilling his or her duties as a member of the inclusive schooling team.

When the team makes decisions about the goals for students and the approaches to be used to reach those goals, all team members *share the responsibility* to reach those goals and use those approaches. The individual discipline of a team member should not determine what responsibilities a member assumes. A special education teacher is not only responsible for the students identified as needing special education. He or she is also responsible for the goals, outcomes, and curriculum strategies being used with the students without disabilities. When in the classroom, the speech-language pathologist is responsible for the student working on a composition assignment as much as for the student with a communication disorder. *All* team members are responsible for *all* students.

The inclusive schooling team members also have *shared tasks.* If the team has decided that a specific behavior management approach will be used with the classroom, all the team members share the task of using that approach. When the team decides that no food or drink will be consumed in the classroom because of the temptation it triggers for a student with Prader-Willi syndrome, who is significantly obese and has a severe eating disorder, then all team members, core and consultative, share the task of keeping food and drink out of the classroom setting. When the team decides that a student with spina bifida should be encouraged to use her walker to go from one place in the classroom to another, the paraprofessional and classroom teacher must promote this behavior in addition to the physical therapist. Only by sharing tasks among all the team's members can consistency of intervention techniques be ensured and the needs of all students be met.

The assumption of shared responsibilities and shared tasks among team members leads to *shared techniques.* While all team members will not be versed in the techniques that any one specialist has at his or her disposal, the techniques of specialists must be shared with all team members, especially when those techniques are the core of an intervention or curriculum approach. Special educators can share with other team members such techniques as partializing activities or using multiple-sensory cues for students with cognitive delays or processing disorders. Regular educators can share techniques for developing literacy or problem-solving skills for reading and social studies lesson. Specialists such as nurses can share with teachers and paraprofessionals techniques for gastrostomy feeding or other specific health care techniques. Through the sharing of these techniques, all team members will be able more efficiently to meet the educational needs of all students.

Finally, all inclusive elementary school team members should have *shared status.*

No one member of the team is more important than another team member. Because each team member has unique perspectives, skills, and understandings, each is indispensable. A fourth-grade teacher will not be able to meet the needs of students with disabilities without the input and assistance of a teacher with special education training. A special educator will not be able to meet the curriculum needs of typically developing students without the insights and strategies that a teacher trained as a regular educator brings to the team. And no team member will be able to optimally meet the needs of the students for whom they are responsible without the input and insight of students' family members.

Requirements of the Inclusive Schooling Team

The basic goals and assumptions of providing education to all students in inclusive elementary school settings includes a number of requirements of the team members. These include: a transdisciplinary mode of service delivery, individual discipline competency, an openness to sharing the specific discipline skills, the openness to learning new skills from different disciplines, and the ability to give and receive feedback about one's implementation of techniques.

The use of a *transdisciplinary* service delivery approach in inclusive settings is essential. The transdisciplinary approach assumes that skills from specific disciplines and specialties can be taught to and implemented by professionals not originally trained in those specialties. For example, although a teacher may not have been trained to suction a student's tracheostomy, he or she can be taught by the student's nurse and can perform the task once properly trained. Likewise, a special education teacher may not have learned about the use of whole-language approaches to teaching literacy skills but can learn these approaches from a second-grade teacher.

The use of the transdisciplinary approach ensures that all team members use the same techniques. In essence, it increases the impact that a specialist has on the students by spreading that knowledge among many of the professionals, paraprofessionals, and family members working with the students. For example, a physical therapist cannot be present to position a student with cerebral palsy on every occasion that the student needs to change position. However, if the physical therapist teaches the regular education teacher basic positioning strategies, the PT's impact and skills are used throughout the classroom day, even though he or she is not present. This transdisciplinary approach allows the team members to efficiently and effectively implement the strategies that have been decided upon and to be more likely to reach the goals established by the team.

Finally, in order to participate in this transdisciplinary approach, the team members must feel *competent* with their specialty and discipline skills (Garner, 1988; Hanson & Wiederstrom, 1993; Rainforth, York, & McDonald, 1992; Sugai & Tindal, 1993). They must feel that they know their skills well enough to give them to others.

GUIDELINES FOR INCLUSIVE
EDUCATION TEAMS

Team Member 1 The picture communication board doesn't seem to be working for Claire. She can't point to things fast enough for the other students and she's stopped using it.

Team Member 2 Is it because she can't point to things?

Team Member 1 It seems like she doesn't want to say anything. Even when she's with me, she won't use the board.

Team Member 2 She tries to make me understand. It seems like she wants to tell people what she is thinking and feeling. I've seen her throw the board at least once.

Team Member 1 Me too. I wonder if we have any feeling statements or emotional-affective symbols on the board.

Team Member 2 Let's look. Nope. Looks like we only have functional items like "Eat," "Bathroom," and "Play."

Team Member 1 I think we may have found the source of the problem. Let's get rid of some of these functional symbols. Claire can usually sign those to people and most of the third-graders know the signs. Let's put on some feeling statements and see how she does with them.

The day-to-day operation of any team is highly unique. There are, however, a number of guidelines that can be followed by professionals working to serve all students in inclusive elementary settings. These include the frequency and form of team meetings, team members' access to each other, the process of decision making, and ongoing evaluation of the programming for students.

Team Meetings

Team meetings should be held regularly, at least once every two weeks, and include both core and consultative team members. The team meeting should be the highest priority of the team members and the most important event of their work week (Garner, 1988). Only with full attendance and full participation in the team meetings can effective inclusive education take place.

The team meeting agenda should always contain two categories: whole-classroom concerns and individual student concerns. Because the team is concerned with the education of all students, any team member who has a concern about an individual student can place that concern on the agenda. The team can discuss the concern, generate possible strategies, and come to a consensus regarding which strategies will be used by all team members.

The team must also address the overall functioning of the class being served and how any new instructional strategies may affect the class as a whole. By consciously discussing the operation of the whole class during each team meeting, the team will not fall into the trap of only addressing individual student concerns and end up ignoring the needs of the group.

The actual structure and process of a team meeting may vary from team to team. Garner (1988) has an excellent structured agenda for team meetings (pp. 27–35). Whatever structure is used, it is essential that all team members feel free to bring up concerns and that full consensus is reached regarding any intervention approaches used by the team.

Access to Team Members

During day-to-day teaching, concerns and crises may occur when all team members are not in the school building. After all, crises do not follow team meeting schedules. Sometimes it is necessary to reach team members as soon as possible regarding an intervention strategy or to provide information about a specific student. This necessitates that team members have ready access to each other.

Core team members should be able to contact each other because they are usually working in the same building. The core team can schedule time during each day to briefly review any concerns that have arisen and to fine-tune any instructional strategies they are using. This communication might take place at the beginning of the school day; at the end; or during a lunch, recess, or break period.

The parent members of the core team should be able to be contacted by telephone or some type of daily communication device such as a notebook or notepad that can travel back and forth from school to home. It is essential to include the family team member in the day-to-day changes that might occur. Because the parent is not in the school building, it can be easy to leave him or her out of daily operations. The core team should make great effort to include this member in any decision making that takes place between full-team meetings.

Access to the consultative team members is equally as important. A nurse who discovers new medical information about a student should be able to get in touch with the core team as soon as possible. If a teacher notices that a student is walking very differently than he did before a fall on the playground, the teacher should be able to contact the physical therapist for information.

This need for access to all team members means that core members should have time during their school day when they can use the telephone to call other team members or can receive or return telephone calls. Consultative team members who work in more than one school building can leave their schedule and telephone numbers with all team members. Because itinerant team members can be extremely mobile and busy, they may want to indicate a time (and place) during each day when they will be able to receive telephone calls and provide information.

Short-Term Decision Making

Because of the sometimes critical need to make an intervention decision before the next team meeting, a short-term decision-making procedure is sometimes necessary. In the case where a new concern occurs, an exciting learning opportunity arises, or an agreed-upon strategy creates a dangerous or chaotic situation in the classroom, the core team can be used to make a short-term decision.

The core team is usually composed of a regular educator, a special educator, a paraprofessional, and a student's parent or guardian. Since all of these individuals are usually in the same building or easily contacted, a consensus decision about curriculum programming can be made among these members. This decision is considered a stop-gap measure, and the situation that precipitated the change in intervention strategies should be brought to the next team meeting for full discussion.

Evaluation of Instructional Programming and Making Changes

Teams serving students in inclusive educational settings should make a point of periodically evaluating the effectiveness of their instructional programming. During team meetings, members should examine how effective their strategies are for all the students they are serving. If it is determined that changes may be necessary for one student or for the class as a whole, they should be discussed. The present strategy may be retained or a consensus may be formed regarding a new strategy. Changes to instructional strategies should be made only with the consent of the whole team.

A point should be made about changing instructional strategies. While change for change's sake may not be the best curricular strategy, the team should not fear change. If a program or method is not working, change is usually appropriate. The vast resources of the team can provide many different approaches to programming. When necessary, those resources should be tapped.

Evaluation of the Team's Functioning

Finally, and perhaps most vital to the team's operation, regular evaluation of how the team is functioning should take place. Periodically or as any team member feels it is necessary, the team should review the decision-making and implementation process for determining programming for students. Each member should address how he or she thinks the team is meeting their stated goals and how effectively the process of addressing concerns is taking place. If concerns about how the team is operating are raised, the team as a whole must address those concerns until they are resolved to the satisfaction of all team members.

CHALLENGES

Providing educational services to all students in inclusive elementary-level settings is itself a huge challenge. There are, however, some very specific challenges that occur for teams in this setting.

Establishing Common Goals

Special educators are taught to obtain students' goals as established by the IEP. Regular educators are taught to work for the advancement of all the children in their classes. Regular educators are trained to have a focus on the group and the group's advancement and acquisition of skills. Special educators are trained to focus on the individual needs of students with disabilities. While both outcomes result in learning for students, the focus is decidedly different. When working as team members, regular and special educators must come to understand each other's point of view. This is also true of all team members from other disciplines. The challenge is to see the benefits of the many different perspectives of various disciplines while remembering that all team members have agreed-upon, common goals for all students being served.

Maintaining Clarity of Goals and Roles

Team members serving students in inclusive settings must keep clear the goals and roles of the team. In many instances it may be easy to slip into disciplinary roles that are concerned with disciplinary goals. When providing services in an inclusive setting, disciplinary goals may be secondary or not addressed at all. Departmental meetings of all one discipline may make it easy to focus on discipline-specific concerns. This must be avoided to ensure that the goals of the team are accomplished.

The primary role of a professional serving students in inclusive elementary settings is that of a team member serving a group of students. It is often difficult to cast aside one's discipline-specific roles. Ultimately, however, the role of team member must come first. By keeping the team and students as each member's first priorities, all possible methods of intervention can be entertained and implemented, rather than limiting oneself to disciplinary-specific strategies.

Teaching Consultative Skills to Team Members

Because all team members will be sharing information and teaching other team members their specific discipline skills, each member will need to learn how to act as a consultant. Related service personnel (physical, occupational, and speech therapists) have often been placed in this role and may be comfortable with it. Regular and special education teachers, however, may not have any experience with consultation and teaching their skills to other professionals.

Luth and Harvey (1992) found that many teachers who were in a consultative role in their jobs felt that they had not been trained to be consultants. These teachers stated that they needed information on how to work with other adults. All staff members who will be part of a team can benefit from learning basic principles of adult education and adult learning styles and implementing them as they teach fellow team members about their discipline.

Students with Challenging Behaviors

Questions often arise about the ability of inclusive school settings to serve students with emotional or behavioral concerns (Forest & Pierpoint, 1990; Hitzing, 1992). While this group of students may be the most difficult to provide support for, this is also the group for which a team approach to inclusive schooling is most needed.

Students with great emotional and behavioral needs necessitate settings where their behaviors are understood, where staff acknowledge and support their positive skills, and where instructional strategies are implemented consistently. Through using a team approach with students with challenging behaviors, the team may better be able to understand why certain behaviors are being exhibited. The multiple views of team members may help the classroom teacher realize that Jamal's consistently aggressive behavior toward the other boys on the playground is his way of trying to be part of the group. Once this is understood, the team can work to generate strategies that will allow Jamal to indicate that he wants to be included in the game.

Because consistency of intervention strategies is often important with students with challenging behaviors, the team approach will minimize staff behaviors that are contradictory. The team will also be able to provide support to those team members who will be working closest with the students. This support may be the resource needed to ensure that positive, supportive intervention strategies are implemented, rather than seeing the student as "hopeless."

The "Re-Merger" of Regular and Special Education

In many elementary schools, grade-level teams are composed of teachers who have the reputation of being wonderful teachers of reading, math, or composition. These teachers also are competent in all other content areas. They are strong generalists who have a specialty. The grade-level teams often collaborate, and teachers trade ideas and approaches.

With the teaming of special education and regular education, perhaps the future will erase the labels of "special" or "regular" teachers. Instead, we may have teams that have members who are excellent at working with children with physical disabilities, cognitive delays, or communication disorders. All of these teachers will also be competent generalists at their grade levels, knowing the specific content information that must be communicated and the instructional strategies to do so. Schools will have teams made of teachers who all have excellent skills and will be specialists in what to teach *and* how to teach it.

The result of these teams will be schools that can address complex content areas and teach all types of skills but will also be able to teach all types of children. The result then will be truly inclusive schooling.

Ortiz (1993) has said that "forging the regular-special education partnership is the challenge of the decade." While it may be the challenge of the 1990s, establishing inclusive partnerships is also the way to return educators and schools to a point where we are *all* responsible for *all* students.

SUMMARY AND CONCLUSIONS

Using teams to educate all students in inclusive elementary settings is essential. Providing education to students with and without disabilities in inclusive schools necessitates considering vast amounts of information, incorporating family needs and information, and coordinating numerous specialized education personnel. In order to do this, a comprehensive team of professionals and the family must collaboratively develop goals and methods for reaching those goals. The inclusion team can then consistently implement the strategies necessary to reach the established goals.

As with other teams working with children, an inclusion team in an elementary school is able to address the varied needs of many students, both with and without disabilities. The team does this by ensuring that the members have control over the goals set for the students, share all available information, teach each other skills from their respective disciplines, and consistently implement agreed-upon educational strategies. As integration of students with disabilities in regular elementary schools becomes more common and as truly inclusive elementary settings develop, the use of teams to support students, their families, and the staff serving the students will greatly increase the success rate of these programs.

REFERENCES

Braaten, S., Kauffman, J., Braaten, B., Polsgrove, L., & Nelson, M. (1988). The regular education initiative: Patent medicine for behavioral disorders. *Exceptional Children, 55*(1), 21–28.

Education for all handicapped children act of 1975, PL 94-142. (August 23, 1977). Title 20, U.S.C.1401 et seq: U.S. Statutes at Large, *89,* 773–796.

Forest, M., & Pierpoint, J. (1990). Support for addressing severe maladaptive behaviors. In W. Stainback & S. Stainback (Eds.), *Support networks for inclusive schooling: Interdependent integrated education* (pp. 187–197). Baltimore, MD: Brookes.

Garner, H. (1988). *Helping others through teamwork.* Washington, DC: Child Welfare League of America.

Gersten, R., & Woodward, J. (1990). Rethinking the Regular Education Initiative: Focus on the classroom teacher. *Remedial and Special Education, 11*(3), 7–16.

Hanson, M., & Wiederstrom, A. (1993). Consultation and collaboration: Essentials of integration efforts for young children. In C. Peck, S. Odom, & D. Bricker (Eds.), *Integrating young children with disabilities into community programs: Ecological perspectives on research and implementation* (pp. 149–168). Baltimore, MD: Brookes.

Harris, S., Handleman, J., Kristoff, B., Bass, L., & Gordon, R. (1990). Changes in language development among autistic and peer children in segregated and integrated preschool settings. *Journal of Autism and Developmental Disabilities, 20,* 23–31.

Heller, H., & Schilit, J. (1987). The Regular Education Initiative: A concerned response. *Focus on exceptional children, 20,* 1–6.

Hitzing, W. (1992). Support and positive teaching strategies. In S. Stainback & W. Stainback (Eds.), *Curriculum considerations in inclusive classrooms: Facilitating learning for all students* (pp. 143–158). Baltimore, MD: Brookes.

Jenkins, J., Odom, S., & Speltz, M. (1989). Effects of social integration on preschool children with handicaps. *Exceptional Children, 55,* 420–428.

Luth, F., & Harvey, J. (1992, April). Survey of early childhood special education teachers in Virginia. Paper presented at the Annual Early Childhood Special Education Conference, Fairfax, VA.

Miller, L. (1990). The Regular Education Initiative and school reform: Lessons from the mainstream. *Remedial and Special Education, 11*(3), 17–22.

Ortiz, A. (1993). The future is in partnership. *Teaching Exceptional Children, 25*(3), 4.

Peck, C., Carlson, P., & Helmstetter, E. (1992). Parent and teacher perceptions of outcomes for typically developing children enrolled in integrated early childhood programs: A statewide survey. *Journal of Early Intervention, 16,* 53–63.

Rainforth, B., York, J., & Macdonald, C. (1992). *Collaborative teams for students with severe disabilities: Integrating therapy and educational services.* Baltimore, MD: Brookes.

Salend, S. (1990). *Effective mainstreaming.* New York: Macmillan.

Simpson, R., & Myles, B. (1993). Successful integration of children and youth with autism in mainstreamed settings. *Focus on Autistic Behavior, 7*(6), 1–13.

Strain, P. (1990). LRE for preschool children with handicaps: What we know, what we should be doing. *Journal of Early Intervention, 14*(4), 291–296.

Sugai, G., & Tindal, G. (1993). *Effective school consultation: An interactive approach.* Pacific Grove, CA: Brooks/Cole.

Tomchek, L., Gordon, R., Arnold, M., Handleman, J., & Harris, S. (1992). Teaching children with autism and their normally developing peers: Meeting the challenges of integrated education. *Focus on Autistic Behavior, 7*(2), 1–19.

Turnbull, A., & Turnbull, H. R. (1990). *Families, professionals, and exceptionality: A special partnership* (2d ed.). Columbus, OH: Merrill.

Vincent, L. (1992). Families and early intervention: Diversity and competence. *Journal of Early Intervention, 16,* 166–172.

Teamwork in Middle School Education

Thomas O. Erb

TEAMS OF TEACHERS KEEPING PACE WITH SOCIETAL CHANGE

The world has changed considerably since the departmentalized structure of high schools was created in the early twentieth century. The self-contained classroom structure of the elementary school has even earlier roots in agrarian America. However, the more modern middle school structure featuring teachers working together on interdisciplinary teams mirrors the changing nature of the larger society in the late twentieth century. Departmentalized schools were a good match for the simpler work patterns of the industrial era. At a time when schools were preparing students to carry out jobs in the factories of industrial America, the idea of isolating teachers in separate classrooms to teach their subject specialties to successive groups of more or less homogeneous students seemed compatible with the types of work environments that the students themselves were being prepared for. The expanding job market of the early Industrial Age called for increasing numbers of workers who didn't have to do much creative thinking, but who could follow orders, respect authority, and carry out their assigned job tasks in relative isolation from other workers (Skrtic, 1989, 1991).

However, a number of societal changes began to become apparent in the decades following the World War II. Not only was the departmentalized junior high school structure beginning to reveal its limitations for dealing with the educational needs of a diverse set of young adolescents, but the structure of departmentalized schools was becoming increasingly out of sync with the needs of the larger U.S. society. Several trends that were to have a bearing on the educational needs of the rising generation of young adolescents were becoming apparent. Economic and social factors resulted in young people receiving much less adult attention than they had received a generation earlier. The families that young adolescents were growing up in were much less likely to consist of two parents, one of whom was a breadwinner and the other a homemaker. Two-worker families, one-parent families, blended families, and other nontraditional arrangements came to predominate. The intergenerational extended family was also less likely to be immediately available to assist the nuclear family in raising its young.

At the same time that young adolescents were getting less adult attention, a technological revolution was taking place that greatly altered the ways we communicate. Disappearing were the days when radios and black-and-white TV novelties were turned on a couple of hours a night. Cable television and VCRs have exponentially expanded the influence of media in our homes. The typical eighth-grader now spends four times as much time watching television as doing homework (Office of Educational Research and Improvement, 1990). Computers have shrunk from room-sized calculators to desktop network terminals. There is so much more information bombarding people today.

The demographics of our society are undergoing major changes, some of which are particularly sobering for those of us whose business it is to educate the next generation. In 1950 there were 17 workers supporting each retiree. By early in the decade of the 1990s there will be 3 workers for each retiree (Corrigan, 1990). Enlightened self-interest suggests that educators need to make sure this generation of young people can be gainfully employed in the new economy of the twenty-first century. This challenge is made even more dramatic by the fact that various minorities who in the past have not always been well served by traditional public schools will make up more than half of the school-age population by the year 2020 (Hodgkinson, 1989).

Just as it did when the United States was transforming itself out of the agrarianism into the Industrial Age, the business community is again claiming that young people do not possess the skills necessary to handle the jobs emerging in the new economy. The skills that worked to secure and keep well-paying jobs in the factories of the industrial age are no longer adequate for the Information Age. According to Skrtic (1989, 1991), the jobs that are increasingly available today require workers who can think and share authority in collaboration with others to invent new procedures and innovatively solve problems.

Departmentalized school structures are simply not flexible enough to deal with the diversity of students growing up in an information-rich, attention-poor environment. Departmentalized structures are especially problematic for young adolescents who are going through puberty and starting the personality transformations associated with leaving childhood behind and striving toward adulthood. The problems associated with schools that are organized around departments, where teachers are responsible for teaching each child only one period a day, are compounded by the fact that middle-level schools are often much larger and more anonymous places than the elementary schools that have been left behind. Consequently, just as students are beginning to experience what psychologist Fritz Redl (1966) calls "personality disorganization," we have given them a large, impersonal, and fragmented school organization to relate to. The result is that too many students do not get the recognition and support that they need to succeed in school. A school organized around subject area departments, with no one in charge of looking after the academic and social well-being of each student, is an inadequate structure to provide for students' needs.

Educating students today to live in the world of tomorrow is far too complex a task to be left to individual teachers working in isolation from each other. Interdisciplinary teams are one of education's most significant structural changes aimed at keeping schools responsive to the changing needs of the larger society. By the late 1960s several authors were defining interdisciplinary teaming in its modern form and documenting its use in schools (Van Til, Vars, & Lounsbury, 1967; Alexander et al., 1968). The use of interdisciplinary teaming in middle-level schools has risen steadily since the late 1960s from around 6 percent of schools to around 40 percent by the late 1980s. By promoting collaboration, shared authority, and joint problem solving, interdisciplinary teams are transforming schools into the same types of work environments that characterize other Information Age occupations.

TEAM ORGANIZATION: SEVERAL VARIATIONS ON A FUNDAMENTAL CONCEPT

Well-functioning interdisciplinary teams not only perform educational tasks differently than do teachers in isolated classrooms, but they alter the basic professional culture in their schools. When a school changes from a separate classrooms approach to an interdisciplinary team approach to teaching, the communication patterns in the school are forever changed. Teachers communicate more frequently and in greater depth about students, curriculum, instruction, and other matters of professional concern. Teachers are able to make more and better decisions about student support, classroom management, and instructional issues because they have more time and better tools with which to work. In addition, because of the new communication patterns that include more communication between teachers and administrators, teachers tend to play a more influential role in building governance. In the end, teachers report that their careers are more rewarding and that they feel a greater sense of efficacy in their teaching.

The Core Team

In U.S. middle schools there are several different types of interdisciplinary teams that can contribute to a changed school culture. The most basic form, the one that

Alexander and George (1981) call the keystone of middle school structure, is the core team, which consists of two or more teachers who are responsible for teaching the basic, required curriculum to a group of students. Another type of interdisciplinary team is the exploratory/elective team. These teams consist of two or more teachers who are responsible for teaching exploratory classes or elective classes to all or some subset of students in a middle school. Some middle schools also set up support teams that consist of personnel who are generally not directly responsible for teaching students but who instead support the work of those who do. Such teams are often made up of media specialists, counselors, nurses, social workers, and psychologists. Another type of interdisciplinary team is the special education team. Although special educators are increasingly assigned to serve on core teams, in many schools, teachers of students with learning disabilities, behavioral disorders, mental handicaps, and giftedness serve together on interdisciplinary special education teams.

The core team is what most people have come to associate with middle school organization. Core teams are responsible for delivering that portion of the curriculum designated as the common core. Such classes as social studies, science, English, math, reading, and any other courses that are required of all students are taught by the teachers on an interdisciplinary core team. To be considered a core team, two essential elements must be in place. The teachers who constitute a team must share the same students. In addition, the teachers on a team must have a regular team meeting time—daily is ideal. The power of teaming grows from the fact that several teachers who share the same students meet regularly to jointly plan for their instruction and to monitor their progress in the school setting. These two elements are absolutely essential for the success of interdisciplinary core teams.

Two other elements facilitate the work of teams by giving the teachers on the teams more control over the teaching/learning environment. The first of these elements is a block schedule in which the teamed teachers have control of a block of time consisting of from two to five class periods. When a team of teachers controls a block of time, they have more flexibility in planning for the instruction of the students on their team. Teamed teachers are not constrained, as are departmentalized ones, by the bell schedule. The other element that facilitates the work of the core teaching team is team space, or a team area in the school building. This can be accomplished by assigning team members to classrooms close to each other. By having team members share adjacent classrooms, both informal communications between teachers and the movement of students from one area of the team to another are facilitated.

Core teams may serve a single grade level or serve multiple ages across grade levels. Currently the most typical pattern is for teams to consist of students at a single grade level. In larger schools there may be two or three teams serving the needs of students at each grade level. For example, a school of 900 students in grades six through eight might consist of nine interdisciplinary core teams, three at each grade level containing approximately 100 students per team. Some middle school faculties have implemented cross-age teams to provide multi-year continuity for the instruction of their students. Cross-age teams take the concept of teaming one step further by removing the constraints of grade-level curriculum in addition to those of the daily bell schedule.

Integrating Special Educators into Core Teams

The power of teaming for dealing with the complexity of educating young adolescents in a dynamic, pluralistic society is increased by adding the talents and expertise of special educators to the core team. The interdisciplinary core team is an excellent arrangement for implementing the Regular Education Initiative (Will, 1986a, 1986b). When students identified as having exceptional learning needs (everything from mental handicaps to giftedness) are mainstreamed onto a core team, those special educators trained to meet their particular learning needs become members of the core team along with the traditional subject specialists. Increasing numbers of middle school educators are finding that combining the talents and perspectives of one or more learning specialists with those of two or more subject specialists makes many good things happen for students.

An effective process for implementing this type of interdisciplinary approach to teaching a diverse set of young adolescents is called *collaborative consultation* (Robinson, 1991; Nevin et al., 1990). Robinson (1991) defines collaborative consultation as "an interactive and ongoing process where individuals with different expertise, knowledge, or experience voluntarily work together to create solutions to mutually agreed upon problems" (pp. 445–446). This process for meeting the needs of a diverse set of learners is recommended as an alternative to the disjointed nature of special education pull-out programs, where students are placed in separate classes for part of the day to address their identified needs. Pull-out programs get particularly complicated when students are given multiple labels such as "learning disabled–behavior disordered" or "gifted–learning disabled," which may result in a very fragmented curriculum for these students repeatedly removed from regular classrooms. Nevin and her associates (1990) have argued that collaborative teaching teams could eliminate the need for a separate special education system by allowing all students to gain access to appropriate instructional support within the regular classroom. According to Robinson (1991), collaborative consultation is based on the assumptions that parity exists among all participants; all educators can learn better ways to teach all students; and educators should be actively involved in creating, as well as delivering, instructional innovations. Robinson specifically cites middle school interdisciplinary teams as an organizational arrangement that facilitates collaboration.

The Exploratory Team

In addition to the teachers organized into interdisciplinary core teams, middle schools are increasingly establishing teams of teachers of exploratory and elective classes. Exploratory classes are short courses, usually lasting less than a semester, designed to expose students to new learning experiences, such as exposure to foreign languages, various arts, music, technology, home economics, computers, and speech/drama. After a short exposure to these curricular possibilities, students are typically given the opportunity to elect longer courses in these areas. Most often the teachers who teach the introductory exploratory classes are the same people who teach the full-course electives. Consequently, the term *exploratory/elective* is often used to label the teams made up of teachers who teach this variable part of the curriculum. Even though their classes are required of all students, physical education and health teachers are often included on exploratory/elective teams for scheduling purposes.

Like any other type of team, exploratory/elective teams must have regular, common planning time. Team members cannot discuss mutual concerns, student needs, or curricular issues without a regular meeting time. However, since teachers of exploratory and elective classes may not share students on a daily basis as do core team teachers, they may not need to hold team meetings as often as do core teams. However, if one takes the long view extending over the course of the whole school year, if not the full two or three years that students spend in a middle school, the teachers on exploratory/elective teams also share the same students. Therefore, they are able to provide assistance to each other in understanding the learning needs of the students they share.

The Advisory Team

Another practice that is sometimes followed in middle schools is for advisory teams to be established. Middle schools with advisory programs often find it helpful to organize student advisory groups around the interdisciplinary core teams (James, 1986). However, if only the interdisciplinary core teachers serve as teacher-advisors, the exploratory/elective teachers would be excluded from participation in the advisory program. In addition, by excluding a significant portion of the faculty from participation, the advisory groups would be larger than desirable. In order to take advantage of the existing core teams, include the rest of the faculty, and keep advisory groups in the 15 to 20 student range, two or three exploratory/elective teachers will be assigned to each interdisciplinary core team to create an advisory team. This expanded advisory team may meet once or twice a month to plan and monitor the advisory program for the students on each core team.

Occurrence of Interdisciplinary Teams

The use of interdisciplinary teams in middle-level schools has increased about fivefold in the last 20 years. Alexander and McEwin (1989) found that the use of interdisciplinary teams in grade five increased from 3 percent in 1968 to 31 percent in 1988. The comparable figures for grades six, seven, and eight showed increases from 8 percent to 38 percent, 6 percent to 28 percent, and 6 percent to 24 percent respectively. Cawelti (1988) reports a slightly lower percentage, 16 percent, for the use of interdisciplinary teams where all types of middle-level schools are considered together. However, there were considerable differences in the use of teaming between various types of middle-level schools. The most recent national study of the use of interdisciplinary teaming (Epstein & MacIver, 1990) reports that overall, 42 percent of early adolescents receive instruction from interdisciplinary teams sometime between grades five through nine. Reinforcing Cawelti's findings, Epstein and MacIver also found teaming to be more prevalent in grade six-through-eight middle schools than in seven-through-nine junior highs. The Epstein and MacIver study also echoed the Alexander and McEwin study in reporting that the use of teaming peaks in grade six and declines thereafter, becoming virtually nonexistent in grade nine. Although there is a clear trend away from departmentalized and self-contained arrangements and toward interdisciplinary teaming in middle-level schools, only about a 42-percent minority of students currently enjoy the benefits of teaming.

CHARACTERISTICS OF SCHOOLS WITH INTERDISCIPLINARY TEAMING

Middle-level schools organized around interdisciplinary teams are fundamentally different types of places than are schools organized around traditional departments or self-contained classrooms. Not only is professional practice altered, but also the professional culture of the school is different. Using such practices as rigid student class assignments and bell schedules, traditional school organizations tend to rely more on bureaucratic rules and regulations to control the interactions of teachers and students. However, after studying a dozen middle-level schools where teaming was being successfully practiced, Erb (1987, 1988b) concluded that improved systems of communication and decision making liberate teachers to focus more effectively on student learning needs. Furthermore, Doda (1984) and Ashton and Webb (1986) have documented how the practice of teaming can positively affect teachers' perceptions of their professional competence, or efficacy.

Communication and Problem Solving among Team Members

Communication about student behavior, curriculum, instruction and time management, and staff development is affected by the use of team organization. Interdisciplinary teaming breaks down the isolation that has traditionally been the bane of the teaching profession. By meeting regularly, teachers are able to discuss a wide range of professional concerns. First and foremost, teaming allows teachers to exchange perspectives on the students they share on the team. These exchanges tend to be targeted on those students who are in the greatest need of support. Much earlier than individual teachers working in isolation, teams identify students who are engaging in problematic behavior. When any member of the team detects a problem developing with a student, he or she is able to discuss this concern with several other professionals who also know the young adolescent from the perspective of their classes. Teachers on a team communicate early and often regarding student performance, whether there is a problem with homework, peer relations, working in cooperative groups, willingness to attempt new assignments, or any of the myriad behaviors that may portend trouble if not addressed. Collectively, teamed teachers can devise plans of action to ameliorate problems that they see developing among their students. In the area of dealing with student misbehavior, teams are so successful in handling matters at the team level that office referrals tend to be significantly lower in schools that are organized into teams than is the case in similar unteamed schools (George & Oldaker, 1985). One suburban school district that operated seven middle schools reported a 23 percent drop in short-term suspensions among its eighth-graders over a two-year period after interdisciplinary teaming was established (Erb, 1988a). Talking about more supportive environments for students is just one way teachers engage in new patterns of communication.

Curriculum also is discussed more frequently. A number of people who have studied schooling in the past decade have commented on the curricular fragmentation that characterizes U.S. classrooms (Goodlad, 1984; Boyer, 1983; Sizer, 1984; Lounsbury & Clark, 1990). Interdisciplinary teaming creates the conditions necessary for curricular cohesion and even curricular integration to occur. Teachers on interdisciplinary teams are able to talk about their respective curricular areas. After a team has been functioning together for a year, its members are conversant with the subjects, in addition to their own, that are taught on the team. By frequently discussing activities, objectives, and resource materials that are used in the service of the various subjects taught on the team, all teachers come to understand the curriculum beyond the limits of the specific subjects that they teach. Once discussions of basic curricular matters have occurred, team members are in a position to plan for the various subjects to be reinforced, interrelated, and/or integrated. Teachers may simply coordinate curriculum by teaching similar units simultaneously and helping students draw connections between the subjects. Or they may engage in more cooperative curricular integrations by planning for specific skill reinforcement across subjects or by creating lessons, learning centers, or units that tie together two or more subjects taught on the team. By the second year of operation some teams are even ready to develop interdisciplinary thematic units that fully integrate, for several days to several weeks of study, two or more subjects with a common theme and integrative culminating activities (Erb & Doda, 1989). In recent years some teams have taken curriculum integration to new heights by abandoning subjects as the basis for organizing the curriculum and turning to a curriculum based on personal and social themes (Beane, 1990; Hawkins & Graham, 1994). Interdisciplinary teaming is a necessary condition if curricular cohesion is to occur in schools taught by subject specialists. Only by communicating with each other about their separate subject areas can teachers of the various subjects ever hope to help students see the interconnectedness of knowledge.

Communication also occurs regarding instruction and management issues. Teachers not only share their successes, but they are able to process their failures in the supportive environment of a team meeting. Teamed teachers who also enjoy a block schedule are better able to match instruction to the needs of students rather than to the dictates of a bell schedule. It becomes possible to arrange instructional times either longer or shorter than the inflexible, 45- or 50-minute periods traditional in many schools. Science labs, social studies videos, English writing assignments, and outside speakers for any class can be arranged for the appropriate length of time that these activities require. Time can be combined with student regrouping to make instruction more efficient. For example, all the students on the team can be assembled for one showing of a video and then immediately thereafter regrouped into clusters of 25 to discuss the presentation. In those teams where exceptional students are mainstreamed and one or more special education teachers are members of the core team, communication occurs regularly regarding instructional modifications for the special-needs students. The discussions of all students' instructional needs tend to be richer in these settings. On interdisciplinary teams, teachers communicate regularly about instructional matters.

Teachers on interdisciplinary teams can also form their own ongoing professional development units. Teachers can readily share professional articles they have read or discuss what they learned from attending staff development workshops or professional conferences. Teaming facilitates peer observations and peer consultations. Simply having the opportunity for sharing classroom events provides a regular opportunity for teamed teachers to learn from each other's experiences. Team meeting time provides the opportunity for teachers to communicate with each other on a broad range of professional issues.

Communication with People Outside the Team

Not only is communication in a teamed setting very different from classroom teachers, but communication between teachers and other people is also different. Communication with parents tends to be more positive, more frequent, and earlier than communication between isolated teachers and parents (Erb, 1987). For young adolescent learners it is particularly important to keep communication open between the home and the school. When a member of a team contacts parents, that communication is generally based on a broad perspective of how the student is functioning in school. Not only is the teacher knowledgeable about how the student is functioning in one class, but he or she can convey the perspectives of several other professionals who see the strengths and limitations of the student in several settings. Parents generally appreciate hearing from someone who has a more complete vision of their progeny than that usually offered by an isolated teacher whose view of a given child is generally far more limited.

Home–school communication can be better targeted by teams. By identifying students who are engaging in problematic behavior early in the school year, teams can involve the parents of these children in looking for solutions long before the behavior deteriorates into a crisis. Team meeting time is frequently a time when parent conferences are held, either at school or over the phone when several teachers are available to converse with the parents. In addition to targeting communication about specific students, interdisciplinary teams often send newsletters to parents informing them of life on the team. Students themselves are often involved in the production of these newsletters as an extension of their academic work.

Communication with support staff in a school is greatly facilitated when teachers are organized onto teams. Counselors can regularly meet with teams to discuss students. Counselors are able to bring information contained in the cumulative files and the expertise created by their specialized training to enrich the discussion of a student's instructional or behavior needs. Media specialists are wonderful resources for teaching teams. They can meet with teams to update the faculty on new acquisitions and help plan interdisciplinary units. Nurses can keep teams current on the health needs and important special conditions of students. A whole team can know at once who are the students with asthma, diabetes, and other conditions that may affect their ability to learn under certain conditions. Another use of team meeting time that brings together several professionals to communicate during the regular work day is the special education staffing or even the conference to plan the student's IEP. The team meeting allows for several regular education subject specialists to meet with psychologists, various special educators, administrators, and parents to discuss a student's IEP and reach a common understanding of each person's role in implementing that program.

Communication between teachers and administrators also tends to improve when teachers are organized into teams. In smaller schools, building administrators may meet once every week or two with each team during its regular meeting time. Alternately, and more commonly in larger schools, the team leaders of all teaching teams form an advisory committee that meets regularly with the principal to discuss matters of mutual concern. The agendas for these meetings are formed by both teachers and administrators. Consequently, two-way communication occurs between teams and administrators, either of which can bring up items for discussion.

The radical changes in communication patterns that occur in schools where teachers are functioning on teams and meeting regularly lead to a number of other changes that can readily be observed in such schools. Life for teachers, students, and administrators tends to be more satisfying in teamed settings.

Student Support

Team organization can provide a more supportive learning environment for young adolescents than is possible in a departmentalized setting. Students in an elementary school setting typically have one teacher who functions as "their" teacher. Even in schools with some degree of subject specialization in the upper elementary grades, students typically spend more time with one of their teachers, who is regarded as "their" teacher by both the students and their parents. This teacher tends to know the students in his or her charge fairly well. They are "persons," not just "students," to him or her. Interdisciplinary teams provide the means to extend the supportive aspects of the self-contained classrooms into the middle grades while adding the greater subject matter expertise of specialists.

The interdisciplinary team represents a major advance in school organizational structure for creating a safe environment where each student is well known by each adult and by the student's peers on the team. In schools with interdisciplinary teams, students are talked about much more than they are in departmentalized, and often compartmentalized, schools. Because a team of professionals who share students is able to meet regularly to discuss any problems that may be developing, students' needs are addressed sooner and in a more consistent manner. Teams are able to hold conferences with students to discuss problems and work out action plans for correcting those problems. Meetings with parents or other school support people are facilitated by the fact that the entire team of teachers has a regular meeting time.

Not only are teams more effective in identifying and addressing student needs than are isolated teachers, but also they are able to perform proactively to promote a supportive environment. From the outset, teachers are able to establish a consistent set of expectations for student behavior. Students will know from one period to the next what is expected in terms of homework, hall behavior, academic performance, and classroom deportment. Consistency of expectations provides a more supportive learning environment for the students on a team. Beyond a set of commonly under-stood and enforced expectations, teams often plan assemblies or social events to promote the notion that the team is a learning *community*. Teams often plan annual events such as field trips or even overnight experiences that are tied to academic objectives but also promote the spirit of community where every child knows that he or she is known and cared about at school. In addition, teams frequently establish criteria for rewarding the positive behaviors that they want to foster among the young adolescents in their charge. The teachers on a team will systematically reinforce a wide variety of student behaviors, including but not limited to academic performance. They will set up opportunities to recognize these behaviors through awards assemblies or various social events rewarding students who have performed up to teacher expecta-tions.

Recently published empirical research supports the conclusion that teamed schools create a more supportive environment for students. Arhar (1990) found that school organization had measurable effects on students' ability to bond with peers, with teachers, and with their schools. In matched pairs of teamed or nonteamed schools, Arhar reports finding that students had higher levels of social bonding in teamed schools versus nonteamed schools by a ratio of 5 or 6 to 1. In another study, Stefanich, Wills, and Buss (1991) concluded: "Students at middle schools with higher levels of use of interdisciplinary teaming reflected higher self-concept scores at each grade level for both males and females when compared to students at schools that did not employ interdisciplinary teaming" (p. 414). It is encouraging to see research that compares student outcomes in schools with interdisciplinary teaming to those without it and shows the expected positive outcomes for young adolescents. Teaming provides the opportunity for teachers to create a supportive, family-like environment that is so important for young adolescents going through the increasingly difficult task of negotiating the transition from childhood to full adolescence. In addition, that opportunity is beginning to result in demonstrably positive outcomes for students.

Curricular Cohesion

Critiques of curriculum delivery in general (Goodlad, 1984; Boyer, 1984; Sizer, 1984) and middle-level curriculum in particular (Beane, 1993; Lounsbury & Clark, 1990) have pointed out that so much of what students are asked to learn is taught in fragmented ways without connections being made either to other areas of learning or to meaningful applications outside of school. Yet teachers in a departmentalized school can hardly be held accountable for this state of affairs. How could teachers be held accountable for failing to integrate the curriculum when they have only been educated to know one subject and they are provided no systematic way to communicate with teachers of other subjects? Clearly, the departmentalized junior or senior high school is structurally incompetent to address the problem of curricular fragmentation.

Cross-curricular connections are an increasingly common occurrence on interdisciplinary teams. However, what evidence exists points to the conclusion that curricular collaboration tends to lag behind other types of collaboration in teamed settings (Lipsitz, 1984; Arhar, Johnston, & Markle, 1988; Beane, 1993). Yet team organization does provide the opportunity for teachers to play a significant role in designing and delivering a coordinated, if not integrated, curriculum. Erb and Doda (1989) have provided an annotated bibliography of thematic units that have been reported in the professional literature, mostly in the *Middle School Journal*. Arnold (1990) has contributed descriptions of a number of multidisciplinary and interdisciplinary projects that have been successfully carried out by interdisciplinary teams. While curricular coordination has to this point been less of an accomplished fact than other results of interdisciplinary teaming, there appears to be a renewed interest in curricular integration (Dickinson, 1993; Brandt, 1991) that teachers on interdisciplinary teams are in a position to take advantage of.

Teacher Decision Making

Teachers who function on interdisciplinary teams report involvement in collaborative decision making. Not only are teachers involved in more types of decisions that affect the operation of the schools in which they work, but the processes by which those decisions are made tend to be more intricate. Erb (1987) has reported the results of his interviews with over 200 teachers working on interdisciplinary teams in 12 different schools. These teamed teachers worked together to reach joint decisions about team goals. After setting team goals for the year or semester, team members were able to set expectations and draw up rules of conduct for students. Later, when specific problems arose, teachers collaboratively decided how best to support a student in need. Teachers had joint input into such decisions as athletic eligibility and retention. Teachers also collaboratively designed such things as student reward systems.

One of the most powerful areas of decision making occurs in the area of student placement and student grouping. Teachers can decide to group and regroup students within the team for academic or behavioral reasons in a way that departmentalized teachers cannot do without upsetting the master schedule. Not only can teachers shift individual students to the best class grouping, but they can regroup whole classes or even the entire team to accommodate different types of instructional strategies. For example, the entire team of 100 to 150 students can watch a video or listen to a speaker at one time. There is no need to repeat a film five or six times or to break up a 100-minute presentation into two or three sittings. Students can then be regrouped into smaller, class-sized groups for debriefing or followup activities. Furthermore, interdisciplinary units can be taught in such a way that students throughout the entire team can be regrouped by interest area or task function into interdependent collaborative learning groups. Because they are no longer constrained by such bureaucratic devices as master schedules and bell schedules, teachers on teams have more control over instructional decisions than do those confined to isolated classrooms. Lipsitz (1984) sums up the perspectives of the teachers in one of the teamed schools she reported on by saying that teachers who have the capacity to make decisions about curriculum, allocation of time, grouping of students, and student choice see themselves as true professionals.

In teamed schools the decision-making process is improved. The critical difference is provided by the team meeting time. The opportunity to incubate ideas in the context of the team meeting really sets teamed schools apart from nonteamed ones. Several heads *are* better than one when it comes to decision making in a school setting. Different teachers see things slightly differently because of their different backgrounds and experiences with the subject being discussed. When teams work together in a climate of trust, the open communication results in the whole being truly greater than the sum of the parts. Larson and LaFasto (1989) have concluded that trust is produced in climates that include four elements: honesty, openness, consistency, and respect. When these elements are present on a team, its decision-making capacity knows few bounds. The team meeting provides the time for full discussion of ideas. Team members are comfortable proposing creative, tentative ideas; listening to feedback; combining different ideas; and going beyond their immediate comfort zones to risk unique solutions to instructional and managerial problems. Teachers on teams not only have the advantage of interacting with other classroom teachers, but they can also bring into their deliberations other perspectives as appropriate. This additional expertise may come from counselors, media specialists, administrators, community resources, teachers assigned to other teams, parents, or other selected experts who can contribute to the discussion of the issue being decided. Teacher decisions tend to be better thought out because of the balance of perspectives brought to bear during the decision-making process. Finally, because team members have a shared commitment to their mutually arrived-at decisions and to each other, the team's decisions tend to be carried out.

Governance/School Improvement

Established interdisciplinary teams fit beautifully with reform efforts aimed at promoting site-based management. A teamed school that has team leadership in place and that has regular meetings of these team leaders with administrators has the structure to involve the entire faculty in building-level decision making. Though additional task forces or committees might be deemed appropriate, a collaborative environment already exists. With team structure in place, every faculty member—whether on a core team, an exploratory team, or a support team—has access to team meetings where groups of from three to eight team members can discuss issues and make proposals for change. Each of these teams is in turn represented on the schoolwide governance committee by its team leader. Though interdisciplinary teaming and site-based management arrangements can exist independently from each other, they complement each other very well. Though considerations in establishing effective team leadership and administrative supervision for teams is beyond the scope of this chapter, the reader who wants to learn more about these issues should consult either Erb and Doda (1989) or Merenbloom (1991).

Teacher Satisfaction with the Work Environment

While it is true that not everyone is cut out to work in a collaborative environment, most teachers report much greater job satisfaction when they are assigned to work on interdisciplinary teams. Typical are these comments from two middle grades teachers in the Midwest. A math teacher just completing her first year on an interdisciplinary team related: "A year ago I was fighting this thing tooth and nail. The 'Bright Boys' were trying to force something else down our throats. But, you know, teaming is the best thing that ever happened to my teaching" (quoted in Erb & Doda, 1989, p. 7). An English teacher in her second year of teaming proclaimed, "If they do away with teaming, I'll quit teaching" (quoted in Erb & Doda, 1989, p. 7). One of the biggest satisfactions with teaming is that it breaks down the isolation that teachers in non-teamed schools feel so strongly. Lipsitz (1984) reported that the teachers in teamed schools felt a greater sense of professionalism as a result of having the opportunity to work together on important professional concerns. Larson and LaFasto (1989) concluded that when those with the technical skills and the desire to contribute work together in collaborative settings, "the observable outcome is an elevated sense of confidence among team members. This confidence . . . translates into the ability of a team to be self-correcting in its capacity to adjust to unexpected adversity and emergent challenges" (p. 71). A collaborative working environment is more supportive of its individual members. Being on a team will not eliminate problems in the workplace, but it will provide an environment that breeds confidence in the teachers' abilities to deal with whatever problems may arise.

Further evidence that teachers working in teams feel a greater sense of confidence in their ability to solve problems and deal with the pressures of their jobs can be found in the work of Ashton and Webb (1986) and Doda (1984). A teacher's sense of power to influence student learning, or efficacy, is a complex concept. It involves not only a personal sense of competence but also a general sense that teachers can influence student learning, regardless of diverse student backgrounds. Doda (1984) compared teacher efficacy in teamed and nonteamed middle schools and found that teachers who were organized as teams showed higher levels of confidence in their own sense of teaching competence. Ashton and Webb (1986) found that teacher efficacy is related to student achievement in the areas of mathematics and language arts. The combined work of Doda and Ashton and Webb points to the conclusion that teaming improves student performance in at least some academic areas by elevating the teachers' feelings of efficacy, or confidence in their ability to influence those factors that promote learning.

Team organization has the power to transform the schools in which it is tried and nurtured. Its implementation often leads to the creation of collaborative learning communities. Teachers engage in much more professional communication that leads to a greater sense of efficacy for teachers and more support, both academic and social, for young adolescents. However, successful teams do not function by magic. They can encounter problems or even create some problems that did not exist before. Let us turn our attention from the functioning of successful teams in middle-level schools to focus on some of the things that can go wrong with an attempt to implement learning. Awareness of these potential problems can increase the chances for success of those who want to try teaming.

POTENTIAL PROBLEMS AND ISSUES ASSOCIATED WITH IMPLEMENTING TEAMING

Evidence continues to mount that schools in which teachers are organized into teams are very different places from those organized along more traditional patterns where teachers tend to work alone in isolation from professional colleagues. While teaming holds much potential for rejuvenating schools as true learning communities, it is still practiced in only a 20- to 30-percent minority of middle-level schools in the United States and hardly at all in elementary and secondary schools. In schools where teaming has been tried, it is not without its problems. Assigning teachers to teams is hardly sufficient to make teams work well. There are a number of things that can go wrong in the effort to establish and maintain effective teams. Some of the problems are associated with the change process itself, and not directly with teaming per se. Another set of potential problems is associated more directly with the working teams.

Too Much Change at Once

The problem of too much change at the same time can be interpreted in two ways. One common way that change can frustrate people is that in transitions from junior high school organization to middle school organizations several innovations may be implemented simultaneously. Teaming may be coming at the same time that advisory programs are being started, at the same time that an exploratory curriculum is being introduced, at the same time the student activities program is being revamped, and at the same time that the core curriculum is being revised. To make matters more stressful, there may be a significant change in personnel due to shifting a grade level from one building to another or the closing or opening of schools in conjunction with the transformation to middle schools. Any change is difficult. Larson and LaFasto (1989) put it this way: "[C]hange requires a shifting away from the comfort of the status quo. This is usually when the antibodies come out and resist any effort to 'do it differently.' The effort required just to overcome this inertia is enormous" (p. 127). Bringing about any change in an organization or its procedures will create resistance. Trying to implement several innovations at once may sink the whole ship. If a more complete shift to middle school organization is desired, it may be wise to establish a three- to five-year plan that staggers the implementation of innovations so as not to stagger the faculty!

The second way that trying teaming can be too much at once is the attempt to implement advanced phases of teaming before the more basic aspects are in place and functioning. Even in the best of circumstances, it takes two to four years for a team of teachers to evolve into a fully functioning interdisciplinary team. There are several ways of viewing the evolution of teaming. Some of the original work on this evolution was done at the University of Texas and resulted in the creation of the Concerns-Based Adoption Model (CBAM) (Hall et al., 1975; Hord et al., 1987). This model posits six levels of use of an educational innovation and the accompanying stages of concern that characterize the users (i.e., teachers). As an innovation is implemented with ever increasing intensity, teachers go through a series of concerns that progress from being focused on self, to being focused on the task, and then to being focused on the impact of the innovation on students. This model suggests that until teachers understand teaming and have some initial successes in managing the mechanics of teaming they are not ready for high-impact outcomes like cooperative teaching and curricular integration.

George (1982) and Plodzik and George (1989) have identified four phases in the development of interdisciplinary teams. Teams start with an *organizational stage,* then advance to a stage of *community.* After a sense of community develops, teams are in a position to evolve into the *team teaching* phase. However, until a sense of community is achieved, team teaching is not a viable possibility. Finally, George argues that teams can emerge into a *governmental* stage that is akin to the site-based management possibilities that were discussed earlier in this chapter. Pickler (1987) provides a five-stage description of team evolution based on his observations. In his system the stages represent an evolution from organizational functions in the first stage to instructional applications in the fifth stage. Erb and Doda (1989) provide guidance for teachers to help set priorities on the team so as to avoid attempting to do too much at once. An intact team, one without new members each year, can expect to spend about three years working together before they evolve into a fully functioning team.

Students Caught in Transition

At the time of transition to team organization some students will invariably be caught in the transition. They will have started junior high school in a departmental format. Either because of, or in spite of, the struggles they had in adjusting to departmentalization in seventh grade, many of them will view the transition to teaming to be a "return to elementary school." They view themselves as having survived departmentalization in seventh grade and feel they are ready to be treated as high school learners. In the first year of transition one should be prepared to hear from the eighth-graders that they are being treated like babies and that teaming is too restrictive for the lifestyle they have become accustomed to. This problem will pass when the eighth-graders pass on to the high school. The grief that teachers will suffer from the eighth-graders may be more than made up for by the positive feedback that the parents of seventh-graders will heap upon the team for knowing and caring about their children.

Teachers Caught in Transition

Not all teachers who wind up on teaching teams are ready or willing to function in a collaborative environment. If some personnel have been moved around as part of the transition to middle school and team organization, there may be some teachers who would rather be teaching at the high school. They are not interested in teaching young adolescents nor in sharing this experience with teachers of other subjects. Other teachers don't mind being at the middle level, but they have spent the last 10, 15, 20 years becoming the best science, English, or math teacher that they can become. They do not see how teaming is going to make life better for them. In fact, they are sure it is going to make life more miserable. Some of these people will reveal themselves to be like the math teacher quoted above who fought the transition to teaming until she experienced it and then became a convert and advocate. However, others will never be ready to function in a collaborative environment.

Dealing with these personnel issues is seldom easy. While a certain percentage of the initial "nay sayers" will come around during the first or second year of teaming, some teachers will never be good team members. To reduce the impact of this situation, some schools may want to phase in teaming with a couple of pilot teams made up of the risk takers who are eager and ready to move ahead. Then, as other members of the faculty see the benefits of teaming, more of them will be ready to try it. Eventually, those who cannot make the transition need to be helped to find teaching positions for which they are suited in nonteamed schools. Others may be at a point in their careers where retirement is a viable option. On the other side of the coin, once the decision is made to go to teaming, all new faculty hired can be screened on the basis of their suitability to work with colleagues in a team setting.

Staff Development

Another factor that can help alleviate some of the anxiety over a transition to teaming is to provide a wide variety of staff development opportunities related to teaming. A majority of teachers are willing to try teaming if they are shown the way. About a year before teaching teams are to begin functioning with students, the staff development program needs to begin. This program will need to include work on teaming skills such as interpersonal communications, group decision making, and the organization of effective meetings. In addition, such teaming practices as goal setting, record keeping, and evaluation will need to be studied and experienced. Various team-building activities will need to be used that promote group cohesion. Without an ongoing staff development program, teachers on teams will lack the skills and direction that they need to make teaming work.

Cross-Team Communication

Earlier we discussed how teaming can change the communications patterns for the members on the team. However, teaming itself raises the expectations for improved communication among all faculty members. It is quite common for exploratory/elective teachers to complain about the difficulties that they have communicating with the core teachers about students and other issues of mutual interest. In departmentalized schools one very seldom hears complaints from an art teacher about poor communication with the science teacher or from the band teacher about never being able to discuss students with the English teacher. Few people even consider such communication a reasonable possibility in a departmentalized setting, so the issue seldom arises. However, when teaming begins with its great potential for transforming the communications patterns in a school setting, teachers across all curriculum areas want improved communication with teachers on other teams as well as with the teachers on their own teams. This is as it should be since core, exploratory, and support teams all share responsibility for the education of the young adolescents in the school. Consequently, means must be devised to keep channels of communication open among teams as well as within teams. Part of the solution resides in the aforementioned advisory committee made up of team leaders who meet regularly with the building administrators. Team initiatives can be shared in this forum. In addition, developing conflicts between and on teams can be aired and resolved.

It will also be necessary to develop a system of direct communication between teams. The location of team mail boxes or team leader mailboxes needs to be known to all teachers in the building. Procedures need to be established that allow for any teacher to get an item on another team's meeting agenda when a mutual concern exists. A home economics teacher is having a problem with a student and wishes this matter to be discussed in the core team meeting where four or five other perspectives can be brought to bear on the topic must be able to indicate to the core team members what the concern is and whether the teacher wishes to be present for the discussion of the student or merely to be kept informed of the outcome of the core team's deliberations.

Later, when interdisciplinary units are developed, cross-team communication about curriculum will be in order. If there are multiple teams at one grade level, it may be important for the whole teams or at least similar subject specialists from the various teams to communicate regularly regarding the curriculum, the use of shared materials, or the ordering of new materials. In teamed schools it may also be wise to have subject area departments meet from time to time to discuss curricular coordination across grade levels, ordering subject specific materials, and other items of concern to the various subject specialists. While the use of interdisciplinary teams will greatly alter the roles of teachers in a school, the need for buildingwide subject area articulation will seldom disappear. However, teams meeting daily will take on a much more significant role in the running of a school than will subject area departments meeting perhaps two or three times a semester.

One aspect of cross-team communication that is not recommended is that of having a single teacher serve on more than one core team. While this is sometimes done to spread around rare expertise on a faculty or because student numbers do not work out right for the creation of balanced teams, it is rarely successful. For teams to function well, teachers must regularly take part in the team meetings. Rare is the schedule that allows a teacher serving on two teams to regularly attend the meetings of both teams. Consequently, the functioning of both the individual teacher and the team are compromised when that team member is not regularly present for the team meetings. It is better to consider regrouping students who need the rare expertise onto one team or to create different-sized teams to accommodate odd numbers of students. Within the range of two to eight there is no research-based ideal size for a team. As long as all the teachers on a given team share the same students, two-person, three-person, four-person, and five-person teams can coexist in the same building. Cross-age teams can even coexist with grade-level teams in the same building.

Scheduling Students on the Team

For teaming to be successful at the middle level, two things must occur: Scheduling students onto teams must take precedence over other matters, and each team should represent a microcosm of the school as a whole. As much as possible, provide each team with some block time to allow instructional flexibility for the teamed teachers. Then do not undermine this flexibility by maintaining a number of pull-out programs, such as separate classes for students who are labeled "learning disabled," "gifted," or "at-risk" that take students off the team. Instead, incorporate the teachers of pull-out programs into the teams. Allow subject specialists and learning specialists of various kinds to plan and teach together to reduce, if not eliminate, the need for pull-outs. At the same time, work to make each team representative of the entire student body on all relevant variables: gender, cultural diversity, ability, and socio-economic status. If each team is not perceived as being representative, the school climate will suffer. Teachers, students, and parents will all compete to be associated with the "best" team and to avoid the "dumb" team. Setting up heterogenous teams unencumbered by pull-out programs allows the maximum amount of teacher autonomy for making instructional decisions at the team level to meet student needs. Teachers can group and regroup students *within* the team as often and in as many ways as they see fit to meet the instructional needs of the students. Remember that power in teaming is in the autonomy it provides teachers to make instructional decisions close to the action. The bureaucratic constraints required to operate departmentalized schools just interfere with the operation of a teamed school.

Team Identity

A team is a new entity that is larger than a single class but smaller than the total school. Especially in large schools, teams are created to make the large school seem smaller. Therefore, it is important to support the notion that the team is a unique learning community by taking steps to create a team identity. Just as a successful family has its ceremonies, rituals, and family memories, so too must a successful team. Since these elements are highly personal and unique to individual teams, there is much variation in how specific teams go about creating team identities. Teams create their own names: The Doors, Climbers, Hard Hats, All Stars, Private Eyes. They often accompany these names with slogans such as "The Door is Always Open," "Learning—the Ladder to Life," "Learning under Construction," "Shining with Success," and "Learning Through Invesigation." In addition, to symbolize their teams visually, some groups design logos and adopt colors to represent the team name and slogan. These team symbols are displayed on letterheads, on bulletin boards, on tee shirts, on pencils, and in various locations in the team area of the building. These graphic symbols exist alongside of identity-creating activities such as newsletters for distribution to parents, assemblies to recognize and reward positive student behavior, and special social events to celebrate the family nature of the team.

Setting Goals

An old proverb says that "a sailor without a destination cannot hope for a favorable wind." So it is with teams. One of the biggest mistakes teams can make is not setting any goals for themselves. If teams have not taken time to discuss and decide what they are attempting to accomplish as a team, then their efforts will be unfocused and directionless. Every semester it is wise for team members to reevaluate where they are and where they would like to be four to six months from now. Every team needs to set from one to five goals for the future. Whereas the lack of goals can be devastating for team development, clear, worthwhile, and challenging goals will cause team members to energize and command themselves and fellow team members better than could sources above or outside the team (Larson & LaFasto, 1989). A set of goals arrived at collaboratively by the team members will serve, more than anything else, to motivate the team toward excellence.

SUMMARY AND CONCLUSIONS

With the emergence of the Information Age, interdisciplinary teams are an idea whose time has come. The business of schooling is too complex to be governed by rigid bureaucratic rules and procedures. Industrial Age artifacts such as tracking, bell schedules, rigid groupings of students, and teachers isolated in individual classrooms are no longer adequate to the task of educating the next generation of young adolescents. The expertise of many specialists brought together onto collaborative teams to make decisions close to the action is what is now demanded. Students are too diverse to be educated in the compartmentalized manner of the early twentieth century.

Although interdisciplinary teaming was implemented in a large number of schools as part of the middle school movement beginning in the 1960s, it is increasingly finding its way into restructured elementary and secondary schools. With the benefits of teaming for both students and teachers so well demonstrated in the middle grades, educators at other levels of schooling are adapting the basic concept of teaming to the realities of both elementary schools and secondary schools. More and more high school faculties, which have remained stubbornly departmentalized for so long, are finding that to teach students whose educational needs are becoming increasingly diverse, some form of teaming is necessary to break down the bureaucratic impersonalization of hugh high schools (Sizer, 1992; Foster et al., 1993).

Teaming, like any innovation, takes time to be understood, implemented, and mastered by a broad cross-section of practitioners in our schools. A reading of this book should make clear that the need for time is not just a feature of teaming in middle-level schools, but of teaming in any institutional setting. However, the evidence is strong that interdisciplinary teams in their multitude of forms are becoming a more predominant occurrence in the schools of the United States. By changing the ways in which professionals communicate and make decisions, they hold the potential to transform our schools from being mere processors of learners to being true learning communities where every student is known and cared about and nurtured to his or her fullest learning potential.

REFERENCES

Alexander, W. M., Williams, E. L., Compton, M., Hines, V. A., & Prescott, D. (1968). *The emergent middle school.* New York: Holt, Rinehart & Winston.

Alexander, W. M., & George, P. S. (1981). *The exemplary middle school.* New York: Holt, Rinehart & Winston.

Alexander, W. M., & McEwin, C. K. (1989). *Schools in the middle: Status and progress.* Columbus, OH: National Middle School Association.

Arhar, J. M. (1990). Interdisciplinary teaming as a school intervention to increase the social bonding of middle level students. In J. L. Irvin (Ed.), *Research in middle level education: Selected studies 1990.* Columbus, OH: National Middle School Association.

Arhar, J. M., Johnston, J. H., & Markle, G. C. (1988). The effects of teaming and other collaborative arrangements. *Middle School Journal, 19*(4), 22–25.

Arnold, J. (1990). *Visions of teaching and learning: 80 exemplary middle level projects.* Columbus, OH: National Middle School Association.

Ashton, P. T., & Webb, R. B. (1986). *Making a difference: Teachers' sense of efficacy and student achievement.* New York: Longman.

Beane, J. A. (1990). Toward a middle school curriculum. Paper presented at the annual meeting of the National Middle School Association, Long Beach, CA, November 14–17.

Beane, J. A. (1993). *A middle school curriculum: From rhetoric to reality* (2d ed.). Columbus, OH: National Middle School Association.

Boyer, E. L. (1983). *High school: A report on secondary education in America.* New York: Harper & Row.

Brandt, R. S. (1991). Integrating the curriculum. *Educational Leadership. 49*(2), 4–75 [themed issue].

Cawelti, G. (1988). Middle schools a better match with early adolescent needs, ASCD survey finds. *ASCD Curriculum Update* (November).

Corrigan, D. (1990). Context for the discussion of the collaborative development of integrated services for children and families: The education side. Paper presented at the National Symposium on Integrated Services for Children and Families, Alexandria, VA, March 5–6.

Dickinson, T. (Ed.). (1993). *Readings in middle school curriculum: A continuing conversation.* Columbus, OH: National Middle School Association.

Doda, N. M. (1984). Teacher perspectives and practices in two organizationally different middle schools. Ph.D. dissertation, The University of Florida, Gainesville.

Epstein, J. L., & MacIver, D. J. (1990). *Education in the middle grades: National practices and trends.* Columbus, OH: National Middle School Association.

Erb, T. O. (1987). What team organization can do for teachers. *Middle School Journal, 18*(4), 3–6.

Erb, T. O. (1988a). *Secondary/middle level reorganization, year two, part II: Report to the Shawnee Mission Board of Education.* Shawnee Mission, KS: Board of Education of U.S.D. 512.

Erb, T. O. (1988b). Focusing back on the child by liberating the teacher. *TEAM: The Early Adolescence Magazine, 2*(3), 10–18.

Erb, T. O., & Doda, N. M. (1989). *Team organization: Promise—practices and possibilities.* Washington, DC: National Education Association.

Foster, L., Johnson, S., Serrano, M., Shaw, A., Veach, A., & Westmoreland, J. (1993). *Making one student at a time a reality: The high school task force report.* Panel presentation at the New Directions in Education IV Conference, Texas A & M University, College Station, June 14–15.

George, P. S. (1982). Interdisciplinary team organization: Four operational phases. *Middle School Journal, 13*(3), 10–13.

George, P. S., & Oldaker, L. L. (1985). *Evidence for the middle school.* Columbus, OH: National Middle School Association.

Goodlad, J. I. (1984). *A place called school.* New York: McGraw-Hill.

Hall, G. E., Loucks, S. F., Rutherford, W. L., & Newlove, B. N. (1975). Levels of the use of the innovation: A framework for analyzing innovation adoption. *Journal of Teacher Education, 24*(1), 52–56.

Hall, G. E., & Rutherford, W. L. Concerns of teachers about implementing team teaching. *Educational Leadership, 34*(3), 227–233.

Hawkins, M., & Graham, D. (1994). *Curriculum architecture: Creating a place of our own.* Columbus, OH: National Middle School Association.

Hodgkinson, H. L. (1989). *The same client: The demographics of education and service delivery systems.* Washington, DC: Institute for Educational Leadership/Center for Demographic Policy.

Hord, S. M., Rutherford, W. L., Huling-Austin, L., & Hall, G. E. (1987). *Taking charge of change.* Alexandria, VA: Association for Supervision and Curriculum Development.

James, M. A. (1986). *Adviser-advisee programs: Why, what and how.* Columbus, OH: National Middle School Association.

Larson, C. E., & LaFasto, F. M. J. (1989). *Teamwork: What must go right/what can go wrong.* Newbury Park, CA: Sage.

Lipsitz, J. (1984). *Successful schools for young adolescents.* New Brunswick, NJ: Transaction Books.

Lounsbury, J. H., & Clark, D. C. (1990). *Inside grade eight: From apathy to excitement.* Reston, VA: National Association of Secondary School Principals.

Merenbloom, E. Y. (1991). *The team process: A handbook for teachers* (3d ed.). Columbus, OH: National Middle School Association.

Nevin, A., Thousand, J., Paolucci-Whitcomb, P., & Villa, R. (1990). Collaborative consultation: Empowering public school personnel to provide heterogeneous schooling for all— or, who rang that bell? *Journal of Educational and Psychological Consultation, 1*(1), 41–67.

Office of Educational Research and Improvement. (1990). *National education longitudinal study of 1988: A profile of the American eighth grader.* Washington, DC: U.S. Department of Education.

Pickler, G. (1987). The evolutionary development of interdisciplinary teams. *Middle School Journal, 18*(2), 6–7.

Plodzik, K. T., & George, P. (1989). Interdisciplinary team organization. *Middle School Journal, 20*(5), 15–17.

Redl, F. (1966). Preadolescents—what makes them tick? In F. Redl, *When we deal with children.* New York: Free Press.

Robinson, S. M. (1991). Collaborative consultation. In B. Y. L. Wong (Ed.), *Learning about learning disabilities.* San Diego, CA: Academic Press.

Sizer, T. R. (1984). *Horace's compromise: The dilemma of the American high school.* Boston: Houghton Mifflin.

Sizer, T. R. (1992). *Horace's School: Redesigning the American high school.* Boston: Houghton Mifflin.

Skrtic, T. M. (1989). School organization and adaptivity: A structural perspective on equity and excellence. Paper presented at the third annual School Improvement Institute, University of Kansas, Lawrence, June 12–16.

Skrtic, T. M. (1991). *Behind special education: A critical analysis of professional culture and school organization.* Denver, CO: Love.

Stefanich, G. P., Wills, F. A., & Buss, R. R. (1991). The use of interdisciplinary teaming and its influence on student self-concept in middle school. *Journal of Early Adolescence, 11*(4), 404–419.

Van Til, W., Vars, G. F., & Lounsbury, J. H. (1967). *Modern education for the junior high years* (2d ed.). Indianapolis, IN: Bobbs-Merrill.

Will, M. C. (1986a). Educating children with learning problems: A shared responsibility. *Exceptional Children, 52*(5), 411–416.

Will, M. C. (1986b). *Educating children with learning problems: A shared responsibility. A report to the secretary.* Washington, DC: U.S. Department of Education.

▶ 13

Teamwork in the Transition from Special Education Programs to Independent Living and Employment

Jane M. Everson

During the 1980s a new term appeared in educational literature and federal and state educational policies. The term is *transition,* and it encompasses a vast array of new roles and activities for families, educators, and other human service providers concerned with the quality of life of adults with disabilities.

Transition has been defined in various ways by numerous professionals and policy makers, but all the literature and policies have at least three common themes. First, transition is a multi-year planning process (Will, 1984) resulting in a comprehensive adult lifestyle for youth with disabilities (Ludlow, Turnbull, & Luckasson, 1988). Second, the transition planning process requires collaboration from multiple agencies and professionals (Everson, 1992; Wehman et al., 1988). Third, successful transition requires the development of family and professional partnerships (Turnbull et al., 1989).

Public Law 101-476, the Individuals With Disabilities Education Act (IDEA) defined transition as "a coordinated set of activities for a student, designed within an outcome-oriented process, which promotes movement from school to postschool activities including postsecondary education, vocational training, integrated employment (including supported employment), continuing education, adult services, independent living, or community participation" (IDEA, 1990). To assist students, families, and professionals in successful transition planning, IDEA further stipulates that individualized education plans (IEPs) must now include

> *a statement of the needed transition services for students beginning no later than age 16 and annually thereafter (and when appropriate for the individual, beginning at age 14 or younger), including, when appropriate, a statement of the interagency responsibilities or linkages (or both) before the student leaves the school setting. (IDEA, 1990)*

Stated in many definitions of transition and implied in many others are such key concepts as collaboration, coordination, interagency linkages, empowerment, and partnerships. Like many goals that are easy to envision but difficult to achieve, successful transition planning demands incorporation of these concepts through teamwork. Transition planning undertaken by teams of professionals and parents can achieve increased-quality opportunities for adults with disabilities more effectively than can individual decision making and actions. During transition planning, individual family members and professionals may justifiably feel pressured and say, "It's not my responsibility!", but teams can say with assurance, "We can make a difference!" The premise of this chapter is that transition planning teams can make a difference in developing and achieving quality adult lifestyles for youth with disabilities.

The use of teams and the concept of teamwork are familiar to most special education professionals and family members of youth with disabilities. They frequently participate as members or leaders of interdisciplinary teams whose purpose is to develop and implement written service plans for students. These experiences may range from positive and satisfying to negative and dissatisfying. Student outcomes achieved through teamwork may range from successful to unsuccessful. As a result, most professionals and family members approach the idea of transition planning teams with guarded optimism, at least in part because they lack positive team experiences and effective team skills. Thus, an additional premise of this chapter is that most professionals and family members approach transition planning without the skills or desire to work together as members of transition planning teams as well as without knowledge of comprehensive transition planning.

The purpose of this chapter is to describe the concept of teamwork within the transition planning process. Successful transition planning is a visionary, individualized, and longitudinal process that draws from interdisciplinary, interagency, and transdisciplinary activities and expertise.

UNDERSTANDING A TEAM APPROACH TO TRANSITION PLANNING

The use of teams has been well described in transition literature (e.g., Everson, 1992; Everson, Rachal, & Michael, 1992; Wehman et al., 1988). Comprehensive transition planning encompasses a three-tiered approach to service planning, delivery, and evaluation. The top tier consists of a state-level interagency team. This team is composed of the commissioners (or their designees) of all agencies providing state-wide services to transition-age youth with disabilities. For example, representatives from special and vocational education, postsecondary adult education, rehabilitation, mental health, and mental retardation services are key members. Other agencies and statewide programs may be chosen for representation depending upon the make-up of a particular state. In addition, parent and family representation is essential. The primary purpose of this state-level interagency team is to establish and promote a state's vision of transitional services. Its members assume interagency roles and responsibilities—sharing information with other team members about legislative mandates, state plans, and agency priorities and initiatives and coordinating person-nel and fiscal resources through state interagency agreements designed to promote increased-quality local transitional services efforts.

The middle tier consists of multiple local transition planning teams. These teams are defined by county, district, regional, or other agency catchment areas. The teams are composed of local representatives from each of the key agencies involved with transitional services for youth with disabilities along with parent and family representatives. The primary purpose of these teams is to design and adopt local transition planning activities, within the broader framework established by the state-level team. Members assume both interagency and interdisciplinary roles and re-sponsibilities—sharing information with other team members about legislative man-dates and state plans, informing other team members about agency priorities and initiatives, coordinating personnel and fiscal resources through local interagency agreements designed to achieve increased-quality transitional services, and cooper-ating in data collection and management efforts to evaluate transitional service activities.

The final tier consists of multiple individualized transition planning teams. These teams are convened around the specific needs of individual transition-age students and their families; thus, membership is driven by the needs of the student and family. The primary purpose of these teams is to develop and implement individualized transitional service plans for specific youth with disabilities. Members assume interagency and interdisciplinary roles and responsibilities, but, more importantly, they *must* assume transdisciplinary roles and responsibilities if comprehensive transitional services with individualized quality outcomes are to be achieved.

Each of these levels of teams plays an important part in the design of compre-hensive transitional services. But the roles and responsibilities of state-level teams (e.g., Bates, Bronkema, Ames, & Hess, 1992) and local-level teams (e.g., Everson, 1992) have been described in detail elsewhere. Thus, this chapter will describe the interagency and transdisciplinary roles and responsibilities, as well as specific transitional services activities engaged in by individualized transition planning teams.

USING TEAMS TO INDIVIDUALIZE THE TRANSITION PLANNING PROCESS

Five major steps are necessary in individualizing the transition planning process. These steps are engaged in by individualized transition planning teams as part of a comprehensive approach to transitional services delivery. Each step is characterized by specific team member and leadership skills and activities. Table 13-1 summarizes many of the skills necessary to accomplish effective transition planning for special education students. Each of the steps involved in individualized transition planning is discussed in detail in the following pages.

Step 1: Convene Individualized Transition Planning Teams

Beginning no later than age 16, and whenever possible by age 14, interdisciplinary teams should be convened to address transition issues and concerns as part of students' educational programs. Although teams should be identified based on the transition needs of individual youths, they will generally consist of education, related services, and adult service personnel along with the students and family members. One or more team members, typically special education professionals, must identify team members who are compatible with the needs of specific students. Effective leadership and team skills are essential during this initial transition planning step.

For most students between the ages of 14 and 17, the IEP team will provide the foundation for the team's membership—the special education teachers or resource teachers, regular education teachers who provide instructional support, therapists and other related services personnel, instructional assistants or classroom aides, guidance counselors, school social workers, and administrative representation. These professionals, who have worked with individual students and their families for one or more academic years, will be most familiar with the youths' educational and therapeutic needs. These team members will also be familiar with the skills and activities needed to function as an interdisciplinary team and perhaps will have some experience as members of transdisciplinary teams. In addition to these team members, the young adults and their families must also be involved in all transition planning meetings and provided the support they need to be effective team members and leaders.

These team members are frequently referred to as "senders" from school to the adult service world. Their primary role is to prepare special education students for the complexities and challenges of adult life and, after this preparation, to send them to the adult service providers and supports they have identified as part of the individualized transition planning process. Because they know the youths well, they must assume responsibility for preparing students and identifying their capacities and support needs. In order to prepare students for the vast array of adult settings and opportunities, they will need to move from an interdisciplinary to a transdisciplinary approach to delivering transitional services.

TABLE 13-1 • **Examples of Leadership and Team Skills[1] Employed by Transition Planning Teams**

Activity	Leadership/Team Skill
Step 1: Convene Individualized Transition Planning Teams	Propose new ideas
	Give and seek information
	Clarify and expand information
	Summarize information
	Bring in all team members
	Record and distribute information
Step 2: Develop Personal Profiles	Propose new ideas
	Give and seek information
	Clarify and expand information
	Brainstorm
	Bring in all team members
	Reward behaviors and ideas
	Provide feedback
	Summarize information
	Record and distribute information
Step 3: Specify Desired Transition Objectives and Activities	Give and seek information
	Clarify and expand information
	Agree and disagree
	Brainstorm
	Bring in all team members
	Reward behavior and ideas
	Provide feedback
	Compromise and negotiate
	Summarize information
	Record and distribute information
Step 4: Implement Transition Objectives and Activities	Give and seek Information
	Clarify and expand information
	Agree and disagree
	Reward behavior and ideas
	Provide feedback
	Compromise and negotiate
	Summarize information
	Record and distribute information
Step 5: Monitor, Evaluate, and Revise Objectives and Activities	Give and seek information
	Clarify and expand
	Agree and disagree
	Reward behavior and ideas
	Provide feedback
	Compromise and negotiate
	Summarize information
	Record and distribute information

[1]Leadership and team skills suggested from materials developed by The O'Neil Group, 1990.

For example, special education teachers, occupational and physical therapists, and speech-language pathologists will need to coordinate the scheduling of therapy and speech-language services to allow students to spend time in community-based training sites. They will also need to develop therapeutic and instructional programs that integrate therapy services within functional community-based activities. Occupational and physical therapists may need to share their knowledge of assistive eating and dressing devices and wheelchair transfering techniques with special education teachers to ensure appropriate placements of students in group homes and employment settings. Speech-language pathologists may need to share strategies for developing augmentative and alternative communication with special education teachers to ensure social integration of students in community-based settings. Special education teachers may need to assist therapists with behavior management strategies and instructional strategies.

As students approach their final years in school, other team members will need to be invited to join and assimilate with this initial team. As these new team members are added, all team members' roles and responsibilities will change. These new professionals,—the "receivers"—include rehabilitation counselors, job coaches and other supported employment personnel, postsecondary educators, and residential services providers. These new team members will represent a diverse set of agencies and disciplines, ranging from departments of rehabilitation services, social services, and mental retardation services, to postsecondary education programs and the business community. Their primary role is to receive the young adults prepared by the senders and negotiate the services and supports they will be able to provide. As adult service providers join students' transition planning teams, the teams become interagency in nature. Now teams must face interagency team challenges along with the earlier challenges raised by interdisciplinary and transdisciplinary planning issues.

Unlike educational services, which are entitlement programs, most adult services are eligibility programs. Therefore, senders must also initiate the service negotiation process with adult service providers. For example, special education teachers and other education personnel may need to assist students and their families with compiling informational profiles, such as employment résumés. These résumés should describe students' demographic data, and outline their significant vocational training experiences and skills, as well as paid and nonpaid employment experiences. These résumés will help transition planning team members negotiate services from rehabilitation counselors by providing functional vocational assessment data. Communication is an important part of negotiation between senders and receivers. Special education teachers will need to ask questions: "What kind of vocational experiences does a student need to be accepted into your supported employment program?", or "If I gather this type of data, will it assist with eligibility determination?"

Once teams have been organized, one or more team leaders, again typically special education professionals, must schedule team meetings at the convenience of both professional and family members, run effective transition planning meetings on an annual or more frequent basis, and assimilate new professional and family members as well as students with special communication needs into transition planning activities. These organizational activities lay a foundation for visionary, individualized, and longitudinal transition planning. They require complex interpersonal skills such as proposing new ideas, expanding the ideas of others, bringing in more reticent team members, summarizing discussions, and coordinating followup activities (e.g., The O'Neil Group, 1990).

Team organizers may find it useful to send letters inviting members to attend initial meetings in which transition planning is described as a milestone in the youth's life, and an opportunity for future thinking and planning. A brief description of who is being invited to the meetings and the anticipated roles they will play will also assist in fostering transdisciplinary and interagency collaboration.

Step 2: Develop Personal Profiles

The purpose of transition planning teams is to develop and implement personal profiles of the accomplishments, dreams, and support needs of individual students. These profiles are typically titled statements of transition services, personal futures plans, or another individualized service plan title. There are a variety of transition planning forms and documents commercially available, any number of which may be adopted or adapted to focus a team's planning activities. The form or document used for transition planning is not important as long as all team members, including the family and students, understand and feel invested in using the planning form.

In addition, the selected transition planning forms should enable team members to consider *all* major adult lifestyle areas, such as employment opportunities, postsecondary education opportunities, community living arrangements, homemaking/personal care activities and supports, financial/income needs, use of generic community resources, recreation/leisure activities, transportation activities and supports, medical services, advocacy/legal needs, and friendships and other relationships. These lifestyle areas should guide teams in setting specific objectives to assist in achieving desired future profiles for specific students.

One or more team members will need to accept responsibility for chairing or leading the team through the development and implementation of personal profiles. Special education representatives may be the obvious choice because of their need to incorporate transition objectives within students' IEPs, but teams may also elect to rotate leadership across meetings or have a parent or family member co-chair the team with a professional.

With input from the most critical team members—students themselves and their family members—teams should address each lifestyle area. A personal profile should answer these questions: What is the youth's life story? Who are some of the important people and what are some of the important places in the youth's life? What are the youth's likes and dislikes? What opportunities does the youth have for choice making? How, when, why, and with whom does the youth communicate and socialize? What does a desirable future look like for the youth? (Mount & Zwernik, 1988). Teams will quickly recognize the benefits of transdisciplinary planning and service delivery as they seek to respond to these questions.

Teams may wish to post these questions on a large sheet of paper for all team members to refer to during planning activities. Whenever possible, the youth whose life is being planned should attend along with key family members and play an active part in the meetings. When the youth's attendance is not possible, teams may find it helpful to either display a photograph of the individual next to the questions or to have the individual attend a portion of the meeting, such as a break or introductory activity.

While developing personal profiles, teams will need to employ additional leadership and team member skills—encouraging all team members to dream and focus dreams on a specific, desired future vision. Team members will need to propose new ideas, expand the ideas of others, bring in more reticent team members, summarize discussions, and coordinate followup activities.

Families are essential in defining a future vision for the transitioning young adult. But the idea of dreaming and envisioning may be difficult for them, as past history with professionals may have focused more on accepting limitations than on proposing ideas and dreams. Team organizers may find it useful to hold transition planning meetings at a family's home or at other informal settings such as libraries, churches, or restaurants. In addition, asking family members simple questions, such as "What do you want for your son or daughter? or "How do these plans fit into your future plans?" will help maintain family-driven transition planning.

Dreaming and envisioning may be equally as difficult for professionals who are used to planning around budget limitations, program waiting lists, and eligibility criteria. Teams may find it useful to practice brainstorming, in which all ideas are recognized without making value statements. Another strategy may be to define team "ground rules" for each meeting that include using active listening skills and valuing all team members' contributions. Remembering to focus only on the specific youth being considered at each meeting will also assist visionary and individualized thinking without being stymied by overwhelming numbers of students, clients, and data.

Step 3: Specify Desired Transition Objectives and Activities

During this component of transition planning meetings, teams will need to employ additional leadership and team member skills —encouraging all team members to identify resources and obstacles in achieving the desired vision, negotiating professional and family responsibilities and timelines, and guiding each other in attaining and supporting the vision.

For example, a transition planning team may define a desirable future living situation for a young woman who is deaf-blind as a two-bedroom home with a screened-in porch, located in a neighborhood no more than 15 miles from her family and no more than one block from a bus stop. As the team's dream unfolds, all team members are able to envision the desired home. But all team members are also able to identify numerous barriers to achieving the dream—staffing, housemates, funding, zoning ordinances, physical accessibility, and so on and so on. Transdisciplinary and interagency planning and service delivery will be essential in identifying potential resources to overcome seemingly insurmountable barriers.

It would be easy for the team's dream to be forgotten at this point. Instead, team members will need to determine objectives, activities, timelines, and team member responsibilities for maintaining and ultimately achieving the vision. If funding is a barrier, *who* will explore the use of low-income housing tax credits and Medicaid waiver funds, and by *when* will they do it? If finding a housemate is a barrier, *who* will assist the young woman and her family with interviewing potential housemates and by *when* will they do it?

Teams will need to develop very specific transitional services objectives and activities in order to achieve the future visions developed in the personal profiles. Many objectives and activities will enable teams to measure the accomplishments of specific students, but many other objectives and activities will enable teams to measure the effectiveness of the teams in guiding the student and family toward the desired vision. For example, student-oriented objectives may include: *"Martha will participate in a YWCA swimming program on Saturday mornings with peer support from a classmate, Yolanda,"* or *"Darrell will participate with three classmates in a community-based vocational training experience at Super Store three mornings a week for two hours where he will learn to stock shelves, sweep, wet mop, and buff floors."* Team-oriented objectives may include, *"The rehabilitation counselor will visit Darrell twice at Super Store and will review task analytic data, supervisor evaluation data, and job production data with the special education teacher to assist with eligibility determination."*

Step 4: Implement Transition Objectives and Activities

A transdisciplinary approach is characterized by: (1) assessment and service delivery in natural settings, (2) sharing information and skills across disciplinary boundaries, and (3) assuming primary service delivery roles in conjunction with consultative roles (Orelove & Sobsey, 1987). An interagency approach is characterized by multiple agencies with differing eligibility criteria, policies and procedures, arrays of services, staffing patterns, budgets, and monitoring and evaluation criteria. Transdisciplinary and interagency collaboration is essential in implementing transition objectives and activities. The diversity of professional backgrounds and experiences, variable family demographics and visions, the eligibility restraints of adult services, the funding patterns of multiple public sector and private sources—these can all be viewed as resources if teams choose to collaborate.

Transdisciplinary, interagency collaboration requires teams to develop an interdependency of transition objectives and activities. Collaboration incorporates complex leadership and team member skills such as honest and trusting information and skill sharing, team brainstorming and problem solving when obstacles appear insurmountable, resource negotiation in a give-and-take atmosphere, and team commitment to completing agreed-upon objectives and activities within specified timelines.

Once personal profiles are developed for students, team members must recognize that their work has just begun! It is relatively easy to develop individualized and visionary transition profiles for students. It is much more difficult to reach the vision through achieving student-oriented objectives. Team members will need to practice and refine a variety of leadership and team member skills as they seek to send and receive students.

Many teams find it helpful to begin by simply acknowledging potential barriers—different education and disciplinary preparation that results in specialized language and skills, competition among agencies for scarce resources, unclear roles and expectations from supervisors, and limited professional reinforcements for collaboration. Team leaders may elect to begin initial team meetings with five-minute "ice breakers" or other team-building activities that allow members to share terminology, regulations, initiatives, and resources. Teams may also wish to establish meeting ground rules that address listening to one another, respecting each other, and maintaining confidentiality outside the meetings. Most importantly, most teams will find it necessary to review and practice active listening skills—no matter how many times they have heard the information during in-service training or other professional development workshops! And, finally, teams will need to recognize that all teams will have strong and effective leaders and members as well as weak and ineffective leaders and members who will need encouragement and training.

Step 5: Monitor, Evaluate, and Revise Objectives and Activities

The effectiveness of a transdisciplinary and interagency transition planning team can be measured by the team's success in sending and receiving young adults with disabilities into the adult world of employment, community living, and recreation and social activities. Transition planning meetings will need to be held annually, and probably more frequently as youths approach the age of graduation. At these meetings, team members will need to review objectives for all adult lifestyle areas, write and revise objectives as needed, monitor progress on long-range objectives, and problem solve resources for troublesome objectives.

SUMMARY AND CONCLUSIONS

Transition planning, like all team efforts, requires hard work and commitment. No one person—professional or family member— or one agency can accomplish the goal of sending or receiving well-prepared youths into adult opportunities. The planning and

TABLE 13-2 • **Common Transition Planning Problems and Team Strategies**

Problem	Team Strategies
Obtaining commitment from professionals to endorse interagency team approach	Written endorsement from state-level and local-level teams
	Interagency inservice training on the purpose and goals of transitional services
	Brief, written materials distributed to invited team members prior to initial meeting
	"Ice-breaker" and other team-building activities during initial meetings
	Development of a team purpose or mission statement during initial meeting
	Carefully developed and followed agendas, allowing both team discussion and resolution
Obtaining parent/family participation	Parent/family involvement on state-level and local-level teams
	Parent/family training using parents as trainers and multi-media and culturally sensitivematerials
	Scheduling meeting times and locations with sensitivity to family needs
	Developing and practicing team skills that include treating all team members as equal partners
Understanding interagency roles and responsibilities	Interagency inservice training on the purpose and goals of transitional services
	Development of a team purpose or mission statement during initial meeting
	Agenda items and team activities during initial meetings to discuss current and desired roles and responsibilities
	Use of brainstorming, "force-field analysis," and other structured problem-solving activities
	Development of transition plans with interdependent objectives and activities
Management of team meetings, including preparatory and followup activities	Team co-chairs who rotate responsibilities across meetings
	Designated roles and responsibilities for each meeting and followup monitoring through transition plans
	Meeting "ground rules"
	Carefully followed agendas, written pre-meeting and followup communication
	Pre-meeting student demographic profiles to ensure availability of assessment and other data, and signature release forms
	Standardized transition planning forms that enhance visionary transition planning in all adult lifestyle areas
Developing personal profiles, including ability to dream and focus dreams	Standardized transition planning forms that enhance visionary transition planning in all adult lifestyle areas
	Presence and participation of students in transition planning meetings
	Use of flip charts, photographs, personal profile questions, and other informal strategies to focus team members on individualized planning
	Developing and practicing team skills that include treating all team members as equal partners
	Review of personal profiles and other visionary transition planning materials from other localities and states

Continued

TABLE 13-2 • *Continued*

Problem	Team Strategies
Developing transition objectives and activities to achieve vision described in the personal profile	Use of brainstorming, "force-field analysis," and other structured problem-solving activities
	Development of transition plans with interdependent objectives and activities
	Inclusion of both student-oriented and team-oriented objectives in transition plan
	Team adoption of one student at a time; individualized planning approach
Monitoring, evaluating, and revising transition objectives and activities	Establishing communication mechanisms between meetings to monitor transition plan progress
	Meeting annually as a full team to monitor, evaluate, and revise plan and more frequently (as needed) with appropriate individual team members
	Development of transition plans with interdependent objectives and activities
	Inclusion of both student-oriented and team-oriented objectives in transition plan
	Use of brainstorming, "force-field analysis," and other structured problem-solving activities

implementation activities required to achieve interagency and transdisciplinary collaboration are tremendous, but the results can be fulfilling both professionally and personally. Table 13-2 looks at one composite transition planning meeting and summarizes some examples of transition planning problems and transdisciplinary and interagency team strategies to address them.

REFERENCES

Bates, P., Bronkema, J., Ames, T., & Hess, C. (1992). State-level interagency planning models. In F. Rusch, L. DeStefano, J. Chadsey-Rusch, L. Phelps, & E. Szymanski (Eds.), *Transition from school to adult life. Models, Linkages and Policy* (pp.115-130). Sycamore, IL: Sycamore.

Everson, J. M. (1992). *Youths with disabilities. Strategies for interagency collaboration.* Stoneham, MA: Butterworth Heinmann.

Everson, J.M., Rachal, P., & Michael, M. (1992). *Interagency collaboration for young adults with deaf-blindness. Toward a common goal.* Sands Point, NY: Helen Keller National Center, Technical Assistance Center.

Individuals with Disabilities Education Act (IDEA) Amendments of 1990. 20 U.S.C., 1400. (P.L. 101-476).

Ludlow,B.L., Turnbull, A.P., & Luckasson, R. (1988). *Transition to adult life for people with mental retardation.* Baltimore: Brookes.

Mount, B. & Zwernik, K. (1988). *It's never too early. It's never too late. A booklet about personal futures planning.* St. Paul, MN: Governor's Planning Council on Developmental Disabilities. (Publication #421-88-109).

The O'Neil Group. (1990). *Interactive behavior skills and meeting effectiveness.* Simsbury, CT: Author.

Orelove, F. P. & Sobsey, D. (1987). *Educating children with multiple disabilities.* Baltimore, MD: Brookes.

Turnbull, H. R., Turnbull, A. P., Bronicki, G. J., Summers, J. A., & Roeder-Gordon, C. (1989). *Disability and the family. A guide to decisions for adulthood.* Baltimore, MD: Brookes.

Wehman, P., Moon, M. S., Everson, J. M., & Barcus, J. M. (1988). *Transition from school to work. New challenges for youth with severe disabilities.* Baltimore, MD: Brookes.

Will, M. C. (1984). *OSERS programming for the transition of youth with disabilities: Bridges from school to working life.* Washington, DC: Office of Special Education and Rehabilitative Services, U.S. Department of Education.

► 14

Generic Teamwork

Mark Krueger   Mary Drees

INTRODUCTION

In 1983 five child and youth care workers, a teacher, and a social worker were hired as youth development generalists to work in a residential treatment program with a group of 10 children and their families. They were paid equally for their previous experience and education and expected to share their expertise and cross into each other's professional domains to help one another. This new transdisciplinary team approach was called *Generic Teamwork*. Following is an overview of why it was developed, a description of how it works, the results of a 10-year study, and suggestions for implementing a similar approach at other agencies.

The Problems

During the 1970s, studies revealed that team members (social workers, teachers, and child care workers) in residential treatment centers often faced four major hurdles. First, they had to be accountable to a department as well as to their team, and this having "one foot in a department and one on a team" hindered communication and kept them from making a commitment to the team process (Garner, 1977, 1980). Second, based solely on their professional background they were often paid differently as well as assigned varying degrees of decision-making authority, which led to disharmony and/or resentment (Vander Ven, 1979). Third, their creativity, productivity, and opportunities for involvement were often limited by professional boundaries and/or "turf issues" (Garner, 1980). And, finally, the demanding nature of the work often created turnover that changed the composition and effectiveness of the team (Rosenfeld, 1978).

The Approach

After an extensive study in 1981 of interdisciplinary teams at four residential programs revealed similar problems (Krueger, 1982). Generic Teamwork was developed by representatives from the Child and Youth Care Learning Center, University of Wisconsin-Milwaukee, and St. Charles Youth and Family Services (a site in the 1982 study) as a possible solution. The idea was relatively simple: One central discipline—youth development generalist—would be created. Then people with the necessary backgrounds in social work, education, and child care would be hired as a team of generalists to work with a group of 8 to 10 children in residential care. Sharing their knowledge, learning new techniques, and helping each other, their goal would be to weave as much counseling, learning, and care as possible into each daily interaction.

Support for this idea came from two major sources. First, Garner (1977, 1980) and Vorrath and Brendtro (1974) had demonstrated in their respective models of Total Teamwork and Teamwork Primacy the positive results of eliminating departments and making the team the central unit of administration and treatment. Second, educateur (Linton, 1969), re-education (Hobbs, 1967), and child mental health specialist (Reiger & Devries, 1974) approaches, which focused on preparing generalists to meet the wellness and holistic developmental care needs of disturbed children, had been receiving considerable attention as an alternative to the existing system, which focused on pathology and professional specialization. In advocating these approaches, Linton (1969) also argued that the United States and Canada were perhaps the only technologically advanced countries where professionals who were almost totally removed from the lives of the children and whose previous training was not related to the re-educational tasks at hand made most of the decisions about how programs were operated and children treated.

Generic Teamwork, like the educateur, re-education, and child mental health specialist programs, was designed to have the staff who were closest to the children more involved in making significant decisions. It was not felt, however, that a new preservice education program was necessary. Instead, the goal was to bring together on equal ground individuals with experience and education in teaching, social work, and child care and youth care and have them explore how they could best put their skills to use in meeting the specific as well as general needs of emotionally disturbed children (Krueger, 1983; Krueger et al., 1987). Additional skills, it was believed, could be developed through a comprehensive program of inservice training.

THE YOUTH DEVELOPMENT CENTER

The generic approach was first implemented in 1983 at the Youth Development Center (YDC), a new, model program for 8 to 10 emotionally disturbed boys at St. Charles, a multifaceted agency with an in-home treatment program, a shelter care facility, and the residential treatment program for 48 troubled adolescents that had been part of the initial study (Krueger, 1982).

Initial Staffing and Responsibilities

Originally the YDC was staffed with seven youth development generalists, all of whom had some experience and at least a bachelor's degree. Their starting salaries were based on the same scale, with equal recognition given for education and experience. They received weekly team and individual supervision (the program supervisor was a generalist with child care experience and social work education) as well as over 100 hours of inservice training convering developmental care (Maier, 1987), re-education (Brendtro & Ness, 1983), educateur (Linton, 1969), social learning, psychodynamic (Redl & Wineman, 1957; Long, Morse, & Newman, 1976), and total team (Garner, 1982) concepts and techniques. Approximately 1000 hours of consultation on treatment planning, special education, family work, and evaluation were also provided by faculty from the Child and Youth Care Learning Center.

The generalists designed and implemented individual care, education, and treatment plans for the children and their families. Although they each had an area of professional expertise (i.e., social work, education, and child and youth care) to which they devoted most of their energy, they all spent some time in school, with families, and on the unit. Where and how much time they spent in each area was based on their readiness to take on new responsibilities and the needs identified in the treatment plans.

The Generic Model in 1994

Although the roles of the generalists have been redefined according to lessons learned from experience and the skills of new workers, the model has maintained most of its original characteristics. Team members continue to share their expertise and cross into each others' domains to help one another whenever possible. For instance, two generalists, one with a child and youth care background and one with an education background, come in together in the morning and get the children up. Then they go to school together, where they both participate in instruction. In the afternoon and evening, several generalists are present to participate in family, group, and individual work. Following are some of the specific details about the model and how it is implemented.

Program Structure.   The YDC is housed in a separate building with individual bedrooms, a central living area, kitchen, recreation area, and offices for the generalists and program supervisor. The program serves 12 emotionally disturbed and/or troubled boys ages 12–17, who come from dysfunctional families and have been emotionally, physically, and/or sexually abused. Most of them are functioning below their grade level in school and have had prior out-of-home placements.

The average length of stay is 12 to 14 months. Specific treatment, education, and care plans are developed for each youth by the generalists, the referring agency, the youth, and the family. In addition to a variety of individual developmental care, re-education, psychodynamic, and family approaches, which are woven into daily interactions, the program offers 10–12 hours per week of group work (covering social skills, recreation, human sexuality, independent living, and group counseling), 1–2 hours a week of family counseling (usually in the parents' home), and 1 hour of individual counseling. Addiction counseling and vocational training are also available.

Progress is monitored by daily and regular formal reviews of the goals and objectives in the individual case plans and the results of psychological and educational tests. The fee for the program is $3,467 per month.

The Staff.   There are eight, as opposed to the original six, youth development generalists, four women and four men, all of whom have met the minimum requirement of a bachelor's degree. Their educational backgrounds and prior experience include social work, sociology, psychology, special education, marriage and family counseling, recreation, and art. Six have completed child and youth care continuing education courses at the University of Wisconsin-Milwaukee. One has a master's degree in social work. An undergraduate student in social work is also completing a field placement.

Paperwork and preparation time is divided equally among all the generalists. Although each generalist has a set schedule, which consists of a mix of first, second, and weekend shifts, schedules change according to the daily and long-term needs of the program. For example, the generalists can easily replace each other in school or on the unit, or fill in for special activities such as taking a child to a court appointment or a home visit. In certain situations they can also fill in for one another in family sessions or in leading a group meeting.

Shared Responsibilities.   Four generalists spend the majority of their time on the daily living unit involved in group work, recreational activities, individual counseling, and daily living programming. They also help in school and with families on an as-needed basis.

One generalist (teacher) spends the majority of his time in the on-grounds school serving as the primary teacher (all the boys, except for those who go off grounds to school, are in the same class at the St. Charles school). He also interacts each day on the living unit before and after school. For instance, he helps get the children up in the morning and participates in after-school group meetings. Previously this generalist worked mostly on the living unit. He has a secondary education degree with a provisional ED license. In addition to supervision from the program supervisor, he also receives guidance from the school principal.

Another generalist (family worker) with a master's degree in social work is the primary therapist for 8 of the 12 families, spending 75 percent of his time in family sessions, writing reports, managing cases, linking services, and coordinating treatment plans with individual workers (each generalist serves as an individual case manager for at least one child). The remaining 25 percent of his time is spent on the living unit, where he assists with routines, discusses cases with generalists, and participates in a variety of individual and group activities.

Another generalist divides his time equally between family and individual work, as well as in child care. He has a bachelor's degree in psychology and experience in child care. He is also the staff member who has been with the program the longest—four years. Finally, one generalist divides her time equally between the school and living unit, where she is also involved in group, individual, and sometimes family counseling.

Program Supervision.   The program supervisor monitors the day-to-day treatment program and provides on-line supervision, direct services, training, program development, supervision, and administration. She also serves as team leader and provides one-to-one supervision.

The generalists and the supervisor meet informally every day and formally at least three hours a week to develop and review treatment plans, share information or ideas, and continue to evaluate and develop the overall program. They make all day-to-day care, education, and treatment decisions. Final decisions regarding the intake and unplanned discharge of youth, annual budgets, and hiring and firing are made by the director of residential services based on recommendations made by the supervisor and team. The supervisor and the director meet on a regular basis to review decisions and the decision-making process. The director and supervisor also oversee the general operation of the program.

Training of Staff.   Approximately 100 hours of consultation in family work and treatment planning are provided annually to this program by the Child and Youth Care Learning Center. In addition to the training the generalists and supervisor provide for themselves on the line and in team meetings, the Learning Center also provides approximately 65 hours of training. Topics covered include behavior management, recreational programming, chemical dependency abuse, physical and sexual abuse, family work, special education, human growth and development, human sexuality, teamwork and communication, and social learning. St. Charles provides approximately another 20 hours of training covering first aid/CPR, group and family work, and crisis intervention. St. Charles also has a consulting psychiatrist and art therapist, who are used by the YDC on an as-needed basis.

One can read descriptions of the different roles, responsibilities, schedules, and training of the generalists; however, in order to understand how the generic model actually works, one needs to spend a day at YDC.

A DAY AT YDC

Wake-Up Time

Monday, 6:30 A.M. The overnight worker wakes three boys who attend public school early and helps them clean their rooms and prepare breakfast. Two generalists, Dan (who is also the teacher) and John, arrive at 7:00 A.M. They review the logs and talk with the overnight worker about how the night went. Then the three of them get the rest of the boys up and assist them with dressing and cleaning their rooms. They also dispense medications.

Eventually the remaining nine boys casually come together in the common living area. This is the main gathering place, where they hold meetings, play table games, watch TV and work on arts and crafts projects at various times during the course of the day. As they arrive, Dan and John talk with them and set the tone for breakfast. The goal is to provide as much individual help and attention as possible. On those days when one child or another is having difficulty, either Dan or John handles the situation on an individual basis, using a crisis intervention and/or counseling method. Today everything goes smoothly.

At 8:00 A.M. they walk together to breakfast in the cafeteria, which is about a block away (on weekends they prepare their own breakfast in the unit). As they eat, Dan and John try to make sure they get the day off to a good start with a healthy breakfast. The conversation is about a visit from a local TV weatherman later in the week.

When they return to the unit, they put the finishing touches on getting organized and ready for school. Then they meet again as a group to review the day before walking together to the school building at 9:00.

School Time

Dan and John continue with them in school. Unlike in many programs where the teacher and an assistant teacher wait in school for the children to arrive, they have been with the boys before school and have a good sense of how they are doing. This allows for a much needed sense of continuity as the boys shift from one learning environment to another. Dan serves as the primary teacher. He has overall responsibility for preparing and implementing the individual education plans. John is with him three days a week and is on the unit in the evening on the other two days, when he is replaced in the classroom by another generalist. This morning, as most mornings, they teach the boys as a group, in subgroups, and individually. For example, Dan gives a history lesson to the entire class; then John works with two boys on a math problem while Dan works with the others on a problem that is matched to their abilities.

At 11:30 they all go to lunch in the cafeteria with Dan and John, who are once again able to provide continuity and deal with specific behavior problems as they occur. Then they all return to the unit for a quiet period. Some of the boys go to their rooms, while others stay in the common living area where they listen to music and take a break from school. Meanwhile Dan and John record the morning observations in the log books, help those boys who need assistance, and dispense medications. Dan also makes phone calls to monitor the boys who are in public schools and to explore options for future placements.

Afternoon Schedule

Around 12:30 P.M. the art therapist comes for her usual Monday visit to the unit. The project this week is sculpture. Sue, another generalist, arrives about 1:00 P.M. She acquaints herself with what has happened by reading the logs and talking with John. Then, since there are four adults present, John takes some time to work in the office on a treatment review that is due in a few days.

As they work, the supervisor arrives and joins them. She has been at a meeting with one of the referring agencies. Later she will have to go to an administrative meeting. While on the unit, however, she is engaged with the staff and children, who know her well and interact with her as they do with the other generalists. Sometimes she takes a child shopping for clothes or for unit supplies. She often observes and reviews daily interactions and treatment plans with the generalists. She may also sit in one of the social skills, feeling, or daily groups. She stops a moment now to meet with Dan to review the day.

At 2:30 P.M. Gabriel, another generalist, arrives, and the boys come together for "community group." The boys and generalists begin by expressing their high and low points of the day. Then the boys review progress on their treatment, education, and daily living goals. While listening, Gabriel, who will work the night shift, gets a sense of how the day has gone.

Tom, another generalist who will work with Gabriel and Sue on the night shift, arrives at 3:00 P.M. When the group meeting is finished, Dan and John pass on additional information to Gabriel, Sue, and Tom. Then Tom meets with one of the boys for an individual counseling session. Gabriel, John, and Sue divide the rest of the group. Sue goes outside sledding, and Gabriel and John stay inside to supervise model building, table games, and watching cartoons (this is the only time during the week that television is on other than for special educational programs, movies, or events).

Gabriel greets the boys who are returning from public school and gets them engaged in an activity. After they have finished with their reports and meeting with the supervisor to review the day (individual cases, special situations, and events for tomorrow), Dan and John go home.

Dinner and the Evening

Gabriel works with a couple of boys to set the table while another one goes to pick up the prepared food from the cafeteria. Just before dinner at 5:30 P.M. the group comes back together to clean up and review the evening activity—social skills group. Then they all circle the dining table, engaged in conversation.

After dinner the generalists and boys clean up. The next hour or so is spent on homework and chores. Tom also meets with one boy for an individual counseling session while the supervisor reviews the plan for social skills group with Gabriel.

At 6:00 P.M. the group gathers to watch the news. Meanwhile Sue, Tom, and Gabriel make final plans for the evening. Jacqueline, the generalist who works mostly with families, also arrives after meeting with a new family in their home to acclimate them to the program. In between writing reports and making phone contacts with parents and community agencies, she catches up on what's been heppening. Being there gives her a better sense of how the boys' days are going. Her familiarity with the program also allows her to assist with chores such as handing out medications or getting paper and pencil for a boy to do homework. She talks with one of the children for a few minutes, then leaves with Sue for a family session at 6:30 P.M.

Meanwhile Gabriel and Tom gather the boys for social skills group. They break into dyads and practice the skill of "introducing others" before coming back to present in front of the larger group. At 7:30 P.M. the group ends and evening free time begins. Gabriel takes four boys to the recreation room to play foosball and listen to music. Tom works on models with three boys while the other four play cards.

At 8:00 P.M. Jacqueline and Sue return from the family session and assist with the final evening routines. AT 8:15 P.M., snacks are prepared, the lights dimmed, and tones of voice are lowered as the generalists begin preparing the boys for bedtime.

The first group of boys leaves for their rooms at about 8:30 P.M. The generalists give them hygiene supplies, hand out medications, and go quietly with them to their rooms. The other group of boys heads off for bed about 9:00 P.M. Sue also goes home at this time, while the others stay to read stories and help the boys get ready to go to sleep. On many evenings she stays to help resolve a crisis. Tonight, however, like the rest of the day, things go smoothly. When everything is quiet, the remaining generalists write their logs, periodically returning to the boys' rooms to make sure everyone is okay. Gabriel leaves at about 10:30 P.M. Tom stays to fill in the night time worker, who stays until morning, when another day begins.

Reflections on the Day

One of the distinctive characteristics of the generic model is the fact that staff members work side by side throughout the day and frequently cross traditional lines between disciplines. Child care workers teach and teachers work in the residential units. The traditional turfs of the social worker and counselor become aspects of the program in which all generalists are involved. Role release, one of the distinguishing features of the transdisciplinary model, occurs throughout the day. In short, the team members share responsibility for planning and supervising the "whole" program—including residential, educational, and therapeutic.

Communication is essential. Much time and energy are committed to both face-to-face and written communications. Transition time between team members is carefully scheduled with a strong emphasis on continuity, conflict resolution, and preventing problems from either occurring or escalating. Social skills training and group problem solving occur during various parts of the day, in both school and residence. The emphasis in the generic model is to serve the needs of the whole child and to avoid fragmentation and inconsistency.

This informal observation of a day at YDC gives one a better understanding of how the generic model works. Research was conducted to evaluate how well it works.

EVALUATION OF THE GENERIC MODEL

In addition to ongoing program, treatment, education, and individual performance evaluations, three major evaluations of the generic model were conducted: (1) the initial study of interdisciplinary teamwork at St. Charles and four other residential centers (Krueger, 1982); (2) a three-year progress report (Krueger et al., 1987); and (3) a study of behavior, self-esteem, and parent satisfaction outcomes conducted by a psychology doctoral student and an independent university research consultant in 1988 (Berger, 1988).

Findings of Success

Five sets of findings pointed to the success of the program. First, most of the past as well as present generalists, many of whom had previously worked on traditional teams, reported their belief that the generic model was a more efficient and effective way of working together. This was borne out by observations; a review of their performance evaluations; a comparison to the notes of interactions at team meetings during the initial study of interdisciplinary teams; and interviews with the executive director and director of residential services, who both said the approach had streamlined communication and improved accountability.

Second, during interviews and team meetings the generalists expressed a general feeling of mutual respect, with the most experienced generalists, regardless of professional background, seen as leaders and positive role models. They also tended to speak about each other in terms of their philosophies and styles of intervention as opposed to their roles, domains, and status as family workers, teachers, and child and youth care workers. In other words, although there were differences of opinion during their team discussions, they were able to focus most of their energy on the human issues, values, attributes, and skills that influence treatment, education, and care.

Third, according to observations and comments from the executive director and director of residential service, the approach had helped create a sense of stability and structure that easily accommodated new children and staff. In comparing the approach to the traditional interdisciplinary team efforts at St. Charles, both administrators said generic teamwork had helped improve the orientation of new workers and the intake of new children as well as the transition period when workers and children left the program. Further, this, along with the other findings here, led to the decisions to use the approach in other programs—in an intensive home-based services program in 1983 and a continuum of care for girls in 1987, and then, just prior to the writing of this report, in the remaining residential programs.

Fourth, according to observations and a comparison to other programs at St. Charles and elsewhere, the generalists were able to offer a complete schedule of daily activities. Their ability to help one another in school, with families, and on the unit provided additional coverage, support, learning, counseling, and care opportunities without sacrificing quality in any single area. For example, in comparison to the other residential programs at St. Charles, more time was spent interacting in social skills, counseling, and activity groups.

Fifth, the results of consumer (parent) surveys, self-concept (Piers & Harris, 1964) and behavioral assessments (Achenbach, 1979), and treatment plan evaluations indicated gains had been made (Berger, 1988). Most of the children left the program feeling better about themselves, having reached a higher level of academic achievement and having developed new social skills. They also returned to parents and foster parents who in general were more equipped to care for them. Perhaps the greatest testament to their success with clients were the decisions by the referring agencies to use the program. Throughout the 10 years, YDC had operated at or near capacity, which could not be said for many other programs in the state.

Two Significant Challenges

Among the many challenges in implementing the program, two stood out. First, the generalists had to constantly encourage one another to stretch their boundaries beyond what was familiar (e.g., school, the unit, and families) and search for a proper balance of duties and responsibilities to meet their clients' needs as well as their own. Although they entered the program with considerable enthusiasm and desire to expand their professional boundaries, overcoming their natural tendencies to be territorial or stick with what they knew best proved for most to be more difficult than anticipated.

Second, the supervisor had to have the skill and knowledge to help them. He or she also had to be accessible. As might have been anticipated, the program worked best during those periods when the supervisor was able to challenge and support the generalists on a daily basis and had the skill to be a positive role model, teacher, and leader.

Areas Needing Improvement

There were two major areas in which the approach fell short of expectations. First, despite the introduction of many of the structural variables that had been shown to be predictors of longevity and commitment (Krueger et al., 1987), the approach did not help reduce turnover. The demanding nature of the job and/or more attractive job offers caused several generalists to leave earlier than the three to five years it had initially been hoped they would stay. A goal for the next five years is to try to reduce the demands without sacrificing the quality of the program.

Second, the pressure to increase salaries for generalists with social worker and education backgrounds to remain competitive with market forces eventually led to the creation of a salary scale in which the ranges for generalists with teaching and social work backgrounds was raised slightly above the range for generalists with child and youth care backgrounds. Although some of the generalists in this latter category were able to make as much (because of their years of experience and years of education) as teachers and social workers, this still compromised the original intent of having equal salary ranges. This is currently being reviewed to see if a more equitable system can once again be developed.

Finally, workers expressed some concerns about the label of *generalist,* which was often misunderstood by others to mean they were not skilled or trained to meet the specific education, treatment, and care needs. A new name is currently being considered, as is the possibility of changing the name from *generic* to *transdisciplinary teamwork* or some other, more appropriate name.

SUMMARY AND CONCLUSIONS

Over a 10-year period, Generic Teamwork proved to be more effective than interdisciplinary teamwork at St. Charles. Although turnover was not reduced, improvements in communication and service delivery were sufficiently improved to encourage the administrators to use the approach in other programs.

Generic Teamwork is an example of the transdisciplinary model of teamwork in action. It uses many of the concepts of the educateur model as well, in which one professional uses the skills and knowledge of education, social work, counseling, child care, and recreation. The generic model demonstrates how information sharing, goal setting, and collaboration can be improved by eliminating some of the unnecessary professional role boundaries in human services. It can also be suggested, based on the similar success in the intensive in-home and continuum of care for girls programs at St. Charles as well as in a new Independent Living Program at the Child and Youth Care Learning Center, University of Wisconsin-Milwaukee, that the approach holds promise for a variety of interdisciplinary programs.

For those who are interested in implementing the approach the authors offer the following general recommendations:

1. Form a partnership with a university or college to help with research, training, and consultation.
2. Make an extensive effort to find a leader who, in addition to a sound knowledge

of education, child and youth care, and social work, has good supervisory and management skills.

3. Allow the program time to grow at a pace that is based on the generalists' abilities and readiness to accept new responsibilities.

4. Provide as much ongoing training in teamwork, education, child and youth care, and family work as possible, focusing on those methods, such as re-education, psychodynamic, developmental care, and social learning methods, that have applications in all three areas.

5. Provide ample time for generalists to meet on a regular basis to develop individual care, education, and family plans (2–4 hrs. a week) as well as informal time to communicate daily information.

6. Create as many opportunities as possible for team and individual supervision.

7. Maintain an equal and fair salary and benefit structure.

Clearly, the generic team model applies many of the principles of teamwork. It focuses on the needs of the whole person. It is based on communication, common goals, coordination, and cooperation. It seeks to avoid fragmentation and inconsistency. It emphasizes what the staff share in common and allows generalists to benefit from that unity in their collective effort to serve the needs of youth with challenging behaviors.

REFERENCES

Achenbach, T. M. (1979). The Child Behavior Profile: An empirically based system for assessing children's behavior problems and competencies. *Journal of Mental Health, 7,* 24–42.

Berger, B. (1988). A report on the results of the Achenbach, Piers-Harris, and consumer satisfaction surveys at YDC. Unpublished.

Brendtro, L., & Ness, A. (1983). Reeducating troubled youth. New York: Aldine.

Garner, H. (1977). A trip through bedlam and beyond. *Child Care Quarterly, 6*(3).

Garner, H. (1980). Administrative behaviors and effective team functioning. *Residential Group Care,* Spring, 2–5.

Garner, H. (1982). Teamwork in programs for children and youth. Springfield, IL: Thomas.

Garner, H. (1990). Helping others through teamwork. Washington, DC: Child Welfare League of America.

Hobbs, N. (1967). The reeducation of emotionally disturbed children. In E. M. Bower & W. G. Holister (Eds.), *Behavioral sciences frontiers in education.* New York: Wiley.

Krueger, M. (1982). Implementation of a team decision-making model among child and youth care workers. Doctoral dissertation, University of Wisconsin-Milwaukee.

Krueger, M. (1983). Careless to caring for troubled youth. Washington, DC: Child Welfare League of America.

Krueger, M. (1987). Making the team approach work. *Child Welfare, 66,* 447–458.

Krueger, M. (1990). Child and youth care organizations. In M. Krueger, & N. Powell, *Choices in caring*. Washington, DC: Child Welfare League of America.

Krueger, M., Fox, R., Friedman, J., & Sampson, J. (1987). The generic team approach. *Child and Youth Care Quarterly, 16,* 131–144.

Linton, T. (1969). The European educateur program for disturbed children. *American Journal of Orthopsychiatry, 39,* 125–133.

Long, N., Morse, W., & Newman, R. (1976). Conflict in the classroom. Belmont, CA: Wadsworth.

Maier, H. (1987). Developmental group care of children and youth. New York: Haworth.

Piers, E., & Harris, D. (1964). Piers-Harris children's self concept scale. Nashville, TN: Counselors Recording and Tests.

Reiger, N., & Devries, N. (1974). The child mental health specialist: A new profession. *Orthopsychiatry, 44,* 7–18.

Rosenfeld, G. (1978). Turnover among child care workers. *Child Care Quarterly, 8,* 67–69.

Redl, F., & Wineman, D. (1957). Controls from within: Techniques for treatment of the aggressive child. New York: Free Press.

Vander Ven, K. (1979). Towards maximum effectiveness of a unit team approach in residential care: An agenda for team development. *Residential and Community Care Administration, 1,* 287–297.

Vorrath, H., & Brendtro, L. (1974). Positive peer culture. Chicago: Aldine.

Index